55.⁓

D0078536

Greek and Roman Folklore

Greek and Roman Folklore

A Handbook

Graham Anderson

Greenwood Folklore Handbooks

GREENWOOD PRESS
Westport, Connecticut • London

2975411

Library of Congress Cataloging-in-Publication Data

Anderson, Graham.
  Greek and Roman folklore : a handbook / Graham Anderson.
    p. cm. —(Greenwood folklore handbooks, ISSN 1549–733X)
  Includes bibliographical references and index.
  ISBN 0–313–33575–3 (alk. paper)
  1. Folklore–Greece. 2. Folklore–Rome. I. Title. II. Series.
  GR170.A543 2006
  398.20938—dc22   2006011151

British Library Cataloguing in Publication Data is available.

Library of Congress Catalog Card Number: 2006011151
ISBN: 0–313–33575–3
ISSN: 1549–733X

First published in 2006

Greenwood Press, 88 Post Road West, Westport, CT 06881
An imprint of Greenwood Publishing Group, Inc.
www.greenwood.com

Printed in the United States of America

The paper used in this book complies with the
Permanent Paper Standard issued by the National
Information Standards Organization (Z39.48–1984).

10 9 8 7 6 5 4 3 2 1

For Jack Zipes

Contents

Preface

It has been some 80 years since William Halliday produced a short account entitled *Greek and Roman Folklore.* To attempt to cover the same ground now has presented this author with a challenge of compression. The amount of material available to Halliday and to H. J. Rose in the early part of last century was intractable enough, but the increase since the 1920s in theory alone has made a further survey increasingly necessary and increasingly beyond the scope of any single volume. This is all the more evident because classicists, in particular, tend to classify folkloric materials in so many other ways and tend to avoid folklore as a subject in its own right.

I have set out to offer some overview of definitions of folklore and some limitations, ancient and modern, in the way we tend to approach it. It is then possible to view the basis or bases on which we are able to understand ancient folklore, from both written accounts, literary and nonliterary, and from the material survivals themselves. It is necessary also to discuss the problems of transmission over time of materials much older than those normally considered by folklorists and from societies considerably more remote than, say, the rural populations of nineteenth-century Europe. On the materials themselves we can begin with transmitted myths, folktales, legends, both local and migratory, and fairy tales: here a great deal of selection is necessary as well as continuous discrimination over the classification of items as myth or folktale in particular. Less problematic, but even more varied, is the repertoire of smaller popular forms—jokes, riddles, anecdotes, and fables—which offer the small change of ancient popular culture but are very patchily documented for antiquity. We can then go on to examine some of the most distinctively folkloric characters—tricksters, satyrs, nymphs, demons, and bogeymen—who populate the world of ancient folklore and make its operations possible. We must also attempt to construct a series of overlapping contexts for the narrative material: we shall examine a cross section of traditional customs and their relation to popular belief and superstition and look, in a limited way, at the people who believe in them, as often as not through the distorting mirror of fiction. We need also to examine some of the concepts relating to the animal, vegetable, and mineral aspects of that world; this will lead us, in turn, into the overlap between popular medicine and magic.

The whole enterprise has given rise to a series of interlinking questions that recur, whatever the precise topic: What underlying assumptions can we notice in ancient attitudes to folkloric material, however we define it? How often do conflicting methodologies prove a hindrance rather than a help? What tendencies are inherent in popular material and the way it is passed on? Some such questions may be no more capable of definitive solutions than questions like "why do we read horoscopes?" But they are always worth bearing in mind.

The present work owes a great deal to friends and colleagues, past and present, and to others farther afield. Thomas Williams and Alex Scobie first harnessed me to the study of folklore, while colleagues at Kent have greatly assisted in a variety of ways. I have also benefited enormously from the published work of William Hansen, Daniel Ogden, John Scarborough, and Roger French, in particular, as I have felt myself trespassing into specialisms well beyond my own. I also owe a great deal to the students in several years of classes on tale-telling and storytelling. AHRB and Leverhulme Awards specifically on Arthurian and ancient kingship projects have also helped on the fringes. I also owe a great debt to the courtesy and patience of George Butler at Greenwood Press, who commissioned the book and supported it through numerous delays; to my wife Margaret, who knew when to distract me; and to the dedicatee, Jack Zipes, who has encouraged my forays into folkloristics from an early stage.

Graham Anderson
School of European Culture and Languages,
University of Kent

Abbreviations

AT	Antti Aarne and Stith Thompson, *The Types of the Folktale*, 2nd ed. (1961)
EM	*Enkyklopaedie des Maerchens*, ed. K. Ranke
FGrH	F. Jacoby, *Die Fragmente der griechischen Historiker*
IG	*Inscriptiones Graecae*
JFR	*Journal of Folklore Research*
JHS	*Journal of Hellenic Studies*
LCL	*Loeb Classical Library*
LIMC	*Lexicon Iconographicum Mythologiae Classicae*
OCD	*Oxford Classical Dictionary*, 3rd ed. (1996)
PGM	*Papyri Graecae Magicae,* ed. K. Preisendanz and A. Henrichs
RE	*Realenkyklopädie der klassischen Altertumswissenschaft*
RIB	*The Roman Inscriptions of Britain*

One

"Or So People Say": Some Definitions and Approaches

Before we even begin to attempt a definition of folklore, I should like to offer what I hope all readers of this book would regard as a clear example of it:

Ovid, *Metamorphoses* 8.617–625, 719–724

Lelex spoke, mature in years and wisdom: "The power of heaven is immense and boundless, and whatever was the will of the gods has been accomplished. And to dispel any doubt, in the Phrygian uplands there stands an oak side by side with a linden tree, and surrounded by a little wall. I myself have seen the site, for Pittheus sent me once to the lands ruled by his father Pelops. Not far from this place is a marsh, though at one time a place where people lived, but now water. . . . To this day the Bithynian peasants of the area point out neighbouring trees from twin trunks. Sober old men told me this (they had no reason for wishing to deceive). Indeed I myself have seen the garlands hanging on the branches; placing fresh ones there myself I said: 'those the gods look after are gods themselves; and those who worship are objects of worship.'"

Ovid's account of a local flood in Phrygia is given to Lelex, the ancient friend of Theseus, who claims to have seen the sacred trees into which Philemon and Baucis, the sole survivors of the disaster, were claimed to have metamorphosed. An almost identical story is told of a woman who survived a local flood in the folk tradition of Yorkshire as being the only inhabitant of the district who had shown piety to a divine visitor.[1]

It should not take long to isolate what elements of this tale might qualify it as folklore: it is an ancient and anonymous traditional story, delivered by a revered elder whose very name was synonymous in later antiquity with "aboriginal," and it was orally transmitted, according to its frame story, in the hearing of some very mythological figures, including Theseus and the personified river god Achelous, as a tale of ancient piety rewarded; it was then commemorated when the metamorphosed couple were honored in their own right with what amounts to a tree cult. An ancient wisdom tale, then: it might be difficult to find an example that we could record as more "folkloric" than that. But how do we actually *know* it is folklore? Or how can we define folklore in such a way that this example will be securely included and much else left out?

TOWARD A DEFINITION

To find a foolproof definition of folklore is as frustrating as trying to define such elastic concepts as myth or magic, both of which it is often taken to include. Maria Leach, in Funk and Wagnall's *Standard Dictionary of Folklore, Mythology and Legend,* disconcertingly collected no fewer than 21 attempts at definition, spreading over 11 columns of the 1949 edition. It is useful to juxtapose some of the shortest:

> Folklore is that part of a people's culture which is preserved, consciously or unconsciously, in beliefs and practices, customs and observances of general currency; in myths, legends, and tales of common acceptance; and in arts and crafts which express the temper and genius of a group rather than an individual . . . it is distinct [from more formal literature and art] in that it is essentially of the people, by the people, and for the people. (Theodore Gaster)
>
> The term folklore as used today is ambiguous. The context in which it appears reveals whether the user is referring to all the unwritten narratives of primitive people and thereby drawing a line between the literature of primitive and civilised peoples. . . . A connotation which adds to the confusion is a hang-over from the earlier European use of the word folklore to cover peasant customs, beliefs, and narratives—the anthropology of peasants. (Katherine Luomala)
>
> Although the word folklore is more than a century old, no exact agreement has ever been reached as to its meaning. The common idea present in all folklore is that of tradition, something handed down from one person to another and preserved either by memory or practice rather than written record. (Stith Thompson)
>
> The entire body of ancient popular beliefs, customs and traditions, which have survived among the less educated elements of civilized societies until today. It thus includes fairy tales, myths and legends, superstitions, festal rites, traditional games, folk songs, popular sayings, arts, crafts, local dances and the like. (John L. Mish)

These approaches are typical of the level of variation we are likely to find. Only the fourth reflects an explicit preference in favor of regarding folklore as survival of the primitive, a now rather unfashionable angle. The middle two are more convinced of the flexibility or ambiguity of the term than the others. There is some hesitation between the catchall formula and the cautious enumeration, in case we accidentally leave something out. There is at least some room for further argument.

It is often advanced that orality is a condition for the transmission of folklore, but in nonliterate cultures, as Alan Dundes long ago pointed out, absolutely everything is transmitted in this way, and much of it is not folklore, any more than much oral instruction in literate cultures.[2] If orality were to be a condition for folklore, then any history of folklore going back more than three generations would automatically be disqualified, along with, of course, practically all evidence from the ancient world at all. A number of folkloric channels of communication—epitaphs, improvised verses in autograph books, or any other forms of written ephemera—can scarcely be discounted as sources of folklore. Moreover, such features as traditional gestures and dance movements can scarcely be discounted either but cannot be said to be oral. Some will wish to compromise by suggesting that folklore has to be transmitted from individual to individual, but even that, in the case of folk art, may not happen directly.

Some attempts at reduction are possible. Francis Utley[3] attempted to isolate the common factors in Leach's 21 definitions: besides the term "oral," key words such as "transmission," "tradition," "survival," and "communal" recur, not always positively, while the word "superstition" tends to be regarded as outmoded. As to content, some disagreements arise as to whether to include language, beliefs, and crafts, and a good deal depends on the background or loyalties of the definer (whether or not his allegiance is anthropological, for example); a mounting problem has been the proliferation of folkloric traits in popular mass media (as opposed to person-to-person communication). This Utley has summed up as follows:

> The statistical weight of authority is for the exclusion of bad science, mass culture, survival, the communal, and matter of origin, and for the inclusion of oral (verbal, unwritten), tradition (transmission), primitive culture, and the subcultures of civilised society both rural and urban. As for the materials of folklore, art and literature are a clearly unanimous choice, custom and belief win the suffrage of about half of the definers, and crafts and language are generally excluded.

In practice, any writer on folklore in antiquity is likely to touch on just about all the topics touched on almost anywhere in the 21 definitions, including those specifically excluded. The very diversity of the definitions underlines the difficulty, or the impracticality, of weaving satisfactory theory around them: the debate between William Bascom and Samuel Bayard in the 1950s on how to classify rug making or folk music in relation to myth, legend, or proverb only serves to underline the difficulties still further. In terms of the ancient world, the Capitoline bronze of the wolf nursing Romulus and Remus would be folk legend, but not folk art, whereas the Aldborough mosaic, where the mosaicist's competence does not extend to producing a convincing wolf, would be folk art depicting folk legend.

Some prejudices can be misleading: it may often be tempting to think of folklore as the preserve of peasantry or the conservative countryside, especially in antiquity, but we cannot afford to suggest that there was no outlet for urban folklore (as in the conversation of the urban freedmen in Petronius, for example).[4] Nor can we insist that folklore is merely "survival" and cannot be spontaneously generated and regenerated under new cultural conditions. There is already a folklore that attaches to e-mails, the Internet, and text messaging and which would have been inconceivable in ages with different technologies. But that is not to say that many kinds of folklore are not permanently under threat from certain aspects of literary culture.

Folklore is often felt to belong to something definable in terms of a group: one may have a folklore of fishermen, for example, or Kurdistani Jews,[5] or the folklore of a group as small as a family or less, and at the same time an international folklore that relates fishermen of many different cultures on both sides of an ocean, or farmers of many language groups across a whole continent, joined by dependence on the same calendar for their agricultural operations.

It is time to attempt our own definition and formulate our own approach, with corresponding caution. "Whatever is generated by folk" is uncomfortably wide and covers more than merely "lore," but it has the prospect at least of leaving nothing out. It points the way to what we might call "anonymously transmitted culture": what is popular in the sense of being practiced or passed on by "people," no more specifically defined. At its crudest we might suggest "anything that can be prefaced with 'they say,'" where "they" are purveyors of popular wisdom. If we might describe a fairy tale as a "once upon a time story," we might just get off with describing folklore as the ultimate "or so they say" subject: everything about it is doubtful and something we only have someone else's (generally spoken) word for. The phrase "we might just get off with it" tells us much about all such attempts: we are wrestling with an ever-changing Proteus, and we might catch him for just a moment, but much that *someone* might reasonably count as folklore will still somehow have eluded us and will still lie somewhere outside the confines of whatever clever phrase we choose. We may note, too, that some phenomena are more likely to be recognized as folklore than others, and it is always likely to be "lore" that is the richer and more suggestive term of the two. What we tend to retain of widely transmitted customs are more likely to be excluded: the technology of smelting bronze or building long ships, we might argue, is folk culture, but not actually folk *lore,* whereas not bringing a bronze object inside a temple on a feast day would be obviously recognizable as the latter. Much of the material of folklore is transmitted as oral narrative, but by no means all, and when we admit, say, popular proverbs as folklore, we might argue that "neither a borrower nor a lender be" is common sense in the first instance rather than folklore, whereas not jumping on the boundaries between every fifth paving stone is folklore, pure and simple.

If we wish to illustrate folkloric behavior or inheritances that we share with Greeks and Romans, we would not take very long to realize that there is plenty in ancient folklore that is at least recognizable, even if explanations are likely to differ as to why this is so. If we touch wood for luck, we accord with something at least analogous to a widespread ancient practice[6]; likewise if we wish someone a Happy New Year, bless someone after a sneeze, or feel our ears burning if we are being talked about,[7] and if we avoid doing something on an unlucky day of the month (for example, Friday the 13th—the day itself may have changed, though the 13th of the waxing month is unlucky for some things as early as Hesiod).[8] Again, if we tell a story that starts "once upon a time" or about a king who marries a girl because of a shoe that intrigues him, or if we call someone "a dog in the manger" for depriving others of useful things he himself cannot use, then we are passing on materials that were already circulating in the ancient world, whatever may or may not have happened to them in between[9].

But there are difficulties. It is easy enough nowadays to encounter folklore either from a single informant (often about "a friend of a friend") or at a social occasion, a family birthday party, a wedding or funeral ceremony, a christening, or a harvest or Christmas celebration; our problem with antiquity is that ancient informants can no longer be contacted in any of these ways. In some other respects, too, there is a wide gulf between the ancient and modern worlds: we do not have the legal framework of slavery, and the ancients did not have computers or cellular phones (though they had the folklore that would have accommodated easily enough to either—a latter-day Socrates would be easily enough distracted not by his famous *daimon* or guardian spirit, but by his cellular).

It does not help that there were all too many ways of editing out much of the folk material that must once have been familiar. The Roman poet Horace seems to have been amused by the banter of servants—but he probably spent more time making love to his own than recording their banter.[10] Everyone must have known the sorts of things uneducated people would come up with so that no one tended to bother to record it. Ancient customs might be introduced, as they still are, with hearsay formulae and little else, rather than with precisely recorded data.

THE STUDY OF THE RATHER VAGUE

The difficulty of defining folklore and its obvious overlapping position in relation to other areas has considerably distorted its identity as a field of study. At the present time, folklore research is perhaps most likely to be conducted as, or felt to be most closely related to, anthropology, especially where fieldwork is involved; but other disciplines, from linguistics to archaeology, are likely to be interested in folklore in some way or other, and practitioners who come from other disciplines may run the risk of dealing with folklore on the basis of little more than inherited prejudice. The number of times this author has seen questionable statements about "folktale" in books about myth is very high: statements often take the form "this is, of course, pure folktale," without any guarantee that the writer has given the matter a moment's thought. Equally persistent is the devaluing of "folklore" in discussions of ancient religion and society, especially in works on "mythology," where the term is often tellingly absent from the writer's subject index.[11]

One major stumbling block is the problem of separating the usage of the words "myth" and "folktale," in particular. This is especially problematic in dealing with Greek and Roman materials since there is an automatic assumption that all the traditional narratives from the creation to the return of Odysseus from Troy can be labeled *Greek myth*. This is very unsatisfactory since it is possible to argue that there is a world of difference between, say, Hesiod's genealogy of creation and the story of Perseus being told how to cheat the Graeae or avoid seeing the Gorgon.[12] The difficulties are well highlighted by a conventional standpoint like the following[13]:

> Folktales are concerned essentially with the life, problems and aspirations of ordinary people, the folk. They are not aristocratic in tone. Greek myths, on the other hand, when they are not about gods, are about heroes, aristocratic figures far removed by birth and context from the ordinary people. Indeed it is this aristocratic colouring of the content of Greek myths . . . that caused the tales of European peasants . . . to be labelled as 'folktales' or 'household tales'

rather than myths—by which people of those days meant the exalted deeds of Theseus, Heracles, Zeus, Athena and the rest. Folktales are not concerned with large problems like the inevitability of death or institutional matters like the justification of kingship. Their social preoccupations are restricted to the family. Difficulties with mothers or jealous sisters are folktale topics, worries over incest and the limits of permissible sexual encounter are not. Supernatural elements in folktales encompass giants, monsters, witches, fairy godmothers, magical equipment or spells; they do not extend to gods in any full sense, to questions of how the world or society was formed, or to matters of religion.

This position may sound plausible, but it does not work convincingly when applied to even the most obvious examples: the *Odyssey* is very much concerned with the family and with giants, monsters, witches, magical equipment, and spells. Are we to say it is "myth" rather than "folklore" just because it has a full complement of gods, but no fairy godmother? Again, the aristocratic nature of much of the canon of Greek mythology does not really affect the subject matter of the tales. Most could be, and many are, told of nonaristocratic situations elsewhere. And Kirk seems unaware that "Cinderella" and "Snow White" are very much concerned with aristocratic contexts. As to the avoidance of incest or the avoidance of death, the Oedipus story and that of Alcestis are both international folktales in their own right, whatever other disciplines may see fit to lay claim to them.[14] The real distinction Kirk is grasping at is a largely unnoticed historical one. If a polytheistic society becomes monotheistic, the popular trickster tales have to be assigned to a little man who confronts the hero, rather than, say, to a god Hermes who no longer exists. Once such reservations are applied, myth tends to become associated with only the most cosmic of tales. But as most folklorists would include myth among "popularly transmitted" material, it becomes unnecessary to pursue the matter much further. *Mythos* ("tale") as a Greek word covered both, as did its secondary connotation of "not necessarily true."

THE SCOPE OF GREEK AND ROMAN FOLKLORE: A BRIEF HISTORY OF HEARSAY?

The specific terms of reference relating to Greek and Roman folklore require some qualification in themselves. This includes any evidence from Greek and Roman literature and other sources (epigraphy, papyrology, art history, archaeology) covering the traditional historical and geographical range of the Greco-Roman world, from the Mycenaean Bronze Age to late antiquity. But a fair proportion of the material to be discussed will not fit as easily as might be expected into even so wide a framework. Because of the traditional aspect of folklore built into any definition, we can expect to find that evidence from other ancient Near Eastern cultures is relevant: the closeness of the archaic Greek world, and the nature of Alexander's conquests, brings a great deal of borrowed or inherited material already into our survey from the Sumero-Babylonians, the Egyptians,[15] and a wide cross section of other Near Eastern peoples. However separately we might wish to perceive the world of the Old Testament from Greco-Roman civilization, we find Palestine as part of the Roman Empire and the possibility of diffusion of Jewish folklore in a wider Mediterranean context.[16] We likewise find Celts widely distributed within the Roman Empire and, indeed, a general "accommodation" up to a point in the ancient world of "other cultures," with attempts from Herodotus onward to equate foreign deities with Greek equivalents.[17] In these conditions we must be prepared to look at the widest possible trajectory of evidence. We must also be prepared to note that in certain areas at least, such as magic and medicine, there was a strong predisposition to borrow and syncretize at will: anything that might be thought to work might be pressed into use as a matter of course.[18]

Within the wide period we are discussing, of around two millennia, we must also expect a fair degree of historical evolution, which we are ill equipped to chart. Even in such a richly documented area of the past, it is very difficult to produce a short history of hearsay. We should, as a matter of course, tend to assume that traditional customs change slowly and that continuities can be tentatively assumed, except when there are strong grounds for assuming breaks, such as major invasions, cataclysmic natural disasters, and known movements of populations. But we must be prepared for the fact that folklore, or folk literature, may die out or be replaced and that changes may happen invisibly inside or outside any given period we choose to study.

SCHOLARSHIP

Because the word "folklore" itself, as a replacement for "popular antiquities," dates only from 1846, it is not easy to bring together any clear and unified line of scholarship on folklore before that date; more particularly, in antiquity itself the awareness of the whole subject or complex of subjects remained diffuse. What follows is no more than a series of map references to one classicist's view of the main methodologies that can be identified.

The Ancient World

Was there a science of folklore in antiquity itself? We might well be tempted to say, rather evasively, not as such. There is certainly an interest in, and a determination to perpetuate, the memory of the deeds and sayings of ancestors: ancient wisdom literature might be described indeed as self-perpetuating folklore; there is also an interest in groups that is as old as the first travelers. Odysseus gives us a reasonable "ethnographic" description of the gigantic cannibal Cyclopes long before he tells us how he saved most of his crew from one of them[19]: both these interests intersect in what we might call a concern with tradition, a high proportion of which will be both anonymous and popular in some sense.

There has been only piecemeal study, also, of ancient views of what, from the perspective of Greek and Latin authors, could be described as folktale and folklore. This is scarcely surprising since the two terms belong in the first instance to the nineteenth century. But ancient thinking involved acknowledgment of the advent of agriculture as a major watershed in the history of civilization. Views bifurcated as to whether this represented a fall from a previous Golden Age (Hesiod, Virgil's *Georgics*) or a sign of rational progress in the history of constantly developing civilization (Lucretius); ancient moralists could tilt the balance either way.

The ancients themselves were able to see what they took to be primitive survivals in their midst, and certain, often stereotyped peoples, sometimes indeed semimythical, were marked out as "primitive." In particular, the Arcadians, who were seen as a model, in some respects, for the social progress of a people, surface frequently in allusions to the primitive: apart from the idea that they claimed to be proselenic, that is, to have existed before the moon, or that they had once dressed in skins and lived on acorns, we have the following more unusual observations by Polybius[20]:

The first Arcadians adopted music into their whole way of life to such an extent that they made it compulsory not only for boys to study but for young men up to thirty, although in other respects their lives were so very austere. For everyone is well aware that it is practically unknown outside Arcadia for boys from the cradle to be trained to sing hymns and paeans in due rhythms, and in these they celebrate the heroes and gods of each locality in ancestral manner. Afterwards they learn the measure of Philoxenus and Timotheus and sing in annual events in intense competition in the theatres with flute-players associated with Dionysus, the boys in junior events and the young men in the adult contests. And in the same way right through their lives they do not import hired singers to entertain at their symposia but provide their own, inviting one another to take their turn. And they do not think it disgraceful to say they are ignorant of other fields, but song they are unable to say they do not know (since know it they all must), nor can they excuse themselves after admitting their knowledge of it, because among them that is considered so disgraceful.

The predominant materials on foundations of cities and communities can often be seen, at least loosely, as both myth and folklore: myth in the sense that they deal with a larger social theme, and folklore in that they regularly resort to folk motifs such as tricks and tricksters, the interpretation of riddles, and the like.

A good example of the convergence of myth, legend, and folktale and the justification of the term "lore" is the story of the origin of the Scythians in Herodotus 4.5:

> The Scythians, so they claim, are the youngest of all peoples, and they say that they came into being in the following circumstances. The first man in their country, which was previously uninhabited, was a man called Targitaus; they claim that he was the son of Zeus and of a daughter of the river Borysthenes—an incredible claim to my mind, but that is what they say. Targitaus they say had three sons, Lipoxais, Arpoxais, and the youngest Colaxais; and while they were reigning, gold objects fell from the sky into Scythia, a plough, a yoke, a battle-axe, and a goblet. The eldest saw these first, and as he approached with a view to taking possession of them, the gold blazed up. He retreated and the second of the brothers came up, with the same result. When the flames had kept off both the elder brothers, the youngest approached and the fire was quenched, and so he carried the objects home. The eldest brothers acknowledged the portent and handed over the entire kingdom to Colaxais. . . .

It is difficult to pick perhaps an overall meaning out of the story directly. Clearly, it is an acknowledgment of the divine origins of basic attributes of civilization and their being accorded to suitable royalty. The four objects seem to embody the symbols of a warrior culture but also of the beginnings of an agricultural civilization: one thinks of the story of Arcas of Arcadia apparently encountering the celestial chariot of Triptolemus. The youngest son born to rule is a particular cliché of folktale rather than myth—where the two are separable.[21]

Moreover, we still have to ask ourselves, Who exactly are the "folk" whose "lore" we are discussing anyway? Not only do our materials emanate almost exclusively from one gender—male—but also from the upper echelons of society, observing "the folk" from some distance. They may, from time to time, inveigh against the pervasiveness of superstition, even among the educated, but we are all too often dealing with an outsider's view rather than one that comes from "the people" in any meaningful sense. Moreover, we should note that while a term such as "popular" might be, on some occasions, more useful or broader and less association loaded than "folk," it need not always be synonymous: "popular storytelling" might mean something broader and more unwieldy than "folktale." But in modern as well as in ancient experiences of folklore, superstition pervades all classes of society, albeit in varying degrees.[22]

Many of the approaches since the Renaissance have, in effect, focused on myth, whose relationship to folktale and folklore more broadly seems constantly and frustratingly shifting and therefore unhelpful. But the majority of approaches to myth in the late nineteenth and twentieth centuries correspond, in some measure, to patterns in folklore scholarship as well. The scholarly politics of the nineteenth century encouraged a particular tendency in the perception of folklore. This was not only the time of the coining of the word "folklore" itself, as late as 1846; it also saw the emergence of anthropology as a science, with a preoccupation with "cultural evolution." The tendency was to see folklore as a survival of the primitive and a means, however imperfect, to rediscovering the nature of the primitive society it had itself survived. In the hands of Frazer, in particular, evolutionism hardened into an untenable dogma that all peoples evolve from a stage of magic through religion to science, a state of affairs positively at variance with perceptible experience, where all three can comfortably or uncomfortably coexist, as indeed they still do. Much of the subsequent history of folklore scholarship has been tied to that which pertains also to myth: the nineteenth century went through a number of phases, from solar mythology to myth-ritual analysis, and psychology and structuralism have provided still others in the twentieth century. In the meantime, archaeology and anthropology have, in varying degrees and at various times, interacted with folklore scholarship, and current development would lead us to a science of "folkloristics." The latter has been recently defined by Georges and Owen Jones as "the discipline devoted to the identification, documentation, characterization, and analysis of traditional expressive forms, processes and behaviours."[23]

The initial stimulus in the study of folktale has been in the laying down of collections of material, often in the nineteenth century, on a national and nationalist basis. The service of Jacob and Wilhelm Grimm was to form the basis of a German collection of *Kinder- und Hausmärchen* (1812–1857) of over 200 folktales, with the beginnings of a scholarly apparatus. The enterprise did not attain to current professional standards overnight: there has been justified misgiving over such practices as accessing or rounding off literary sources, conflating versions of tales from different tellers, and the like, and the whole idea of a national collection at all set an unfortunate direction in some respects that has persisted ever since. But the overall achievement was still staggering.

A number of approaches through the nineteenth century have not stood the test of time in a way that the material collected by the Grimms has done. No one can now subscribe to the overingenuity behind Max Müller's solar mythology, which tried to interpret myth and folktale obsessively and overingeniously in terms of the heavens and, in particular, the weather. It is not hard to pick out this or that detail, such as Heracles borrowing Apollo's bowl to journey to the West, where a solar interpretation is particularly attractive, or the function of Zeus and his Indo-European cognates as a sky god, but such incontrovertible examples cannot give us a key to the interpretation of all myth. No less dogmatic or convincing were early attempts to study the wider diffusion of tales, in particular, the "orientalizing" theory of Theodore Benfey, whose study of the Indian *Panchatantra* and its sources claimed that India was the source of most European folktale, except for fable. This has been shown to be untenable in quite those terms; it will take a great deal more study of much more ancient Near Eastern materials before any definitive sourcing of this kind can be attempted again.

The Finnish School

The methodology most directly concerned with folktale as such is the approach favoring the "historic-geographic method" and originating with research into the sources of the Finnish Kalevala toward the end of the nineteenth century. It is on the system brought to fruition by Karl Krohn and Antti Aarne that the basic archive describing characteristics of individual folktales is based. His *The Types of the Folktale* (second edition by Stith Thompson, 1961) gives outline descriptions of tales in several segments and an outline of the motifs corresponding to those in Stith Thompson's motif index as well as an indication of the distribution of the tale over national folk archives. The system is not without its drawbacks, mostly due to piecemeal expansion. Not least of such drawbacks was the concentration in the early stages on Scandinavian material and the relative absence of that from the Near and Middle East and farther afield: the index is primarily European and colonial American in focus.

The method has attempted a systematization of a tale's history rather similar to that of a stemma for a manuscript tradition. Date and place of versions was established as far as possible but sadly reaches a vanishing point, in most cases, not long before the start of collecting oral evidence in the nineteenth century, and where ancient evidence is available, it is often at odds with conjectural origins, where such evidence has been ignored. Unfortunately, classicists have shown an almost indifferent attitude to the implications of the school, and few British-based classicists have been able to use it effectively. An exception has been Alex Scobie's work on the ass romance, especially in his *Apuleius and Folklore* (1983). One recent howler has been to confuse the two basic indexes, and this has unfortunately occurred in as standard a reference work as the third edition of *The Oxford Classical Dictionary,* an error perpetuated in its derivative, *The Oxford Dictionary of Classical Myth and Religion.*

Anthropology and the Cambridge Ritualists

The Finnish School was concerned with the taxonomy of folktale in all its aspects but showed little interest, by contrast, in matters of ritual. It was the service of Sir James Frazer in *The Golden Bough* to interpret from a ritual angle in the first instance, taking his starting point from a report of the rites of the shrine of Diana at Nemi. Frazer's eventually multivolume work remained a landmark of misguided erudition in that ancient instances of the *pharmakos* ritual are so isolated that it is impossible to generalize from them as to the status of this rite in the history of human development, as indicating the existence inter alia of a matriarchal society. In this instance the rite is that of a scapegoat, or *pharmakos,* who takes the sins of the community on himself and, in being discarded, leads to the mythology of the hanged god, the concept of a savior who performs a ritual in order to atone for and save others, whether in a magical or nonmagical way.

The legacy of Frazer and his fellow Cambridge scholar, Jane Harrison, was to emphasize what they saw as the priority of ritual over myth. This is very questionable to sustain in practice, if only because for antiquity we so seldom have a full picture of the relationship of a myth and a ritual: we tend to have the evidence for one or the other, as often as not without enough evidence of which has preceded the other in the first place. For this school, ritual tended to be seen as preceding myth so that the myths we have interpret and impose meaning on rituals whose initial myths have been lost.[24] No one is likely to deny that meanings of acts can be lost, although the acts themselves are still performed, but does it really make sense to take this to be the general rule? Suppose we take a story that Adonis is killed because of his love for Cybele. To commemorate the fact, rites and a cult are instituted in honor of Adonis. But according to ritualist logic, what is happening is that people plant a "garden of Adonis" and go up to rooftops to lament; only afterward do they say, "We don't know why we are doing this; let us suppose there must have been someone called Adonis who died, and that will (falsely) explain what we are doing." Some wish, in a revival of ritual speculation, to go back still farther from a new starting point: Burkert[25] claims that "ritual is older, since it occurs even in animals." Unfortunately, any interpretation to that effect is anthropocentric. He also reviews afresh a number of attempts to define the relationship between myth and ritual, but the formulations tend to be equivocal at best.

We might attempt an instance in the institution in the Christian Gospels of the rite of the Eucharist at the so-called Last Supper. In this case the consecration of wine and bread as the blood and body of Christ comes before the actual blood and body sacrifice of which it is symbolic, which would favor both Burkert and Frazer. But in fact, it only does so because the event the ritual commemorates is seen as inevitable, and the commemoration of it will not really happen until it takes place. (And it would be meaningless if the crucifixion were somehow called off!) Even the most obvious instance, then, is instantly controversial. Of still larger import was Frazer's tripartite model of human progress already mentioned. A glance at the evidence for Greece and Rome, which Frazer himself knew very well indeed, would at least furnish cause for hesitation as so much evidence for the three stages, superstition-religion-reason, so obviously coexists at one and the same time, while the prehistory of Greece is complex enough to help little.

Psychoanalysis and Archetype

At least the Cambridge ritualists began from the ancient world itself. But in the first half of the twentieth century and beyond a recurrently challenging interpretation of folktale and myth came from Freudian and post-Freudian psychology, where the basic assumptions were generated by observation of contemporary patients and not heroes of myth or folktale. Freud pioneered the concept of the unconscious and subconscious mind and with it the possibilities that each individual could be motivated by feelings or drives that he need not fully understand or indeed care to acknowledge. The access to these states was felt to be through dreams, and that in itself is unexceptionable. If enough people claim to have similar nightmares in which they experience pursuit, slowed down by some kind of sexually related humiliation (such as trousers falling down), then the patient may well be suffering from dark fears with sexual overtones, whether or not such fears reflect the experience of guilt or shame in remote childhood, which may well be treatable by recalling and confronting such experience. But it is a very large step from accepting the concept of the subconscious mind to using it to explain myth or fairy tale. How many of us have dreams that we have been flying too near the sun when our wings have melted or, in modern terms, that hijackers have thrown us out of an airliner—or that we were in a garden eating an unfamiliar fruit with a partner of the opposite sex when we realized that clothes have not yet been invented, and we fear punishment from some puritan father figure? If larger numbers of people did experience such dreams, then we should be entitled to make a correlation between myths or fairy tales and dreams.

Of course, it was not Daedalus and Icarus or Adam and Eve that Freud related dreams and myths to in the first instance, but the Oedipus story, which is available both as oral folktale and mythologically based literature. Freud harnessed the ancient tale to a subconscious belief that male children regard their fathers as competitors for the affection of their mothers and wish to supplant them. The Oedipus myth would then be a projection of this desire onto the unfortunate tale of a third party, who did not wish to do this: the horror of an unacknowledged desire is then realized in fact. But this does not work. It is impossible to prove, and psychoanalysts have retreated from the theory. But at base Freud has simply not understood the point of the story in the first place. We could well argue that virtue does not always receive its due reward, that misfortunes have to be borne, that there is no escaping destiny, and that any psychological significance lies precisely in its ability to enable us to accept just such a truth. But that is not what Freud set out to do.

It was in his *The Interpretation of Dreams* (1900) that he argued that not only myths, but folktales, sagas, popular tales, and even jokes, are connected to dreams. And in his *Totem and Taboo* (1912–1913) he went further and claimed that myths are "distorted dreams of entire nations." It was the same myth once more which served as the paradigm: he claimed that this one myth embodies the events of the mental life of every individual, which would otherwise appear only in dreams. The development in *Totem and Taboo* was that the Oedipus story did not simply represent wishful thinking, but a kind of folk memory of events in some primeval horde, in which sons of an oppressive father rose up against their oppressor, whom they killed or expelled, in order to take possession of his consort themselves. It is easy to be as sweepingly condemnatory of this amateurish fantasy as Freud himself was dogmatic. But it is certainly worth reflecting on such myths as the castration of Ouranos by Cronos (or the extrabiblical tale of Ham castrating Noah) to remind ourselves of a very overt antagonism between fathers and sons. Genealogically based mythology can indeed be uncomfortably conscious of any generation gap. Classicists have not abandoned the notion of an Oedipus complex altogether: Jan Bremmer notes that Sophocles and Plato do indeed acknowledge the occurrence of mother-son incest in dreams and asks the right question: Why does awareness of this seem to surface in the fifth century B.C.?[26] He suggests that the social revolution of female segregation is responsible: he suggests that in ancient as in modern rural Greece, "the pampering of their sons became one of the foci of [the mother's] life." Bremmer might well be right that this might have contributed to dreams of sleeping with one's mother. But that is something different again: he is equally right to suspect that we will not find a satisfactory answer to the explanation of the Oedipus story itself until we can be more sure of its original form as a story.[27]

More pervasive and difficult to refute have been the myth-inspired theories of the renegade Freudian Carl Jung and his classicist collaborator Karl Kerenyi. Jung was impressed by the recurrence of a number of images both in dreams and in myths and folktales: the wise old man, the earth mother, and the wonderful child suggest themselves. According to Jung, myths draw on the store of these symbols and are thus formed from the products of a collective unconscious of the human race. But if this is due to instinct, then it must be genetically transmitted, and the DNA coding has yet to be found; otherwise, the archetypes are meaningless. Where problems tend to arise is the very moment when the psychologist moves off the ground of the social historian into the world of the subconscious. If it is subconscious, then it is more or less in the realm of the unverifiable. It is very hard to prove an assertion that Cinderella runs away from the ball for some psychological reason—because she wants to be sure of the prince's feelings for her, because she wants to play hard to get, because she is ashamed of her own sexuality, or the like. Folk- and fairy tales, by their very nature, almost seem to preclude the psychological nuance; few storytellers have Cinderella wake up from an anticipatory dream or reveal her conscious or unconscious reflections. Where some versions have her fleeing from the prospect of abuse by her father, that is quite explicit in the terms of the story—her father insists on marrying her, and she finds a way of escape.

Nonetheless, this is not a fruitless approach: dreams are none too far from daydreams and wish fulfillment, and there can be little difficulty in seeking and finding a certain psychological patterning in, for example, the "utopian" plots of Aristophanic comedy, with their allowing individuals to realize their wildest dreams, a state of affairs characteristic of folktale plots that involve the persecuted hero's acquisition of a magic object.[28] The opening of Aristophanes' *Acharnians,* where the rebuffed common man Dikaiopolis is offered three (magic) wineskins, enabling a private peace treaty to take place for up to 30 years, is as good an embodiment of "if only . . ." as we are likely to find.

But this is not the approach we get from the post-Freudian Bettelheim: if something is obvious, then it must be wrong.[29]

> The many stories in which innocent Cinderella is claimed by her father as his marital partner, a fate from which she can save herself only through flight, could be interpreted as conforming to and expressing universal childish fantasies in which a girl wishes her father could marry her and then, out of guilt

because of these fantasies, denies doing anything to arouse this parental desire. But deep down a child who knew that she does want her father to prefer her to her mother feels she deserves to be punished for it—thus her flight or banishment, and degradation to a Cinderella existence. . . .

Bettelheim tends to force interpretations of this kind time and time again: the hunter in fairy tales represents an aristocratic privilege, and so the hunter becomes a father figure; the younger brother in the "Two Brothers" story projects his own desires onto his older brother's wife; and so on.[30]

All in all, twentieth-century psychological approaches have not provided the sought-after key to provide meaning for traditional narrative. But the same hindrances have presented problems for others as well.

Structuralism

Psychological approaches nonetheless show an effort to pose perfectly valid questions from quite a different viewpoint than the Finnish School. After all the taxonomies of tales have been done, why do some themes predominate and others not? Are there preoccupations and thought patterns that are clearly prominent, and what, if anything, can they tell us about the society that has generated the tale?

Such questions are posed from the perspective of later twentieth-century social anthropology through the works of a series of contributors loosely characterized as structuralists. The first of these, Claude Lévi-Strauss, looked, in the 1950s, at myths where we are most likely to find them: in a context uncontaminated by the preconceptions of the civilized world, in this case, in the still subliterate Indian tribes of South America. Lévi-Strauss collected an extensive repertoire of the mythological heritage of such peoples in his three volumes of *Mythologiques,* and his myths tend to be less interested, or indeed uninterested, in what we might see as the linear content of the myths; rather, he attempts to analyze their preoccupations and basic purpose, to explain and come to terms with basic tensions in the ordering of society, with particular reference to issues of kinship and identity and the economic basis of living. We could look in this connection at the biblical tale of Cain and Abel: one of them gives an offering that relates to the harvest, the other to the flock. The Lord finds one offering acceptable, the other not. Cain murders Abel and is punished by being a fugitive on the face of the earth. How will structuralism explain such a story, and how will we know whether it is right? We could say that this story is built on binary opposition, between agricultural and pastoral economies. This explains how the Hebrews come to be pastoral nomads.

It also explains how the murder of one's own brother comes to be prohibited and that this is an offence that society cannot accept—it establishes a basic taboo in kinship relationships.

Let us take a classical example, the tale of the Cyclops: he eats his meat raw, and when Odysseus comes along, he eats some of the latter's companions, but he drinks wine as well as eating the men and is thus tricked into drunkenness. Here is a myth of the ordering of society: this is a tale where the drinking of wine is preferable to the eating of raw meat, demonstrates the superiority of the wise man to the fool, and shows that it is wrong to commit cannibalism. Instances of that kind, we might argue, at least show us that *some* binary oppositions can be teased out of *some* versions of *some* texts and at least may help us to look rather differently at certain particular texts. But how much further can we take such principles? There are a number of potential objections to this kind of analysis. The first of them is Lévi-Strauss's insistence that myth is a form of communication analogous to music or language—just as language consists of an arbitrary succession of sounds that have to be illuminated by some kind of structure (grammar and syntax), so myths are a form of communication in which it is the structure that conveys the meaning. This seems quite clearly a false analogy: the object of language is to convey content, and myth in itself is one content that language is set up to convey.

Still more disturbing are Lévi-Strauss's ideas that the narrative content of myths is not important or is even irrelevant. Moreover, not all binary opposites necessarily are important. What are we to make, for example, of the pattern of the father sending his son to fetch three different kinds of object from dangerous surroundings, as Perseus, Heracles, or Jason might have to do: important or incidental?[31] But how does this kind of analysis work on classical myth? We might look first of all at Detienne and Vernant on the subject of *metis,* cunning intelligence, when they analyze a familiar novella of Ares and Aphrodite.[32] We might have expected the clever trapping of Ares and Aphrodite in bed by her deformed and jealous husband Hephaestus to give rise indeed to a binary opposition between the brain of Hephaestus and the useless brawn of Ares, or even between the divided loyalties of the audience to the guilty couple's humiliation. But no. We have much on Aphrodite's *metis,* not in evidence even in the recriminations of Hephaestus, who could so easily have mentioned it, and a less than illuminating disquisition on the meaning of the "innumerable" magic chains surrounding the couple. And of course, no cross reference to other traditional adultery tales is given. How would we rate this? Does it throw new light on the tale? It does certainly emphasize relationships, but what is the role of Aphrodite as deceiver and trapper? Neither Homer nor Lucian emphasize this side in their tellings of the tale: how far is it really intrinsic to any structure of the narrative? And what of the relationship between Hermes and Aphrodite? Vernant and Detienne link them in marriage ceremonies, but is that specially relevant here? What have they missed?

Some relationships seem to work better. J.-P. Vernant, in *Myth and Society in Ancient Greece,* has a chapter on Prometheus; he compares his treatment in the two major poems of Hesiod and establishes a relationship: Prometheus divides the sacrifice for Zeus/Zeus retaliates by denying it to mankind; Prometheus steals fire from Heaven/Zeus retaliates by sending Pandora to Epimetheus. Here the myth does quite obviously lend itself to some sort of analysis of relationships, but we are still in danger of merely paraphrasing content in a smartly abstract way. It is still more questionable whether the trick of Prometheus, fooling Zeus with bones and fat, corresponds to the description of women as "mere bellies," as applicable to the gift of Pandora. We shall see still further problems in due course.

The structuralists have done little better on the story of Oedipus: there are no obvious binary structures in this story, and it takes considerable effort of the imagination to provide any. Lévi-Strauss used it in his pioneering *Language of Myth* in 1955: his analysis at least has the discipline and academic rigor to look closely at the whole myth (from the foundation of Thebes by Cadmus through family history). He found a number of motifs or themes:

Overestimation/underestimation of family relationships.

Concern with the autochthony or otherwise of man.

A preoccupation with feet.

His own verdict was as follows:

The myth of Oedipus expresses the inability for a culture that holds the belief that mankind is autochthonous, to find a transition from this theory to the recognition that each of us is actually born from the union of a man and a woman. Although the problem obviously cannot be solved, the myth of Oedipus provides a kind of logical tool which makes it possible to build a bridge between the original problem and the derivative problem that might be formulated: is the self born from the same self or from someone else? By this means, a correlation emerges: the undervaluation of blood relationship is to their overvaluation as the attempt to escape authchthony is to the impossibility of succeeding in it.

Vernant (1982) similarly seizes on the problem of feet: he tries to emphasize the odd figure of Oedipus in terms of his gait: "a gait beyond the human, because in rolling, faster and more agile in all directions at once, it transgresses the limitations to which walking straight must submit; but also this side of the normal mode of locomotion because mutilated, unbalanced, vacillating, he advances limping in his singular fashion all the better to fall in the end" (37).

These two interpretations underline the weakness of structuralist approaches: if the binary aspects of a story are not really very obvious, and scholars cannot agree what they are anyway, there is not much point in having them—they are just as unconvincing as the Oedipus complex in elucidating an unusual story. Or rather, obvious binary aspects are missed because the right amount of the story is not taken: the contrast between fall and redemption in *Oedipus the King* and *Oedipus at Colonus* is absent from these interpretations.[33]

Sociological Perspectives

Since the 1960s, there has been an increase in the interest shown in the gender balance in traditional materials, following agendas of feminism in general, and over the decades, these have served to highlight the role of female characters in folk- and fairy tales, in particular: the emotive quotation from Disney's *Snow White,* "Some day my prince will come," goes a long way to suggesting the frustration of women faced with the stereotyping of a woman's life as predestined to end in marriage, childbearing, and subservience to a husband. None of these messages would come as a surprise to any student of ancient social history, with its emphasis on early marriage and general subjugation of women, at any rate in the eyes of vastly predominant male writers. The fairy tale of the oppressed heroine who becomes the good wife reflects both reality and a self-perpetuation of social control. Perhaps the best available example from the Greco-Roman world would be the case of Alcestis (there is, as far as I know, no ancient surviving version of the Griselda story or of the legend of Lady Godiva). Alcestis presents the woman who sacrifices her own life in substitution for that of her not particularly creditable husband. Scholarship on the heroines of folktale has come a long way in a short time—it has indeed come as far as to challenge the description of heroines and women generally in the descriptions of tales in the Aarne-Thompson index, formulated before the emergence of feminist scholarship.[34] Some conventional scholarship has taken to task the passivity of heroines in very well known tales such as those of "Cinderella," "Snow White," and "The Sleeping Beauty," but such an approach needs a good deal of care[35]: less familiar variants of even the most common heroines often have a much feistier side, like the resourceful

Cinderellas who avoid the advances of their fathers in the variants that begin with a motif of incest.[36] But there has been little scholarship on the feminine heroines of ancient folk- and fairy tale, which is often accorded a very limited existence, though the flourishing scholarship on male views of women in antiquity in general offers plenty of suspicion that the same values could be expected in traditional storytelling.[37] It has to be said that the Psyche of Apuleius' *Cupid and Psyche* is not particularly resourceful (while still capable of, in effect, murdering her sisters), but no feminist reading has yet reached the Cinderella-like story of Aspasia of Phocaea, who knows how to deal with even the King of Persia when he tries to touch her breasts.[38] Nor has it, to my knowledge, reached the version in Strabo, where Rhodopis is a courtesan before she takes the slipper test[39]: on the one hand, evidence of women degraded and used, but one has to be aware of the ambiguous and often powerful status of ancient courtesans before making a final judgment.

A further avenue for the development of scholarship has explored social relationships in a different way. Marxist critique of literature in general has drawn attention to class struggle and economic background, and this has not failed to impinge even on the fairy tale: the phenomenon of the impoverished hero going from rags to riches is one scenario; occasional hints like the question, in "Little Red Riding Hood," "will you take the paths of pins or needles?" may even refer to the conditions of work of seamstresses. It is worth remarking that stories of the redistribution of wealth do not really preach social justice but just as often seem to advocate that the poor be content with their lot and that changes of fortune, as in tales of a "three wishes" type, is a matter of whim or luck rather than moral desert; indeed, acquisition of great wealth and a good marriage may be attributable to amiable roguery or folk cunning rather than to the dignity of the peasant.[40] Jack Zipes, in particular, has noted the bourgeois preoccupations of the fairy tale and the increasingly commercial mutations of it, and it is not too difficult to extrapolate a message for ancient fairy tales: Rhodopis, in Strabo's early Cinderella tale, could be said to have "done well for herself" and "found her pharaoh," but we might attribute such a viewpoint to little more than an ancient form of our cult of celebrity.

Classical Scholarship without the -isms

In many respects the study of folklore in antiquity has reflected the general history of both classical scholarship and folklore scholarship itself. It has been conducted for over a century in a more or less piecemeal fashion, by classicists without training in folklore and by folklorists with increasingly less training in classical languages and literatures. It will be seen as a recurrent problem that many approaches that could have profited from basic acquaintance with the work of the Finnish School and the full range of classical evidence have found themselves unable to do so, so that solutions and evidence favorable to their own particular views have often been overlooked. It is no surprise, and sadly typical, that an eminent classicist in the mid-1950s triumphantly claims to have noticed that Hackman's monograph on the Polyphemus sage still had its pages uncut in the Bodleian copy in 1953.[41]

The only direct predecessor of the present book, Halliday's *Greek and Roman Folklore* of 1927, reflects not only the very different outlook of the 1920s, but also the marked paucity of supporting study then available. Right up to the present, classicists are more likely to talk almost exclusively of myth (separately from or in combination with "ritual"); provision of folklore as a study remains very limited in the United Kingdom (in contrast with the United States), especially in academic circles. Folklore may occur on the fringes of archaeology or anthropology but seldom as a discipline or complex of disciplines in its own right. Sadly, too, some of the most important resources in the study of folklore-rich texts, the standard commentaries on Pausanias and Ovid's *Fasti* (and notes on Apollodorus), date from the turn of the nineteenth and twentieth centuries and from Sir James Frazer, whose major contribution to the interface between classics, anthropology, and folklore in *The Golden Bough* is now seen to be seriously flawed.[42]

One of the most obvious missed opportunities is in relation to H. J. Rose's *A Handbook of Greek Mythology*.[43] Two chapters, in particular, were relevant to the study of folktale: the title of the first, "Italian Pseudo-mythology," set a tone of condescension. Always, the unspoken assumption seemed to be that myth is the raw material of tragedy and other great literature, whereas folktale, where it is mentioned at all, is almost embarrassingly trivial or beneath notice. In this context the opportunity is consistently dismissed to note materials in Greek mythology which occur in other situations or cultures as "folktale." Rose did turn himself to serious folklore collection in his collaboration with Argenti in the *Folklore of Chios*, but this, too, is seriously handicapped by the failure to key the folktales to the Aarne-Thompson index.[44]

Generations brought up on Rose and his frequent reprintings did not deviate greatly from his own view, and in the tide of revisionism that swept classical scholarship in the 1980s and beyond, the position, if anything, worsened. Dowden, in his eminently sensible *The Uses of Greek Mythology*, is at pains to take the most negative possible view of the Grimm Brothers and in so doing runs the risk of throwing the baby out with the bath water.[45] Obvious constituents of folklore like the origins of the *Arkteia* are subsumed under Greek religion, and here, as elsewhere, it is difficult to find reference to folktale in the indexes or references to publications by folklorists in the bibliographies.[46] Those coming from classical scholarship to folklore were likely to encounter folklore studies focused more readily on Vladmir Propp,[47] whose work has generated little reference material, than on the Aarne-Thompson indexes, which have.

A number of bibliographical mischances have contributed to the general picture of confusion. Sydney Hartland's massive treatment of the legend of Perseus unfortunately appeared before the full implications of the historic-geographic method had been worked out[48]; Marian Cox's study of "Cinderella" suffers from the same limitation, and it was not until the 1950s that a study to the standard of historic-geographic monographs appeared.[49] Indeed, on the folklore side, very little ancient material tends to be found, partly because so much ancient material that is relevant is in corners of ancient scholarship (fragments, scholia, and the like) that are likely to remain least accessible to any but the most specialized classicists, and partly because the assumption that most folklore is either of recent origin or indeed recent manufacture means that no one is likely to be looking for it anyway. Ranke's multivolume *Enzyklopädie des Märchens,* still in progress since the 1970s, uses very little ancient material in proportion to what is actually available. Very often, quite standard resources are lacking: a Penguin study of fairy tale mentions a ninth-century Chinese version of "Cinderella" as the earliest known, while an American primary school workbook is able to trace it correctly back at least to Strabo in the first century B.C./A.D.[50] Moreover, a recent British study of folklore, spearheaded by Ronald Hutton, has perhaps unfortunately come firmly down on the side of discontinuity: Hutton stresses that Morris dancing cannot be shown to descend from a prehistoric fertility rite, while Trubshaw provocatively stresses the fragility of oral memory. The result, for them, is continued modification and reinvention, rather than continuity. If folk traditions and folk tales are the invention of the nineteenth century, what hope is there of establishing continuity over the centuries?[51] However, the context of what they are studying is different from that of classical antiquity. They wish to dissipate the romantic twilight that has grown up in New Age movements over prehistoric pagan religion: they wish to oppose arguments of survival based on practically no evidence at all, while classicists must seek to master and understand a huge corpus of ancient material that actually exists and is chronologically fixed, whether or not it can be linked to the folk beliefs and culture of subsequent eras.

It is difficult to characterize the response of classical scholarship to more than a century of views of folklore from radically different quarters. There was a time when a classical education or a training in classical languages could be taken for granted as part of the equipment of any scholar in any field of the humanities. It is important in an altered climate to realize the limitations of access that confront nonclassicists, for whom classical scholarship might suggest little more than Foucault's history of sexuality and a few quotations of Aristotle's *Poetics,* in that order. One is certainly struck by the paucity of mention of folklore as a discipline in the works of many key scholars in the field over the past 40 years or more. Classicists tend to associate folklore with Stonehenge and maypole dancing and little else and look to anthropology, postmodern approaches to just about anything, or mantras of culture and ethnicity to fill the gap. Myth has expanded and folklore has contracted since the loss of momentum in the Finnish School at the end of the 1950s. The world of *Fabula* and *Folklore* as professional journals is closed to most.

THE ISSUE OF "BELIEF"

Paul Veyne once wrote a book entitled *Did the Greeks Believe Their Myths?*[52] The same kind of issue needs to be raised concerning folklore of all sorts.

There are some beliefs that we should not really wish to insist upon: Trubshaw[53] illustrates from actions such as cursing a recalcitrant car or computer: such an action does not mean that we expect to change the behavior of either by means of a mere verbal formula, but it does raise the issue of belief in the broad sense. Did someone in antiquity who buried a lead cursing tablet really believe that it would have any effect? Or was it simply a procedure with some supposed therapeutic value for the person performing the action? How could it persist for so long in the face of rational enquiry or empirical attitudes? A valuable insight is afforded, in particular, by the Younger Pliny on the subject of ghosts; it appears that he writes to his friend Licinius Sura on the problem in a genuine spirit of enquiry: do ghosts have some objective reality, or are they simply the product of psychological causes and so "all in the mind"?[54] Pliny's instances are carefully and "objectively" reported, with a number of precautions taken by a "ghost buster" against becoming the product of his own or other people's fears—and yet, by the end, Pliny is still calling for a second opinion. A similar scenario is constructed some decades later by the satirist Lucian, who, in his *Philopseudes,* ridicules philosophically minded intellectuals for their petty and trivial superstitions, especially in respect to their belief in the supernatural—the array of snake charmers, matchmakers, wizards, and mountebanks that have convinced the intelligentsia are paraded with a fine degree of observation.

A very different opinion again comes from the near-contemporary ficti-tious guests of Trimalchio: on hearing a chilling ghost story they are deter-mined to take what precautions they can against the same thing happening to them; at a popular level, there is no doubt that the spirits of the night are assumed to exist.[55]

CONCLUSION

We can at least hope to set out with some notions of what folklore might be, but we may already have the uncomfortable feeling that we only have someone else's word for it and a description modified with "or so they say." We have a wide variety of approaches offered by a breadth of disciplines over the past two centuries to apply to it. But we should set out with a sense of our own limitations. Many of our available approaches were designed for other purposes and have not fully succeeded even in accomplishing the tasks they were designed for. But we must make a start by asking what sort of witnesses from antiquity are still available to us and how far we think we can trust them.

NOTES

1. "Simmer Water," Briggs (1970), part 2.2.349.
2. Dundes (1965), 1f.
3. Dundes (1965), 8.
4. See, e.g., Petronius, *Satyrica* 44, a telling mixture.
5. For the former, see Mullen (1978); for the latter, see Y. Sabar (1982).
6. Kissing the table when afraid (Petronius, *Satyrica* 64.1).
7. For examples, see Pliny, *NH* 28.22ff.
8. *Works and Days* 780f.
9. Once upon a time, Dio Chrysostom 5.5; shoe-test, Strabo 17.1.33; dog in the manger, Lucian, *Adversus Indoctum* 30.
10. Horace, *Satires* 1.5.51–70, 1.7, 1.2.116–119.
11. See, e.g., Rose (1928), 286–304; Beard et al.'s (1998) index is silent, as is that of Beagon (1992). A welcome exception is Page (1955).
12. Hesiod, *Theogony*; Apollodorus 2.3.2.
13. Kirk (1974), 33.
14. Aarne-Thompson (1961), 901, 937.
15. On orientalizing influences, see Burkert (1992); West (1997); Kramer (1981).
16. On ancient Jewish folklore, see, e.g., Rappoport (1937); Ginzberg (1948).
17. On this tendency, see, e.g., Momigliano (1975).

18. See chapter 10.
19. *Odyssey* 9.116–130.
20. 4.20.7–11.
21. For Arkas in this regard, see Pausanias 8.4.1.
22. Hand in R.A. Georges and M. Owen Jones (1995), 47.
23. R.A. Georges and M. Owen Jones (1995), 1.
24. For a wider hindsight on the ritualists, see Csapo (2005), 132–180.
25. Burkert (1979), 57; (1983), 29–34.
26. Bremmer (1987), 53f, citing *Oedipus Rex* 981f, Plato, *Republic* 571C.
27. Ibid., 52f. But treatment as a folktale by comparative approaches needs to be tried before we dismiss it as a mere "bricolage from various mythical motifs."
28. cf. Sifakis (1992), 36–39.
29. Bettelheim (1976), 246.
30. For the latter example, see Bettelheim (1976), 92.
31. cf. Kirk (1970), 76f.
32. Detienne and Vernant (1978), 284f.
33. For a folkloric interpretation, see chapter 4.
34. Lundell in Bottigheimer (1986), 149–163.
35. Useful résumé of trends in feminist theory in Zipes (2000) s.v. "feminism and fairy tales."
36. cf. Stone in Bottigheimer (1986), 230f.
37. Myth has, by contrast, fared better: we now have monograph treatments of Medea and Circe for a start; see Clauss and Johnston (1997); Yarnall (1994).
38. Aelian, *Varia Historia* 12.1; see Anderson (2000), 29–33.
39. Strabo 17.1.33.
40. For the whole subject in relation to fairy tale, see Zipes (1979). For a brief résumé of further Marxist approaches, see Zipes in Bottigheimer (1986), 237–243.
41. Page (1955), 18.
42. See Frazer 1921; 1898; 1929.
43. 1928, with numerous but insubstantial revisions.
44. Argenti and Rose (1948).
45. Dowden (1992), 6f.
46. e.g., Dowden (1989).
47. Propp (1928–1958).
48. Hartland (1894-1896).
49. Cox (1893); Rooth (1951).
50. Philip (1989), 7; Sierra (1992), 5.
51. e.g., Hutton (1991), 325–341.
52. Veyne (1988).
53. Trubshaw (2002), 99.
54. Pliny, *Ep.* 7.27.1.
55. Petronius *Sat.* 64.1.

Two

Fountains of Tradition: Some Sources of Folklore in Antiquity

Ancient folklore has to be picked up from a varied mix of sources, and it is far from easy to form as full or as comprehensive a picture as it is, for example, for the canon of Greek mythology. Classical authors themselves do not package folklore-rich material so that it can be studied by an alien culture some two millennia later on: it may be simply presented as a puzzle in after-dinner conversation, to add curious facts to a collection, to offer an ethnographic footnote to history, or for some completely random reason. The following short selection of extracts and examples is intended as just that and not as an exhaustive list of folklore sources: their purpose is to alert us to some of the most obvious contexts in which we can expect to encounter folklore and the difficulties of extricating and explaining it.

HESIOD

The earliest dedicated collection of "folk wisdom" from Greek literature is to be found around 700 B.C. in the didactic poet Hesiod. The *Works and Days,* in particular, represents a farrago of traditions centered on "agricultural" operations. Their unique value is that the author offers them as *living* traditions—about the right time or the right way to do this or that in the context of a society devoted to subsistence farming.[1] Wisdom, parables, advice, proverbs, prohibitions, and much else are strung together in what is sometimes almost a stream of consciousness manner, and the very absence of strong literary control reinforces the notion that much of Hesiod's information comes in almost as raw a form as he can provide it. The following mix is fairly typical (742–755)[2]:

> Neither should you cut the withered from the living on the five branches with the glancing steel at a cheerful banquet of the gods,
>   Nor ever place the ladle on the mixing bowl when people are drinking, for a dire fate attaches to it;
>   Nor when building a house should you leave the surfaces rough, lest a cawing crow take up its seat there and croak;
>   Nor must you take anything to eat, or wash when the pot has not been charmed, since that too has a price;
>   Nor must a lad of twelve sit on things not to be moved, for that is no better, and makes him lose his manhood; nor should you allow a twelve-month baby to do so, for that produces the same effect. Nor should a man wash in a woman's water; for that has a terrible effect for a time.

First, we are warned not to cut nails at a sacrifice, probably because this is felt to be an affront to nature and hence to ritual purity: this author's mother's generation strictly maintained the taboo against cutting nails on a Sunday. The placing of the ladle may be less like the superstition of crossing knives than we might assume: it may impolitely indicate that the party is over, as this is the out of use position. The croaking of an ill-omened bird was to be avoided and reflects more extensive superstition relating to roofs: modern Greek practice has associated it with a death within the house. There may well be a notion close to our own conception of hygiene in the treatment of the pot, but we do not know what the charming of the pot actually entailed: nineteenth-century extreme Presbyterian sects tended to be very prescriptive about preparing no food on the Sabbath itself, and taboos could extend to the utensils. The twelve-year-old is not to sit most probably on tombs (rather than altars), and the unmanning is a concern when he is approaching puberty; there is probably a subliminal association with unmanning in the communal use of water, which would exchange the attributes of the sexes.

We should note the cryptic, riddling style of some of the prescriptions: the nail paring is described in truly oracular style, as is the tomb—we are meant to be hearing the dispensing of an awesome traditional wisdom, and we must be careful to avoid bad luck or mischief, especially where loss of masculinity is concerned. We are none the wiser on much of this tiny extract, and Hesiod himself may have been scarcely less so. It is this vagueness and lack of full explanation which might be felt to distinguish what is lore from what is not. In Hesiod's world we are not dealing with any clear system, and tiny taboos are all round us in our daily lives, as often as not detached from any attempt at a fuller explanation.

HERODOTUS AND THE PERIEGETIC TRADITION

Hesiod may assemble a kind of folklore which appears to be part of his real-life environment: he cannot see it from the outside. We have a quantum leap forward when we encounter it in the Greek historian and periegete Herodotus (mid-fifth century B.C.). In a very real sense he is not only the "father of history" but the father of modern ethnography, whose digressions in his history of the Persian Wars led him into an equivalent of what we might see as extended footnotes, particularly on the unfamiliar customs of non-Greek peoples as seen by a curious West Asiatic Greek.[3] Some of these are offered as no more than the intelligent asides of the travel writer, for the most part nonjudgmental, about whatever he finds interesting or unusual: he will offer both "data" and analysis and wishes to get to the bottom of what he does not understand, though he can still respect, from time to time, the taboos of others. Here we can see his approach to the origins of the oracles at Dodona and in Libya[4]:

2.54f

Concerning the oracles of Dodona in Greece and Ammon in Libya, the Egyptians give the following account. The priests of the Theban Zeus said that two priestesses had been kidnapped from Thebes by Phoenicians; they had learned that one had been sold in Libya, the other in Greece. These women they held to have been the first to found oracles in the two countries. When I enquired how they could be so sure of their knowledge, they replied that there had been a painstaking but fruitless search, but that they had only later learned the information they were telling me.

That was what I heard from the Theban priests; the following is the account given by the oracular priestesses of Dodona: they say that two black doves had flown from Egyptian Thebes, one to Libya, the other to Dodona itself; the latter had settled on an oak tree, and spoke with a human voice, telling them that there should be an oracle of Zeus there; the people of Dodona realised that their instruction was divine, and complied with the request. They say that the dove that arrived in Libya instructed the Libyans to set up an oracle of Ammon; this is also sacred to Zeus. My informants at Dodona were the priestesses, the eldest Promeneia, the next Timarete, and the youngest Nicandra; the rest of the temple staff at Dodona agreed with their account.

Herodotus' own interpretation (2.56f.) is an ingenious rationalization: the captive women set up oracles of their own deity (the Egyptian Ammon, thus equated with Zeus); the women's language sounded initially like the twittering of birds, and later, the "doves" spoke with a human voice as they learned to speak intelligible Greek. The dove is black because the woman was an Egyptian.[5] It is the element of analysis that heralds both the awareness of differences between cultures and critical responses to what is being clearly perceived as tradition. Herodotus may not necessarily be right, though at least aspects of his explanation are plausible enough, but he has asked the right *kind* of question about a traditional oddity and on such grounds might be hailed as a father of folklore as well. He is also a folklorist before his time in his care over the description of his sources, though even that has been suspected.[6]

In other cases, what we can recognize as folkloric is presented not as digression, but in what the author regards as mainline narrative history without distinction:

1.34

Croesus had a dream which revealed that [his son] Atys should be killed by a blow from an iron spear. When he awoke and reflected on the dream, he was terrified . . . he removed from the men's quarters the javelins and spears and all such implements used in war, and piled them in the women's quarters, in case any hanging weapon should fall on his son. (The boy is still killed by an iron weapon in a hunting accident not long afterwards.)

The tale belongs with Stith Thompson motif M37 ("vain attempts to escape fulfillment of prophecy"). The specific form of it used here occurs in terms most familiar to us in the fairy tale "The Sleeping Beauty," where the king attempts to thwart his daughter's fate by removing all the spindles in the kingdom—with, of course, the same result, that there will always be one remaining, and its effect will be fatal.[7] The story underlines a preoccupation that runs through much of the folkloric material we can expect to encounter: the scrupulous attempts to avoid ill luck and its inevitable realization when it is so fated.

PAUSANIAS

For Herodotus, such materials gradually reduce as the course of his history gathers momentum. But in the second century A.D., when Greece was part of the Roman Empire, we have a guide who puts local tradition at the center of his overall design.

Pausanias, like Herodotus in his digressions, could be described as a *periegete,* or tour guide[8]: he takes us round mainland Greece, in this instance, region by region, often, but not always, using extant monuments as the prompt to record local myths, legends, and folktales connected with them. Sometimes the material has an obviously civic, official, and authored status, but more particularly, in remote rural areas he is able to point to what he regards as immemorial rites and traditions, and he is particularly outstanding for his reliability. He may be occasionally guilty of erroneous interpretation, but falsehood, propaganda, or forgery are foreign to him, and his value as a folklore resource is enhanced accordingly. He describes what he sees and what is locally said about it. On the whole he is interested in the sacred rather than the secular, a preference that again augurs well for information about folklore. He still believed in the traditional gods and made sacrifices on his own account; he also had a belief in oracles and their connection with divine justice.

The pious objectivity of his makeup is implied in the description of a rain-making ceremony in Arcadia:

8.38.4

If a drought lasts for a long period, and the seeds in the earth and the trees are withering, then the priest of Lycaean Zeus prays in the direction of the water, makes the accustomed sacrifices, and lets down an oak branch on to the spring's surface, but not deep into the water. When he has stirred the water a vapour rises like a mist; and after a short period the mist becomes a cloud, gathers other clouds to itself, and causes rain to fall on the land of the Arcadians.

In spite of his own generally rationalistic style of observation, Pausanias will, however, acknowledge the work of what he sees as magical or demonic forces, as when he notes the deterioration in the appearance of Megalopolis and attributes it to supernatural powers:

4.29.9

It is the nature of human affairs to be turned on end, if the *daimon* has allowed the Messenians to rescue the Arcadians in turn, and still more unexpectedly to capture Sparta.

In the periegetic tradition of Herodotus he can also be critical of claims, as when, for example, he disputes the number of the hydra's heads or modifies the claim that werewolves are still found on Mt. Lykaion (there was only the original one, Lykaon himself); he even suggests that Actaeon's hounds were maddened by rabies, not by Artemis.[9] He was quick, also, to point out that a gigantic skeleton uncovered by an earthquake in Asia Minor could not be the body of Geryon, as local guides had been accustomed to claim. He has a similar complaint at Argos over a local claim to possess the Palladium from Troy, when general consensus had it brought to Italy by Aeneas.[10]

It is typical of Pausanias to offer a tight texture of factual information, with the odd skeptical aside, side by side with apparently genuinely pious reverence, for example, for the mysteries of Eleusis:

> They say that the Rarian plain was the first place ever to have been sown or to have borne crops; hence the custom of using barley-grains from that source, and of making sweet-cakes for the sacrifices. Here you are shown the threshing-floor of Triptolemos, as it is called, and the altar. My dream has forbidden me to write what lies within the sanctuary wall, and the uninitiated clearly should not know about the things they are not allowed to see. They say the hero Eleusis from whom the city takes its name is either the son of Hermes and Daeira the daughter of Okeanos, or others have it that his father was Ogygos. When the ancients had no poem to follow, they made up a great deal, particularly on the genealogy of heroes (I.38.6f.).[11]

In common, however, with the other early Imperial writers noted below, Pausanias lived at a point where the ancient world tended already to be suffering from what we might term information overload. One has a sense, all too often, of serendipitous compilation rather than systematic exposition.

PLUTARCH, GREEK AND ROMAN QUESTIONS

So far, then, wisdom and periegesis. But what of the explanation of specific instances? A few decades earlier than Pausanias, we have two invaluable sources, which bridge the gap between scientific and philosophic approaches to the primitive and the presentation of raw data: the *Greek Questions* and *Roman Questions* of Plutarch,[12] not only a biographer in his *Lives,* but a scholar and moralist in a large number of short ethical and other treatises, the so-called *Moralia.* The two sets of questions are collections of self-contained *problemata* or *ainigmata* in little more than note form: the vast majority of them concern the explanation of what we should term "raw" lore, as such. Often, several conflicting explanations are offered, with or without any attempt to evaluate them. Plutarch represents a more intellectual and interactive attitude to folklore than does Pausanias.[13] Much of the information may be random, antiquarian, and arbitrary, but that does not prevent attempts to evaluate it:

Greek Questions 2

Who was the woman riding the donkey at Cumae?

The Cymaeans would bring a woman taken in adultery into the market place and make her sit on a particular stone where everybody could see her. Then they would get her to mount a donkey, and after she had been taken round the city, to resume her place on the stone; and in future to continue in her disgrace, with the nickname 'donkey-rider'. And after this they held the stone to be unclean and conducted a purification ceremony.

In this case Plutarch is well informed about the custom and does not have to resort to conflicting interpretation. He does not have to tell us the actual reason for the choice of animal: the donkey was depicted both in literature and art as having lustful associations and an enormous member. The folkloric aspect of the custom in part resides in the conservative nature of the Cumaeans, who clung to an early and savage form of public humiliation (though scarcely the most brutal known in antiquity): the custom emphasizes the community's collective responsibility for morality, and other variants in antiquity were also known.[14] Unfortunately, the two collections as a whole show us a tendency in later antiquity to collect rather than to systematize: Plutarch maintains the spirit of serious intellectual enquiry, but here, at least, the manner of a miscellanist.

PLINY THE ELDER, *NATURAL HISTORY*

Several decades before Plutarch, we have by far the largest amount of folkloric data from any single source in the Elder Pliny's 37 books of *Natural History:* in a sense, this is intended as an antidote to folklore, since this first-century A.D. Roman scholar, antiquarian, and man of letters is setting out to record information on all aspects of the natural world that is as factual, and therefore as scientifically informed, as possible.[15] The author himself takes stances against incantatory medicine (that is, magical healing) as he does against astrology and much else. But he does tend to record information with enormous industry: his nephew, Pliny the Younger, has left an invaluable memoir of his uncle's working methods and of his excerpting "useful" information from any source whatsoever, once more in the manner of a miscellanist or a literary magpie (*Ep.* 3.5); he was an implacable extractor of information and a workaholic in his amassing of material.

The result is that we have an overwhelming and sometimes apparently indiscriminate farrago of information on all manner of subjects relevant to the concerns of folklore, and of course, inevitably, of "fakelore" as well: Pliny is able to quote C. Licinius Mucianus concerning a temple of Dionysus that was capable of flowing with wine[16] or a temple in Lycia where a letter was preserved that had allegedly been written by a Trojan war hero.[17] But it is here that we can hope to find our most concentrated collection of what we ourselves would slightingly call superstitions:

Pliny, *NH* 28.27f.

These matters have been determined by those who believe the gods to be present in all their dealings and at all times, and so they have left the gods reconciled to us, even to our faults. Indeed it has been noted that a gathering suddenly falls silent, but not unless an even number are gathered, and the harmful effect of this report still extends to each person present. Also, food fallen from the hand is not put back on the table at least between the courses, and it has been forbidden to remove it to clean. And there are auguries relating to what people say or think during such an occurrence, and it is particularly inauspicious if it should happen to a priest officially present at the meal; to put food back on the table and burn it in the presence of the Lar is an act of sacrilege. Medicines put on the table by accident before use are said to be ineffectual. Many feel it to be a religious obligation to cut nails on Nundinae Romanae, and to begin with the index finger; but to cut their hair to ensure against hair loss and headache on the seventeenth and twenty-eighth of the month. The peasant custom in many regions of Italy forbids women to turn their spindles as they walk on a journey, or to carry them uncovered, as this gives rise to disappointment in all things, especially in relation to crops. M. Servilius Nonianus, an important figure in the city, was not afraid of eye-strain until he mentioned it himself or someone else spoke to him about it, but hung a piece of papyrus round his neck inscribed with the two Greek letters PA, and tied round with a thread; while Mucianus, three times consul, used for the same reason a live fly in a little white bag; the two declared that thanks to these cures they were always free from eye-strain.[18]

The passage affords a useful illustration of the diversity of matters that can readily come under the label of folklore, ranging from taboos over simple table manners to recurrent superstitions over nail parings and bizarre remedies, not without an allusion to overarching divine (or possibly demonic) involvement. The notion that sudden silence can be harmful may be because demons are able to approach (they are often kept off by loud noises). Occasional modern instances of associating silence and odd numbers are known; it may be that the odd number was potent enough to ward off demons—on the other hand, a widespread primitive notion was that enchantment by the evil eye was most likely to occur during meals.

Evil spirits were thought likely to make malicious use of hair or nails, which, as part of the living person and still growing, have a special status and could be thought, in particular, to control weather magic. The significance of the 17th or 29th of the month would be after full moon or just before the new moon. The taboo on exposing the spindle on a journey may relate to the prophetic or fatal power of women spinners (by analogy with the fates themselves). Apart from the relative objectivity of Pliny (and his perhaps revealing lack of selectivity), we have some sense from so brief an extract of the extent and variety of superstitions and irrational notions and the thought world of folklore reaching even to the highest ranks of society. We shall notice, from time to time, the trust in aristocratic authority for this or that phenomenon or practice: all too often, educated writers are distrustful of those who could have furnished much more detail about popular belief. Those who recorded folklore in antiquity are least likely to be those we should describe as ordinary "folk."

SOME EVIDENCE FROM FICTION

A number of what we might see as fictional sources can be no less instructive. In the course of a sequence of literary character sketches, Theophrastus, a fourth-century B.C. scholar and pupil of Aristotle, offers the following celebrated vignette of the *deisidaimon,* the superstitious man—after suggesting the definition as "cowardice in the face of the supernatural" the author characterizes his subject as follows:

The superstitious man is the kind who if anything pollutes him will wash his hands, sprinkle himself with holy water, put bay-leaves in his mouth, and walk about like this for the rest of the day. And if a weasel runs in front of him, he will not go one more step until someone else overtakes him or he has thrown three stones to the other side of the road. And if he should see a snake in the house, if it is a harmless one, he invokes Sabazios, but if it is poisonous, he sets up a stone to Heracles on the selfsame spot. When he goes past the smooth stones at the crossroads he anoints them with oil from his flask, falls on his knees, and reveres them before he can go on his way. And if a mouse gnaws through a bag of barley, he goes to the expounder of omens to ask what to do; and if he is told to give the bag to the cobbler to stitch it up, he pays no attention, but turns tail and performs a sacrifice to expiate the omen. And he is adept at frequently purifying his house, claiming that something has happened to attract Hecate. And if he hears the hoot of owls as he walks along, he is in a panic, and exclaims 'Athene is greater' and only then passes on. And he does not like to set foot in a tomb, or go near a corpse or a woman in labour, but says he has to avoid pollution. And on fourth and seventh days of the month he tells his household to boil the wine, while he goes out and buys myrtle-berries, incense, and honey-cakes, and comes home and puts garlands on the figures of Hermaphroditus; and when he has a dream, off he goes to the dream-interpreters, the soothsayers, or the interpreters of birds, to ask what god or goddess he should pray to. When he is intending to be initiated he goes to the Orphic initiators month after month, with his wife (or the nurse, if his wife is too busy) and his children. And I imagine he would be one of those who scrupulously sprinkles himself with salt water on the seashore. And should he ever see Hecate's offerings at the crossroads garlanded with garlic, he goes off, thoroughly washes his head, and calls in a wise woman and asks her to purify him by walking round him with squill or a puppy to sacrifice. And if he sees a mad person or an epileptic, he spits into his bosom with a shiver.

Not only can the great majority of details be supported from other sources,[19] but the author has afforded an entertaining caricature of someone almost unbelievably addicted to the observation of petty taboos. He has also afforded an ethos of the kind of superstitions that might infest the imagination of the man in the Athenian street, as similar modern counterparts do ("avoiding walking under the ladder, he waited for a lucky black cat to cross his path"). An interesting sidelight of the passage is the reference to a whole range of consultants available to interpret the omens and avert any potential bad luck incurred. His authorities range from the relatively reputable Orphic (again, with strong associations with purity, but already derided by Plato), to the wise woman, little more than a fortune-teller. He has to ingratiate himself with any and every deity, including the relative newcomer Sabazius; he needs to flatter Athene as the deity in charge of the (otherwise ominous) owl, which he presumes he has startled; the fourth day is sacred to Hermes, the seventh to Apollo (in whose regard he chews the bay leaves); Hermaphroditus is presumably honored as a son of Hermes; the stone at the crossroads is in honor of Hecate. He is particularly sensitive about potentially ill-omened sights seen en route and so liable to prejudice the outcome of any expedition, hence the throwing of stones against the evil of the weasel or the spitting to counteract an ill-omened human contact. No less revealing is the nuance that his wife may have better things to do with her time than join in the endless round of purifications. One notes, once again, the emphasis on avoidance of bad luck, which far outweighs the acquisition of good: it is fear rather than hope that drives the *deisidaimon,* and that fear is of an obsessive-compulsive kind.

Petronius' *Satyrica* and Apuleius' *Metamorphoses* are able to furnish similar instances, not anthologized in this manner but happening in the context of narrative action in Latin novels of the first and second centuries A.D., respectively. Both authors establish an ambience of the provincial superstition of the lower classes, as viewed by the highly educated and sophisticated observer. The *Cena Trimalchionis,* the central episode in what survives of Petronius' *Satyrica,* furnishes catch songs, games, proverbs, superstitious tales, and the rest—the freedman host Trimalchio himself embodies and perpetuates a whole range of the mannerisms of the *deisidaimon* of half a millennium before, and unsurprisingly, he never listened to a philosopher, as he proudly intends to inscribe on his tombstone, and is defiantly uneducated and prey to any superstition that is going. His freedmen friends are similarly inclined, all of them heavily reliant on the vagaries of luck.[20] The effect, in many cases, is intended by the author to highlight the social embarrassment of more sophisticated guests, but it also illustrates the existence of a lively, popular, and folklorically charged speech among the characters:

Sat. 74.1ff.

As he was saying this, a cock crowed. Trimalchio was thrown by this and ordered wine to be poured under the table, and even the lamp to be sprinkled with undiluted wine. He even transferred his ring to his right hand and said: "This trumpeter didn't give the signal without a reason; for either there should be a fire, or someone in the neighbourhood will be breathing his last—Not one of us I hope! So whoever brings me this informer, he'll have a tip." (The cock is then killed and cooked.)

A rather stranger and part-fictional confection has come down to us from the less familiar thought world of the early third century A.D.: there is a great deal of folklore in Philostratus' quasi-biography of the first-century sage and miracle worker, Apollonius of Tyana:

Philostratus, *Life of Apollonius* 4.11, 4.16

Now Apollonius told his companions to embark, while he himself would spend the night on Achilles' mound. His companions tried to discourage him—for the Dioscoridai and Phaidimoi and the whole company of such disciples were already attached to him: they claimed that Achilles was still dreadful as an apparition; for the people of Troy were convinced of this. But Apollonius reassured them: "I know Achilles well: he is very fond of company. . . . I did not come to converse with Achilles by digging a ditch like Odysseus, nor did I use the blood of sheep as an enticement, but by praying the prayer the Indians say they use to their heroes: "Achilles," I said, "most of mankind declare you are dead, but I do not agree with their account, nor does Pythagoras, the forebear of my own wisdom. If we are telling the truth, show me your own appearance; you would derive great benefit from appearing to me, as you would have my eyes to witness your existence. At that there was a tremor round the mound, and a young man five cubits in height emerged, clad in a Thessalian cloak, but he did not have an arrogant appearance, as some imagine. . . . When I first saw him he was five cubits in height, but he grew to more than twice that height. . . . He spoke to me: 'I am glad,' he said, 'to have met you, since I have long wanted to meet a man like yourself. For the Thessalians have for a long time neglected to make offerings to me, but I do not yet think it right to show my anger against them. . . . I am warning them gently not to violate tradition custom, and not to prove themselves inferior to the Trojans, who . . . make public sacrifice to me and offer me their tithes of fruit, and ask me for a truce with their supplications. . . . So then that I do not reduce the Thessalians to (the fate of the Trojans), serve as my envoy to their assembly on the matter I have raised.' 'I will act as their envoy; it was to save them from ruin that I came to you. But I too have a request to make of you, Achilles.' 'I understand,' he replied 'for you are clearly about to ask about the business of the Trojans. Ask then five questions, on whatever you wish and the Fates approve'. . . . With this and with his final word about the young man from Paros, Achilles departed with a little bolt of lightning, for the cocks were already beginning to crow."

Here we have a complex reconstruction of an encounter between the object of a genuinely attested hero cult and a prestigious holy man who wishes to act as the hero's agent in brokering the renewal of worship rights (under duress).[21] The account is heavily literary, but its hagiographic basis is never in doubt. Underneath a heavily sophistic overlay Philostratus himself is providing propaganda for a local hero cult. The cult itself is attested in nonliterary materials still further afield, in the Black Sea region itself.[22] We are also given one of several detailed descriptions of an act of necromancy, the conjuring up of the dead to produce prophecy (which may, as in this instance, be information about the past rather than the future). The tradition is already present in great detail in the *Odyssey* itself, where Odysseus has received advice on how to communicate with the Otherworld ghosts from the witch Circe in person.[23] The tradition persists throughout antiquity and is still flourishing in fairly similar form in the magical papyri. It receives detailed latter-day description in the chilling scene of the witch Erichtho in Lucan's *Pharsalia*,[24] who activates a corpse to divulge prophecy for the benefit of Sextus Pompeius, or in Heliodorus' description of the witch at Bessa, reactivating the corpse of her own son.[25] Apollonius' actions emphasize the degree of what has been termed performativity in occult practices[26]: professional practitioners, or at least their biographers, enjoy a sense of theater.

The above extracts preserve both a flavor of the forms in which information is to be found in literary sources and some idea of the difficulties involved in interpreting and using the kind of data these sources can provide. Our information is not, of course, confined to those authors whose aims or methods happen to provide us with a rich supply of folklore. Much else, again, comes from others who supply information sporadically or even incidentally: historians, whether or not in the manner of Herodotus, may happen to yield us such invaluable information as a list of portents, as important for the author's own attitude to the list as for the contents it happens to contain.

NONLITERARY SOURCES

There is much emphasis, in any case, in the study of folklore on anonymous sources. Where those are most obviously in play is in often subliterary inscriptions and papyri, which are frequently anonymous or where names mean nothing to us and where the contents are not contaminated by learned or literary mannerisms and inhibitions. Here we can be more confident that people are saying exactly what they mean and not what polite society expects them to say. Such media are especially useful for records of papyrus spells or inscribed curse tablets.[27] Vase paintings and other visual media, whether inscribed or uninscribed, also have something to offer, most notably in supplying versions of well-known myths that are different from those found in the literary versions.[28]

The Archaeological Record

Much of our evidence has no written background at all, but comes from a broad range of archaeological sources, where in many cases, the context as much as the object itself may suggest a clue as to what we have evidence of.[29] Take the case of a mosaic from Brading Villa, Isle of Wight: a god (Iao?) is shown next to a ladder leading up to a house door. Martin Henig takes this to be "an allegory of the straight and narrow ways of God leading to the security of the heavens." There are two griffins depicted on the right of the panel, which he sees as "the demons encompassing man and threatening to destroy him."[30] The other mosaics in the villa have some prospect of establishing at least some context for this one: there is an Orpheus, often depicted with Christianizing associations, and an Ambrosia and Lycurgus, implying that Bacchus looks after his own. A knowledge of the general symbolism of

Gnostic syncretism helps, but all in all, we have to be able to keep an open mind where actual written captions are not provided. Without at least a neb-ulous religious context we should be much more in the dark than we are.

Archaeological evidence in isolation and not depicting anything with a narrative or visual counterpart is a very different matter: a string with a knot in it out of context is scarcely evidence of anything, but in the right context it might well be evidence of magical practice of "binding," either for erotic or more sinister magical purposes. Often, it will take the proximity of a cursing tablet to explain a binding operation or some similar object to confirm it. Sometimes, however, even here we can find the makings of a narrative, as in what seems to be two halves of the same story found around 30 miles apart at Silchester and at Lydney Park in Gloucestershire. The latter site yields a curse tablet of obviously pagan connotation ("To the god Nodens, Silvanus has lost his ring. He has given half its value to Nodens. Do not allow good health among those who possess the name of Senicianus until he brings it right to the temple of Nodens" (tr. D. Ogden)). The Silchester ring seems to be pagan, originally with Venus on the seal, then with "Senicianus, may you live in God" on the loop. The inference is natural enough that the Christian Senicianus (an unusual name in itself) has actually stolen Silvanus' ring and Christianized it. The Christianization was presumably intended as an apotro-paic against the pagan curse.[31] But such conveniently symmetrical evidence is naturally a good deal rarer than we should hope.

On the other hand, much epigraphic material is not too far distinguishable in historical value from literary sources on papyrus, especially where the content is heavily stereotyped. Here is a prohibition against the disturbing of a tomb:

Dittenberger Sylloge 2, 888 (= 3, 1238), *IG* 3.1417.

Near Cephisia, Attica: Appia Annia Regilla, wife of Herodes, the light of the household.

    In the name of the gods and heroes, whoever owns the land [in the future], never remove any of this [i.e., do not disturb the tomb]; and whoever should destroy or remove the carved images and honorific offerings, may his land not bear fruit, nor may he be able to sail the sea, but his family and their prog-eny should come to grief. But whoever guards the site, offers customary hon-ours, and continues to improve it, many blessings are to accrue to him and his descendants. No one is to pollute or damage or break off or destroy the relief and the adornment. If anyone does so, the same curse is to fall on them.

The prohibition against the disturbance of a tomb offers us the real archaeo-logical evidence which would complement ghost narratives of the terrible fate of tomb robbers and other sacrilegious persons at the hands of the dead.[32] In this instance we know a great deal about Herodes Atticus himself, a wealthy and socially preeminent Athenian magnate of the second century A.D. We have complementary literary evidence that he had brought about the manslaughter of his pregnant wife[33] and incurred censure for his obsessive and ostentatious grief on her account: this is much more evidence than we could hope for in the case of the great majority of inscribed curses, a reminder once more of the bias of our evidence as a whole toward the elite and, of course, their susceptibility to the general belief in the practice of cursing.

The Magical Papyri

A rather different world again is implied in a series of subliterary materials on papyri: these deal with magical practice and pose considerable problems of source evaluation. Much of the material is prescriptive: to make a good *daimon,* do the following acts and make the following prayers. Although the materials are anonymous, they are also literate and certainly not the product of, say, illiterate peasants; indeed, many draw on ancient and deliberately learned and esoteric materials. We could, of course, still call them wisdom of a sort:

PGM 1.121–125 (extracts)

Magic to deliver someone, to be said over smoking myrrh.

Let the myrrh smoke on coals and recite the spell.

The spell: "You are Zmyrna [i.e., Myrrh], the bitter and effective one, the one that reconciles people who fight with each other, the one that roasts those who do not recognize the power of love and forces them to love. Everyone calls you Zmyrna, but I call you Eater and Burner of the Heart. I am not sending you far away to Arabia; I am sending you to X, daughter of Y, to serve me against her and bring her to me.

If she is sitting, she may not sit (likewise for talking, approaching, walking, drinking, eating, kissing, enjoying, sleeping). She may think only of me, Z, desire only me, love only me and fulfil my every wish.

Do not enter her by her eyes, nor by her ribs, nor by her nails, nor by her navel, nor by her limbs, but enter her through her soul and remain in her heart and burn her entrails, her breast, her liver, her breath, her bones, her marrow, until she comes to me, Z, to love me and fulfil my every wish.

I urge you, Zmyrna, by the three names Nocho, Abrasax, Tro, and by those that are even more appropriate and more powerful, Kaormeioth, Iao, Saboth, Adonai—to make sure that you carry out my orders, Zmyrna. Just as I am

burning you and you are potent, just so you must burn the brain of X, the
woman I love, burn it completely and rip out her entrails and shed her blood,
drop by drop, until she comes to me Z, the son of A. (tr. H. D. Betz)

The materials constitute folklore in the sense of traditional love magic, as practiced by the end of antiquity and indeed long before in Greek rural tradition of at
least the Hellenistic era (see, for example, the rituals in Theocritus' second *Idyll*).
In spite of the veneer of pretention, it does not greatly differ from the ideology or
indeed the procedure outlined by Lucian in the love magic of *Philopseudes* 14f.,
the comic tale of Chrysis and Glaukias. Of note in this case is the personification
of the Myrrh as though it were a female messenger as well as the tactility, still
more obvious elsewhere, with which the anatomy of the female object of affection is enumerated. The obsessed lover is drooling over his subject.

In the magic materials, there are cases where literary and nonliterary evidence complement one another to a perhaps surprising degree: when Deianira's
nurse in Seneca's *Hercules Oetaeus* waxes eloquent about the powers of her mistress, we tend to attribute the results to typically Silver Age rhetoric[34]:

> Wives often bind their marriages by prayers mixed with magic arts. I have com-
> manded a grove to grow green in the midst of winter frost, and a lightning bolt
> to stand still in mid flight; I have shaken the sea while the wind was still, and
> calmed the swollen waters, and the parched earth has opened with new foun-
> tains; rocks have acquired the power to move; I have torn asunder the gates
> and shades of Hades, and the shades talk when ordered by my prayer; the hell
> hound has been silenced. Midnight has seen the sun and day has seen night.
> Sea, earth and sky and Tartarus are my servants, and nothing maintains its laws
> against my incantations. We will bind him; our spells will find a way.

The boastfulness of the magician empowered with universal control seems to
reflect the kind of boastfulness we routinely find in the magical papyri themselves, where inflated claims to power are the order of the day[35]:

> I am he who shut the double folding doors of heaven and put to sleep the
> dragon whose sight nobody can endure. I stopped the sea, the stream, the flow-
> ing of rivers . . . give me strength, I beseech you, and grant me this favor that,
> whenever I order in my incantation one of the gods themselves to come, he will
> come and show himself to me. (tr. G. Luck)

Other pieces of evidence are even more obviously complementary: if we
have a surviving voodoo doll with the pins still stuck in it, we have archaeological confirmation of the rite of erotic magic known to Theocritus 2 and
Virgil, *Eclogue* 8.[36]

Others, again, however, can be more puzzling and their interpretation more open-ended. Georges and Owen Jones illustrate the changes in the modern depiction of "three wise monkeys" (connected, at times, with the motto "hear no evil, see no evil, speak no evil") and note the changes in the use of the motif over a relatively short period in the nineteenth century. Now, as it happens, we have an equivalent of sorts in antiquity in the form of *genii cucullati* ("hooded spirits"), which often appear as small trios of figurines in Celtic contexts. In this case we have no key, and conjectures are difficult to evaluate. Are they fates? Do they represent the dead? What is their actual purpose? Are they apotropaic, for the warding off of evil? Are they cult objects?[37] In this case we must be cautious: changes in the meaning of the three wise monkeys themselves make it doubly hazardous to use them to interpret the *genii cucullati* in isolation.

CONCLUSION

From this brief sample of major sources for ancient folklore we can form some notion of our own limitations as interpreters. There is, most of the time, no guarantee that any given piece of information will be much older than the date of our source for it, and yet we can find information in late glossaries and scholia that seems obviously authentic and very early indeed in respect to its character and content. Even the most conscientious collectors and compilers of information operate with some degree of bias, as when Pliny the Elder voices his suspicions of Greek medicine, but in any case, compilers are only likely to be as good as their sources. Overall, we are also left with a sense of diffuseness: we have a great many miscellaneous curiosities to handle, but at least we are able to salvage something of the mentality that has put them there.

NOTES

1. Note, in particular, Walcot (1966); West (1978), esp. 3–24 on wisdom literature, 41–59 on composition.
2. For details, see West (1978).
3. For the general character of Herodotus' ethnography, Gould (1989), 86–109; Murray (1987) on oral sources; much of the folklore is collected and discussed in Aly (1921).
4. On the account, Parke (1967), 52–55.
5. cf. Lord (1960), 272; a twentieth-century oral singer sees the scholar Milman Parry traveling from America to Yugoslavia as a gray falcon.
6. Most notably, by Fehling (1989).
7. e.g., Perrault in Opie and Opie (1974), 86: Aarne-Thompson type 410.

8. On Pausanias, Habicht (1985), esp. 141–164; Veyne (1988), 95–102; Alcock et al. (2001), esp. 1–60; for the folklore the six-volume commentary by Frazer (1898) is still invaluable.

9. Pausanias 9.2.3.

10. Pausanias 1.35.7f. (Geryon); Palladium, Casson (1974), 244.

11. Many more examples in Casson (1974), 292–299; cf. Habicht (1985), 65–71.

12. Commentaries by Halliday (1927) and Rose (1924), respectively.

13. For Plutarch's intellectual horizons, Mossman (1997); Russell (1972) remains a classic short exposition.

14. Examples in Halliday (1927).

15. For Pliny's science, French (1994), 230–240; for his place in natural history, French (1994), 240–255; and, in general, Beagon (1992); for folklore, esp. the short commentary of Wolters (1935) on 28.22–29.

16. Pliny, *NH* 2.231, 31.6.

17. Pliny, *NH* 13.88.

18. Detailed commentary by Wolters (1935), ad loc. It is a measure of the concentration of folkloric detail in cc. 22–29 of book 28 *alone* that Wolters's commentary extends to over 120 pages.

19. Commentaries by Jebb and Sandys (1909); Ussher (1960); Steinmetz (1960), ad loc; see also Halliday (1930).

20. Commentary by Smith (1975).

21. For the ambience of the *Life of Apollonius,* see Anderson (1986), 227–239.

22. Hedreen (1991), 313–330.

23. *Odyssey* 10.490–540.

24. Lucan 6.413–587.

25. Heliodorus 6.15.

26. Graf (1997), 16.

27. See chapter 9.

28. The major resource is *LIMC;* Gantz (1993) is detailed on visual sources; for a useful short anthology, see Carpenter (1991).

29. Note Merrifield (1987); Henig (1984), esp. 128–205.

30. Henig (1984), 220f.

31. *RIB* 306; Ogden (2002), no. 187.

32. As embodied in folktales patterned after AT type 366; Anderson (2000), 114f.

33. Philostratus, *Lives of the Sophists* 555f.

34. *Heracles Oetaeus* 452–463. For the supernatural in Seneca's tragedies, see Braginston (1933).

35. From the Paris Magical Papyrus (*PGM* 1.76ff.).

36. On voodoo dolls, see Flint et al. (1999), 71–79; Ogden (2001), 245–260.

37. On the three wise monkeys, see R.A. Georges and M. Owen Jones 141–144; on *genii cucullati,* see Toynbee (1957); O'Neill and Toynbee (1958), 52.3 nos. 4–6.

Three

Passing It On: The Transmission of Folklore

A key part of the study of folklore is the process, or complex of processes, of passing it on. Very occasionally, we have the sketch of a transmission suggested to us[1]:

> I am going to tell you an ancient tale which I heard from a man who was no longer young. For at that time [my grandfather] Kritias, so he said, was close to ninety, while I was round about ten. Now it so happened that it was "Children's Day" at the Festival of the Apatouria. . . . [when Solon was complimented] the old man, as I well remember, was delighted and said . . . "If Solon had completed the tale he brought here from Egypt . . . there would have been no other poet more famous than he." "What was the legend, Critias?" asked Amynadorus . . . "Tell us from the beginning the story Solon told, and how he came to hear it, and who his informants were. . . ." "When Solon travelled to the city of Sais . . . when he asked questions about antiquity of the priests that were best informed about them. . . ."

So begins Plato's telling of the celebrated and still controversial myth of Atlantis, according to Critias who heard it from his grandfather, who heard it from Solon, who heard it from the Egyptian priests, while the (genuine) festival Apatouria has an obvious resemblance to *apate*, "falsehood." Already, we can see an instance of perhaps suspiciously overprecise tradition and the unease it naturally evokes. We must now consider what can be known or surmised about the whole process.[2] Often, the processes of passing on tradition are invisible for the most part, over long periods of time. All too often, the only evidence of it—or indeed, alleged evidence—is the fact that two very similar items, be they stories, material artifacts, children's games, or something else of the kind—turn up widely spaced apart in time, or space, or both, and we are at a loss to explain the resemblance other than through a borrowing of one from the other (or both from a common source).

PASSING THE BUCK

A good illustration of what is at stake is suggested by a game reported for the mid-first century A.D. in Petronius' *Satyrica*[3]:

64.11f

Trimalchio told the boy to get up on his back. Without delay the boy climbed on horseback onto him, and beat Trimalchio on the shoulders with the flat of his hand, calling out with a chuckle "Bucca, bucca, quot sunt hic?" ("Buck, buck, how many [fingers] are there here?")

A commentator on this text in the early twentieth century noted the same game played in Cambridgeshire, with the same or very similar words ("buck, buck, how many am I holding up?"). He could not explain the phenomenon. Here the problem is solved by the collecting of further examples: more cases of the same wording were reported in England (in Yorkshire and Northumberland), and collection in Europe showed that the game is very widely, but not universally, known, in many cases with the same or very similar words. It is reported from England to India, but apparently not in Latvia, Poland, Hungary, Russia, or Finland. This is prima facie a simple matter of diffusion: this was a popular children's game, and the familiar forces that enable children to communicate will have passed the game on within some geographical and/or linguistic areas, but not outside them. How do we know that it did not arise spontaneously anywhere that children play guessing games? Because they will not hit on the words Bucca, Buck, Bock, and so on any more than a typing pool of monkeys typing Shakespeare will hit on "to be or not to be." If a game can spread, so, presumably, can a tale.

One of the major stumbling blocks in studying ancient as opposed to modern folklore is that almost by definition, it is not a living science: it can only be studied as a body of evidence and no longer as a living organism. If any comparison or continuity is to be established with modern folkloristics, we must be particularly cautious about how to treat survivals. Can material survive from antiquity to the present, and if so, what implications must this have for missing links? Georges and Owen Jones suggest a labeling system of survival, continuity, revival, and historical source.[4] For our purposes, each of the first three must somehow entail the evidence of the last. In the case of "bucca bucca" the evidence came to hand from a very large number of modern examples. But what happens to our perception of the probabilities when these are not available?

A debate occurred in the 1970s, when John Henderson challenged the generally received view that a medieval version of "the ass who rescues the lover" by Huon le Roi in Old French must be a very simple story traceable to the first-century fabulist Phaedrus, as reflected in *Appendix Perrotina* 16.[5] The two tales can be paraphrased as follows:

> A poor man and a rich man are rivals for the same girl; the girl is forced to marry the rich man, who hires the poor man's mule to take her to the wedding. The mule bolts back home to the poor man in a thunderstorm, carrying the bride, who promptly marries the poor man instead. (Phaedrus)
>
> An uncle and nephew are rivals for the same girl; the uncle cheats the nephew by winning her father's consent on his own behalf, but the father borrows the palfrey from the nephew: it knows the way home and takes her to the nephew, whom she marries instead. (Huon)

Henderson found himself unable to accept a convincing link because the complex transmission of Phaedrus is not likely to have allowed his version in Latin senarii to have been widely accessible. He discounts that the Old French form could have been derived from a Hellenistic Greek source of Phaedrus, all of 15 centuries before, and he debunks some of the general presuppositions of the Aarne-Thompson method. This was countered by Tom Stinton, who saw no problem in assuming at least some kind of continuity from one version to another and seems to incline slightly in favor of diffusion.[6] How one evaluates such evidence for survivals of ancient tales can rest on our view of the nature and probability of transmission itself. It is indeed feasible that even a real case of a bride being conveyed to her wedding by an ass owned by his poor rival should occur more than once in the natural order of things and that on at least two such occasions the bride is conveyed back to the righteous underdog. But we can just as easily argue that the story is funny and memorable enough to reproduce itself by diffusion (there is at least one other medieval version), both orally and in writing. Can we generalize about other such cases?

In this instance the sheer popularity of fable as a subliterary form should be all that is necessary to ensure *some* kind of continuity of transmission. A similar impasse has occurred over some aspects of the transmission of "Cinderella": it was long assumed that the modern European versions, starting no earlier than

Basile's *La Gatta Cenerentola* in the 1630s, were a far cry from the version recognized in ninth-century China in apparent isolation. But once similar or partial versions begin to be reported for Greco-Roman antiquity, the picture and the balance of evidence starts to change, especially when Strabo reports a very clear case of the slipper test in his tale of Rhodopis at the turn of the Christian era.[7] Nor is time a barrier, especially within the same limited geographical area. The master-thief variant known as "The Poor Man of Nippur" was preserved in a version only edited and published in the 1950s in an Akkadian cuneiform text from Asshurbanipal's library dated to 701 B.C. Yet a form of the same story turned up in an oral version reported from Turkey from the previous decade[8]: this exceedingly complex tale had survived without reference to the cuneiform text for two and a half millennia on end,[9] and a similar tale of survival could be cited for the ancient Egyptian "Tale of the Two Brothers." Those who shake their heads at long stretches of oral memory should acquaint themselves with these cases, in particular that of the Nippur tale, which is irrefutable. A useful indication of speed and duration of oral memory can be adduced from the findings of Iona and Peter Opie in *The Lore and Language of Schoolchildren:* irreverent children's rhymes about the British abdication crisis of 1936 were countrywide within the year; while schoolchildren were telling riddles and jokes familiar in the age of Swift or Shakespeare, and one children's game known to Norman Douglas's informant before World War I is first picked up in the age of Nero.[10] Such cases never guarantee that we can use continuity as the only explanation in every case. But they are indicative nonetheless. It goes without saying that traditions of stable geographical phenomena in a locality are likely to remain constant, as when the modern Libyan Teda tribe preserve a legend about a boiling spring known to Herodotus and the Elder Pliny.[11]

There are a number of ways in which folklore, verbal or material, can be said to survive. It can simply be transmitted from one person to the next, or in the context of a family or other community, from one generation to the next. It can be spread beyond its original confines by invasion, cultural imperialism, or trade, or any combination of the three. It can be transmitted orally or in writing or in some degree of alternation between the two. In the case of Greek and Roman materials we have frequently to raise the question of diffusion of folk materials from the Near East. Where two areas can be shown to have strong links (of trade or military occupation, for example) and are relatively contiguous, then there is a reasonable presumption that survivals, either literary or material, have spread from one to the other. It is perverse to presume that the Babylonians discover the wheel, and that the wheel stops at the boundaries of the Babylonian Empire, and that the Greeks have to wait for a Greek *protos heuretes* ("first discoverer") to rediscover it in

Greece so that it then spreads back to Asia Minor. Yet these are the sorts of implications that result from the facile misapplication of polygenesis, the late nineteenth-century conviction that the same tale was capable of replication under similar cultural conditions. The problem is that polygenesis is tied to a view of cultural evolution that is itself no longer tenable. Of course, instances are regularly cited of fantastic coincidences in the plots of novels, where it is claimed that two writers came up with the same complex plot independently. But such instances are all too frequently tied to questions of plagiarism and profiteering to be taken on trust.

Diffusion Theory

In opposition to polygenesis stands the conviction that folk materials are overwhelmingly likely to have been derived from a common source by distribution. The key premise of the so-called historic-geographic method of folktale transmission held the field from its inception around the turn of the nineteenth and twentieth centuries for some six decades. Folklorists examined both the degree of variation among modern orally collected forms of a tale, co-related these with older forms surviving in written transmission, and on a basis of separative and conjunctive features, set out to find a historical and geographical point from which a reconstructed *Urform,* or archetype, of the tale could have arisen. Since then, the method has been under attack, less in itself than for the fact that the ideal set of conditions in which to operate it are seldom actually there.[12] We tend to find that older forms of any given tale occur randomly, and if they go back to antiquity, they are so anomalous as to be useless in reconstructing an archetype. Or we may find that so many forms of the modern tale are present in antiquity that all we do is displace the *Urform* of the tale farther and farther back in time and never actually reach it.

There are other complications: to the original premises of Krohn and Aarne, the Finnish initiators of the method, Carl von Sydow added the theory of *oikotype,* a strongly established and distinctive local variant of a tale, which does not travel well outside its own tradition area and which may make it very difficult to be certain about the existence of a single unequivocal archetype. Von Sydow also challenged the assumption that tales slowly spread from one community to the next by a sort of steady osmosis and emphasized the likely role of single, gifted performers who might be more mobile and make a sudden difference to the diffusion of a tale. Such complications have eventually encouraged scholars to turn their backs on origins and look for some form of analysis or study that will produce more tangible results more quickly. It must also be emphasized that the method is extremely laborious to conduct and demands painstaking collection of materials from often inaccessible sources and polyglot skills increasingly hard to find in one individual. But that is not a good enough reason for abandoning it.

It should be emphasized that the same material can be literary and folkloric, depending on the circumstances of its transmission. For example, a literary scholar will readily identify "cowards die many times before their deaths" as a quotation from Shakespeare's *Julius Caesar*. As such, it can fairly be described as literary. Yet this author encountered it first as written folklore—in a writing book still surviving in my primary school in the 1950s, in written form, but now anonymized and being transmitted as a moral maxim to young children for their edification. We could say that it had, in the process of complex transmission, *become* folklore. But how did it begin? Did Shakespeare take it from one of his several known literary sources for *Julius Caesar*? If so, was it a genuine dictum of Caesar on the day, correctly reported, and if so again, was he drawing on a popular proverb of the first century B.C.? If this is the case, then this particular saying will have come full circle, popular because of its sheer succinctness and quotability.

TRANSMISSION AND VARIATION

When Odysseus asks Teiresias how to placate Poseidon, he is told to go to where someone mistakes his oar for a winnowing fan (or some such) and there, to offer sacrifice. A classicist in the 1940s heard a version of this from a latter-day wandering sailor on a train: he was to go to where his binnacle was mistaken for a signal lamp, and there, retire (that is, as far from the sea as possible). The story is obviously the same, and indeed, the similarity is so striking that the meaning of the Homeric text is actually clarified by comparison with the modern example.[13] The presumed explanation is less likely to be that this latter-day instance was invented independently: both draw on what was already circulating as a nautical tradition or superstition, and the fact that it is nautical strongly suggests the prospect of its continued history—sailing lore is notoriously conservative and can be conserved and diffused over as wide an area as is covered by sailors.

Very often, in the process of transmission a story can be seen to bifurcate: in the tale of "The Emperor's New Clothes," for example, there is one tradition in which the trickster claims to produce invisible cloth. This goes back at least to a late medieval Spanish tale book of Juan Manuel. The other entails the trickster painting an invisible picture with resemblances to individual royalty, as illustrated by a Renaissance chapbook version of Tyl Eulenspiegel.[14] An ancient version hitherto unidentified is closer to the second than to the first, though there may also be ancient traces of a story where only one out-sider dares to explain the king's impending nakedness to his court.[15] The balance of probability is that the tale is far older in some form or other than the medieval and Renaissance specimens but that the trail cannot be taken much farther without still more examples from antiquity. The important point here is rather that both the royal products are luxury items, but may nonetheless be culture-specific.

The question of transmission applies to artifacts as well as words. In a context of the ancient world we only have to think of *terra sigillata* (Samian Ware), a utilitarian terra-cotta product whose progress from its Arretine ori-gin can be traced and dated on its diffusion by way of increasingly local manufacture through the Roman Empire and whose frequency and use can be correlated with such details as the movements of military units. A sim-ilar process of distribution can be shown for distinctive crossbow-shaped brooches in late antiquity.[16] Georges and Owen Jones note similar processes of diffusion for a particularly unusual type of rural American agricultural apparatus.[17] Roger French, on the other hand, is able to demonstrate that some very everyday things, such as names of fish or vegetables, sometimes do not cross the cultural barrier and that larger cultural themes like philosophy only appear to—Greeks can reconstruct Indian philosophy in very Greek terms, but may have no idea of how to identify items of diet perfectly famil-iar as day-to-day items in India.[18] He hints that this may be the reason why the identity of the phoenix still eludes us.

Some contexts provide us with clues as to how some traditions at least could have been passed on. We have a picture in *Odyssey* 8, for example, of how a blind oral reciter could tell stories: the information is as relevant to the telling of traditional tales as it undoubtedly is to the transmission of oral epic. Despite the suspicion of classicists regarding the continuous transmission of folktale, one celebrated analogue to this has gained more or less unquestion-ing acceptance. That is the comparison made from the late 1920s onward in which the American Milman Parry and his disciple A. B. Lord argued that the formulaic transmissions in Homer used a technique that survives in the oral poetry of twentieth-century Yugoslavia. Parry was able to find singers who could recite orally from a stock of material on heroic themes, embel-lishing and varying in a manner that went far toward recreating the kind of performances implied by the performances of Demodocus in *Odyssey* 8. The implications of this for the folk heritage of the Balkans can then be asked: Are the Yugoslav bards with their one-string guslars in some sense the successors of Homer's bards? Do they, in fact, represent a continuous tradition no longer found in Greece but surviving to the north and west? Certainly, the question can be widened. The medieval Turkish corpus known as *The Book of Dede Korkut* represents a repertoire of heroic tales with a number of more or less striking analogues to Homeric material, this time in a prosimetric medium and again with the central presence of a wisdom-laden didactic reciter, the grandfather figure Dede Korkut himself. With a medieval Turkish figure and the modern Yugoslav material we are a step nearer to a continuous history of heroic tradition.

DISCONTINUITY AND SURVIVAL

There is a constant problem in arguing discontinuity of either a traditional story or artifact: if the chronological period in which a tradition is lost is sparsely documented (for example, the Dark Ages following the collapse of the Roman Empire), it is always, on principle, impossible to prove that a tradition has actually died out altogether (though, of course, a pagan custom can be shown to be formally suppressed by Christianity, for example). It may be impossible to show that the story of Rip van Winkle is directly based on, say, the legend of *The Seven Sleepers of Ephesus,* but it is hardly credible to assert that there was a break in the oral belief of someone living long enough in isolation to miss some major political change. (At the same time, cases do again recur in real life: the Japanese soldier who survives decades in the jungle and reemerges to find that the Second World War is over is a credible version of the story.)

The notion of survivals of ancient folklore is sometimes a treacherous one, given the history of the Balkans and the ethnic diversity of its occupiers since the end of classical antiquity. It is unwise to assume that everything similar is proven to be a survival, though the nature of the evidence all too often makes it impossible to prove conclusively that it cannot be so. There is, for example, late medieval mention of a tomb of Zias (Zeus) in Crete: it would be perverse to assume that this is reinvention of a lost classical tradition, given that the idea of Zeus having a tomb was so foreign to the rest of the Greek-speaking world.[19] It might, of course, be the case that this latter tomb represents popular inheritance of a learned tradition (the tomb figured frequently in educated Christian polemic against paganism), but it is no less possible that learned and popular tradition simply survived side by side.

A very clear case of survival in a modern Greek context is the survival of Charon, the ferryman of the Underworld, as a spirit of death as Charos or Charondas.[20] The example is a good one since here, in particular, we are able to note very clearly how literary borrowing of Charon in subsequent European literary heritage differs from the fortunes of the figure that has survived in Christian popular tradition. In literary borrowings the characteristic of Charon as the ferryman of the dead remains constant throughout classical literature, and this is likewise true of Dante and subsequent Italian learned treatments[21]; in the context of a Renaissance literary tradition the Styx can be borrowed along with the boatman who traverses it. But in the world of popular Christian myth the rivers of the pagan Underworld have themselves gone; we now have Charos as a detached embodiment of Death, sometimes on a horse, like the horsemen of the Apocalypse, and carrying off his victims regardless of age. He has now acquired a wife, Charontissa, and he is able to wrestle or jump victoriously against the heroes who resist him. The gloomy abode is still there, in stark contradiction to any Christian notion of the afterlife.

The Golden Fleece and "Panning for Gold"

Sometimes the locations of literary tradition and artifact can be seen to coincide and complement one another. It has been widely noticed by travelers and makers of popular documentaries such as Tim Severin or Michael Wood that golden fleeces are still to be found in the neighborhood of the historical Colchis at the eastern end of the Black Sea: panning for gold is practiced there by gathering gold dust washed down in river flows by means of a fleece, which, accordingly, does indeed become "golden." Here the accusation that the local populace is simply responding to tourist pressure has not been made. The assumption in the Western literary tradition had always been that the fleece was an entirely mythical object (and so in a sense it is, as a symbol of fabulous wealth). It had not occurred to writers on myth to rationalize this until instances from Colchis were actually reported. It is inherently implausible that gold production by this method of "panning" should have been lost, then rediscovered under the pressures of modern media. There is every reason to continue with a traditional local skill because it is economically rewarding. Indeed, this example shows that what is, in fact, a commonplace economic fact becomes fabulous simply by being put in the singular. It is also useful to note a much earlier analogue to the story: in the Sumerian myth of Inanna and Enki, the obstacle flight story associated with Jason is already tied to the idea of technology transfer when Inanna uses trickery to export priceless attributes of civilization from her father's kingdom to her own.[22] At the same time, other cases have to be seen in a different perspective. For example, Daphnis and Chloe dress the shrine of the nymphs, set in a cave with a spring—one thinks reasonably in a British context of the well-dressing customs of Derbyshire. But the relationship is simply the persistence of a very early and widespread custom widely diffused and capable of both survival and revival.

FOLKLORE AND FAKELORE

The whole question of continuity or otherwise is complicated by the concept of fakelore, which looms large in modern discussions of folklore methodology. Some folklore will survive, some continue, some *appear* to offer revival. The nature of the evidence, especially in predominantly oral contexts, is not easy to date: if we take down a folktale from dictation, and the informant says, "I heard this story from my grandfather, and he heard it from his grandfather," then we can date the story a further two centuries back. But how can we be sure that "I heard this story from my grandfather" is not itself part of the tale and a cliché to establish authenticity or a convention to suggest that the story is not really true in the first place? Sooner or later, the short step is made from "there was an old custom in these parts" (to celebrate Mayday, for instance) and "this must have persisted from time immemorial." We are then faced with an unprovable assumption. It has been the signal service of Ronald Hutton as a cultural historian to note the flimsiness of the evidence for the authentic antiquity of so-called New Age cults, which purport to revert to a pre-Christian paganism for which there is very little support from antiquity itself[23]: we are back to the enormous presumptions that are used to support prehistoric matriarchy or execution of seasonal kings that so dominated the era of Frazer and Jane Harrison.

Moreover, we have ample evidence of a good deal of fakelore in antiquity itself. We know enough about the revivalist aspects of Augustan traditional Roman religion and its political motivations for a start,[24] and we have invaluable testimony on a very dubious, though still controversial, cult invented by a resourceful religious entrepreneur in the second century A.D., the cult of the snake oracle Glycon, as presented by Alexander of Abonouteichos.[25] The oracle was, however, successful, and evidence of its successes was widely diffused. It seems not unreasonable to suggest that in this instance, fakelore legitimized itself rapidly into folklore itself.

In some instances we can immediately guess what form fakelore might take, as when aristocrats date their ancestors back to the period of the Trojan War in order to enhance their prestige. In other cases we simply expect assumptions that anything that goes back before one's grandfather's generation must have existed from time immemorial: the human memory accommodates three generations or so back in time at most. A celebrated nod and a wink at fakelore is, as we have seen, offered in Plato's introduction to the story of Atlantis.[26] Similarly, in the *Phaedrus* Socrates is rightly suspected of making up a myth of how Thoth was criticized by Osiris for threatening oral tradition by the invention of writing.[27] There are similarly times when Herodotus' account of chronology and the integrity of historical legend are themselves suspect: in his accounts of Scythian origins, for example, including the Greek account of Heracles in Scythia.[28]

If historians can be suspected, the most popular and potted history can be regarded as more dubious still. In antiquity, as now, we can suspect that temple and site guides will "make it up as they go along," particularly in the matter of displaying what purport to be ancient relics. A catalog of "mythological artifacts" has survived from Lindos in Rhodes: bracelets of Helen of Troy and her drinking cup, in the shape of a breast; other objects attributed to Minos, Cadmus, or Telephus; weapons from Homeric heroes and Heracles; and indeed, nine suits of armor from the Rhodians themselves. Other places boasted Helen's neck ornament and stool (Delphi) and a sandal in southern Italy, with the egg, of course, at Sparta itself. The inventory could be extended to Marsyas' flayed skin (in Asia Minor, as hung by Apollo himself, to say nothing of the tools Epeius used to build the Trojan horse).[29] The fraudulence of at least some is instantly underlined by duplicates elsewhere (Thebes as well as Delphi boasted Helen's stool, though, of course, any real Helen could reasonably have had two). More than one town in Asia Minor claimed to display Iphigenia's sword for sacrificing Greeks, while the statue of Artemis stolen by Orestes was claimed in Greece and Italy, to say nothing of the Palladium in at least five sites. Argos boasted physical remains of Tantalus, whatever might be his fate in the Underworld.[30] Yesterday's fakelore is today's tourism. Rome was preeminent in acquiring memorabilia, from the robe of Servius Tullius in the Temple of Fortune to the ring of Polycrates in the Temple of Concord. Pilgrims or visitors could view the fig tree at the foot of the Palatine where the cradle had overturned containing Romulus and Remus; even the shepherd's hut was pointed out. The site of Troy in the Roman era enjoyed highly privileged tourist guide status: the fig tree outside the Scaean gates could be exhibited, as, of course, could the tombs of Achilles, Ajax, and Patroclus, to say nothing of the cave where Paris conducted the judgment or the site of the abduction of Ganymede.[31]

Other instances of folklore frauds emerge more sporadically. Perhaps most amusing is the case known to Maximus of Tyre, where a fraudster instructed African parrots to tell the locals to worship him as a god, whereupon a cunning wag reprogrammed the birds to reveal the fraud ("X *told* us to tell you to worship him").[32] But preeminent among the fakelore of antiquity (all the more so because of its ambiguity) is the case history of Alexander of Abonouteichos, as reported or misreported by Lucian in the late second century A.D.: for Lucian, this back street nonentity from a tiny hamlet in northern Pontus had perpetrated a fraud by inventing and manipulating a new cult with strongly traditional roots in the form of a healing oracle operated by a good luck–bringing snake god Glycon.[33] Alexander claims descent from Perseus on his mother's side and from the Homeric physician and son of Asclepius, Podalirius.[34] Indeed, he later implied some form of identity—suitably mysterious and ambiguous—with Asclepius himself and could give clients of the oracle accounts of their previous transformations. Not that Lucian himself was above dabbling in fakelore himself, spreading false information about having witnessed an apotheosis of Peregrinus Proteus when the latter immolated himself at the Olympic Games of 165 A.D.[35] Much less explicable than either of these instances was a case recorded in the early third century A.D. by Dio Cassius of a figure who appeared to have reenacted some sort of pilgrimage through the Danubian provinces to Troy with a band of hundreds of followers, apparently reenacting Alexander's impersonation of Dionysus and culminating in nocturnal rites at Troy.[36]

Christian tourism in late antiquity continues the emphasis on finding the exact spot, this time of acts in the Bible rather than Greek myth and folktale— as early as the reign of Constantine himself, the emperor's mother visited Palestine and claimed to discover the true cross. Jerome's friend Paula visited inter alia what was supposedly Abraham's tree and the hut where Isaac's swaddling clothes were shown. The late antique Spanish nun Egeria, on a tour documented in great detail, climbed Mount Sinai to where Moses had received the tablets and saw the burning bush and the rest; she could report a tour not only of the biblical sites themselves, but even a pilgrimage to Edessa to inspect the correspondence, now long discredited, between its ruler Abgar and Jesus Christ.[37]

STORYTELLERS AND THEIR CONTEXTS

But storytelling in the oral tradition entailed much more than the opportunistic yarns of cunning site guides. Some of the best evidence we have for the transmission of folklore is in the widely scattered scenarios and incidental remarks relating to direct oral storytelling and its occasions: the level of "did you hear the one about. . . ?" There is a strong sense of its association with children, either to reward, console, or scare them ("the bogeyman will get you!"),[38] and correspondingly, it is regarded as childish and therefore out of place in a sophisticated adult world,[39] a fact which helps to limit the evidence available to us. And there is a strong sense of its belonging to the less well-educated sectors of society, and in particular, to older women, who might pass it on at the level of the nursery.[40] Professional storytellers could also ply their trade, usually at an unsophisticated marketplace level, though evidence is, predictably, rather limited.[41]

We have a number of instances in Apuleius' *The Golden Ass* of different occasions for oral tales: at an elite dinner party in Hypata in Thessaly a man is politely requested to recount a misadventure from his own experience for the benefit of the first-person narrator, a stranger in these parts:

> And so with the covers piled in a heap Thelyphron propped himself up and reclined half upright on the couch, stretched forth his right arm, and turned his fingers in the manner of orators: he closed the last two and held forth the rest, with a threatening thumb, then rose gently to begin:
>
> "When I was still a young lad I set out from Miletus to be a spectator at the Olympic Games: as I wished to come to this area of the celebrated province, I made my way all over Thessaly and came with ill omens to Larissa. And as my travelling funds were quite run down I looked all over for some way to relieve my poverty, and I saw a tall elderly man in the middle of the forum; he was standing on a rock and declaring in a loud voice that if anyone was prepared to guard a corpse, he should name his fee. . . . (2.21)
>
> The moment Thelyphron had ended his tale, the revellers, deep in their cups, renewed their chuckling. . . . (2.31)

Here we have an after-dinner storyteller telling a lengthy and incredible yarn about witchcraft, lust, and mutilation and functioning as a *gelotopoios,* a joker, with considerable and deliberately delineated panache. The innocent opening has the air of "a funny thing happened to me on the way to the forum," though already with an ominous hint of the horror to come: this is emphatically folktale in performance. The overall context is that of the local Risus festival, or festival of laughter, where a practical joke is to be played on the narrator. It is also quite emphatically to be seen as contemporary urban legend: Thessaly may be conservative in its beliefs in ghosts and witches, but this episode is set in the principal town among an audience of urban elites.

A still more striking example is the social occasion of *Cupid and Psyche* in the same novel: here an old woman who serves as the moll to a gang of robbers is talking to their young female captive who has just had a disturbing dream:

4.27f, 6.24f

"Cheer up, mistress, and don't be afraid of the empty fictions in dreams. . . . But I'll take your mind off them with nice old wives' tales." And she began: "There was a city with a king and queen, and they had three beautiful daughters. But the two elder ones, although they were so very lovely to behold, were thought worthy of mere human praise. But the youngest girl was so amazingly, so superbly beautiful that our poor human tongue could not do her justice. . . .

. . . And so Psyche was duly married to Cupid, and she had a daughter when her time came, whom we call Pleasure." Thus did the raving, drunken old woman tell the tale to the captive girl.

Here we are close to the world of "once upon a time . . . happily ever after" in the tale itself, that of a princess who breaks a taboo and loses her supernatural husband, to regain him after much trial and tribulation. The teller herself describes the tale disparagingly as an *anilis fabula,* an old wives' tale: the tale is told as consolation, just as the Athenian victims destined for Minos' Crete are told stories to keep their spirits up, and the audience, this time, too, is little more than a child.

TRADITIONAL TALES: ASPECTS OF PERFORMANCE

The phrase that best characterizes traditional narratives, long or short, is perhaps "it's how you tell them." Since the 1960s, folklorists have been increasingly interested in the manner of delivery of tales, in contrast to the search for archetypes of content that characterized the historic-geographical method. The work of Alexander Falassi and Linda Dégh, in particular, signaled the change; the focus is not unfamiliar to classicists used to the Parry-Lord descriptions of the informants who provided them with the Yugoslav folk epic.[42] This is, of course, a kind of scholarship where genuine and objective evidence is close to unattainable for the ancient world: we cannot ask Aristides of Miletus how he heard or recited his Milesian tales, for example.[43] But in a number of cases, especially where folktales or other traditional narratives are encased in longer narratives, there will be some account of the speaker and his mannerisms. The two Latin comic novels helpfully supply a number of glimpses, no more, of just such storytellers' mannerisms, as in the following[44]:

Trimalchio looked in the direction of Niceros and said, "you used to be more fun at a party. Now—I don't know why—you're saying nothing, not a word. I'm asking you—make me happy and tell me that adventure that happened to you." Niceros was delighted at his friend's affable approach and replied, "I hope I don't make another penny if I don't jump for joy seeing you in such a good mood. And so just for a laugh, even if I'm afraid those school-masters will laugh at me. Let them look on, I'll tell it anyway. For what do I care who laughs? Better to be laughed at than laughed down." When "thus he had spoken" he began a tale like this:

> While I was still a slave, we used to live on a narrow street; now it's Gavilla's house. There, as the gods will have it, I began to fall for Terentius the innkeeper's wife. . . .

The story proceeds about traveling to see his beloved in the company of a man who turns into a werewolf and ends with, "It's for others to see what they've made of this: if I'm telling a lie, may your guardian spirits be angry with me."

The sophisticated Roman author Petronius has been very careful to characterize his storyteller Nikeros: he is telling the tale for entertainment but is conscious of the intellectual snobbery that better-educated guests are likely to bring to bear on it. He has Nikeros tell the story as if he genuinely believes it, and corroborates it with tiny, trivial detail in a leisurely and discursive style. It does not matter at all to the outcome of the story that Gavilla owns the house now—but that is the loosely associative way people talk. And at the end, as at the beginning, the informant is still defending himself against the skepticism of the sophisticated. We can rarely get closer to the effect of taking a tape recorder into a pub. He interlards the texture throughout with lively speech mannerisms: "as heaven would have it" or "a friend in need is a friend indeed."[45] At the point of metamorphosis into the wolf he has to give us an assurance: "Don't think I'm only joking; I'd rather lose a whole fortune than tell a lie, but as I started telling you, after he changed into a wolf. . . ."

There is also a tailpiece on audience reaction:

63.1ff

> Everyone was thunderstruck in wonder. Trimalchio replied: "Your story's absolutely true! Honestly, I really felt my hair stand on end, because I know Nikeros doesn't talk any nonsense. On the contrary, he's absolutely reliable and never tarts things up. And now I'll tell you a horror story of my own: an ass on the roof! When I still had long hair. . . ."

Here we have the infectious effect of chain storytelling ("that reminds me. . . ."). We can see similar forces at work in a passage of Aristophanes' *Wasps:* here a sophisticated son Bdelycleon is trying to "educate" his father, Philocleon, into telling the "right" repertoire of stories for polite company. The unsophisticated parent falls back on much more earthy material, exposing the snobberies of the next generation as he does so. The point is clear: rudely vigorous folk material is not for the upwardly mobile.[46]

> B: Well then, will you know how to tell proper stories (*logous semnous*) in front of educated, sophisticated people?

Ph.:   I will indeed.

B: So what story would you tell?

Ph.:   No end of them. First of all how the Lamia farted when she was caught; then how Cardopion did his mother—

B: None of your *mythous!* But some human interest stories, the sort we're used to telling at home.

Ph.:   Alright, one that's very homely—"So there was this mouse and this ferret. . . ."

B: "You ignorant lout!" as Theogenes said to the dung-collector, and that was meant as an insult. Are you going to talk about mice and ferrets in the company of grown-ups?

Ph.:   And what sort of stories should I tell?

B: Important ones, like how you were on a state delegation with Androcles and Cleisthenes.

Ph.:   But I've never been on a state delegation to anywhere, except to Paros, and then I only got paid two obols.

B.:   Well, at least you ought to say, for example, how Ephudion fought well in the free-style event against Ascondas, when he was already getting on and grey-haired but still had his huge rib-cage, great arms and flanks, and a marvellous trunk.

Ph.:   Stop, stop, you're talking rubbish. How could he fight free-style carrying his trunk?

B: That's the way the clever people tell stories.

The coarser side of fairy tale, and the animal fable, are for the lout who will show up himself and his son in "proper" society; they also lack the patriotism of the good citizen.

CONCLUSION

It is wise not to lay down too rigid rules for this critical stage in the life of folk material. In the end, little can be proven absolutely in the life of a folktale, where the early examples are few, scattered, and widely varied. But the forces that drive popular material underground and beneath the notice of polite literature are also just as likely to keep it alive. Everyone likes to hear a good story, and few forget to pass it on; with that in mind we should allow the laws of probability to take their course.

NOTES

1. Plato, *Timaeus* 21A–22A. (Partenie 99f.)
2. Illuminating examples of memory from an archaeological perspective are in Alcock (2002), 1–35, 176–183.
3. Data in Brewster in Dundes (1965), 338–368.
4. R. A. Georges and M. Owen Jones 59–89.
5. Henderson (1977), 17–31.
6. Stinton (1979), 432–435.
7. Texts in Anderson (2000), 24–42.
8. Jason (1979), 195.
9. Gurney (1956, 1972); Jason (1979).
10. Opie and Opie (1959), 6, 2; praef. vf.
11. Kronenberg (1955).
12. See, e.g., *JFR* vol. 34 (1997), in particular, Dundes (1997), 195–202.
13. Hansen in Edmunds (1990), 241–272; Halliday (1927), 86f., had actually anticipated the analogy.
14. Juan Manuel, *El Conde Lucanor* 7; Tyl Eulenspiegel 27; Uther in Ranke 7.852–7 (Kaisers neue Kleider).
15. See Anderson (2003), 94f.
16. On *terra sigillata* and pottery in general, see Salway (1981), 641–651; perhaps only here does the great amount of surviving material enable mapping to be done with the quantity of data available, say, for nineteenth-century folktale; on brooches, see Swift (2000), 43–50.
17. On hay derricks, see R. A. Georges and M. Owen Jones 132ff.
18. French (1994), 303.
19. Rose (1959), 139f.
20. Lawson (1910), 100–109.
21. Terpening (1985), 243.
22. e.g., Kramer and Maier (1989), 57–68.
23. e.g., Hutton (2003), 87–135 (among others).
24. e.g., Beard et al. (1998), 1.181–210, on the replacement of Roman religion.
25. Commentary by Caster (1938); see also Jones (1986).
26. *Timaeus* 21A–25D.
27. Plato, *Phaedrus* 575B.
28. Herodotus 4.5–12.
29. These and other examples listed by Casson (1974), 243.
30. Ibid., 243–246, passim.
31. Ibid., 249 (among many further examples).
32. *Oration* 29.4.

33. Lucian, *Alexander*, on which see Jones (1986), 133–148.

34. Lucian, *Alexander* 11.

35. Lucian, *Peregrinus* 39.

36. Cassius Dio 79(80).18.1ff.; for discussion, see Millar (1964), 214–218; Anderson (1994), 2f.

37. Casson (1974), 300–329, passim.

38. Delight, Julian, *Oration* 7.207A, (*LCL* 2.278f.); consolation, Apuleius, *Met.* 4.27; scaring, e.g., Plutarch, *Moralia* 1040B.

39. For the condescension, see Anderson (2000), 9f.

40. Hence the term *anilis fabula* ("old wives' tale").

41. e.g., Dio Chrysostom 20.10.

42. Dégh (1969, 1989); Falassi (1980); esp. Lord (1960), 99–123.

43. For the problem, see Walsh (1970), 10f.

44. *Satyrica* 61f.

45. Ibid., 61.6, *quomodo dii volunt;* 61.9, *in angustiis amici apparent.*

46. *Wasps* 1174ff.; excellent discussion in Edmunds (1990), 2–15, passim.

Four

Traditional Forms: Folktale, Myth, Fairy Tale, Legend

When we approach such categories as folktale, myth, fairy tale, and legend, we are generally confident that we can define the boundaries at least approximately and that we should be able to recognize examples of each when we encounter them. This chapter sets out to define and illustrate these principal genres, but I also suggest that it is not always easy to maintain a consistent distinction between myth and folktale, or between folktale and fairy tale, or indeed, between any such categories and legend. One approach to definition favored by folklorists is in terms of belief: myths are believed; legends carry at least a shadow of doubt; and folk- or fairy tales are felt to be fiction.[1] The problems will come when dealing with actual examples: is an early "Cinderella" to be treated as legend when told by Herodotus without the slipper test and fairy tale when told by Strabo with the test included?[2] We might well say so, but it does not really enhance confidence in the definition system. Ancient myths are nurtured by popular tradition, as urban myths still are; in particular, a good deal of the material collected from religious sites by Pausanias can be readily assigned to either myth or folktale.[3] Another way of approaching the two is to define them in terms of typical content. Perhaps the most simplistic definition would be that myths are concerned with gods, heroes, and society at large, often in an explanatory way, while folktales are concerned with ordinary, usually anonymous individuals. If they are often concerned with magic and the supernatural, they tend to be preoccupied with private concerns, but very often, a tendency is about as much as we can hope to establish.

FOLKTALE

It is probably least controversial to define folktale as "anonymous narrative transmitted in a popular milieu." But whatever our primary definition, there are a number of secondary characteristics that tend to present themselves again and again: we might note the characteristics of the trickster on the whole looming larger in folktale and folklore than in polite literature[4]; the presence of magical themes, especially the use of a magic object as a means of resolving problems,[5] is a motif that we might associate particularly with fairy tale. At the same time we can often note the presence of a simple primitive wisdom element, suggesting a relatively simple cultural origin: folktale heroes may have their wits about them, but they are very seldom city educated or pupils of philosophers, even when society has moved on sufficiently to make them so.

Example: Polyphemus

Some folktales have long been recognized, or at least partly recognized, in an ancient context. The most obvious case is that of Homer's tale of Polyphemus, the cannibal ogre who traps the cunning hero but is blinded by him before the hero escapes, in this case, under a sheep.[6] It is useful to note by comparison with numerous orally transmitted folktale versions what is different about the Homeric version of this in *Odyssey* 9. It is not primarily a matter of scale as such, as still early versions in the medieval Turkish *Book of Dede Korkut* and the Arabic *Third Voyage of Sindbad* are spun out to similar length. There are certain fixed features in the story and a number of variables: when the story is told in isolation, the number of companions can be reduced, or indeed, the hero can act alone, but at least one companion is useful as the ogre's first victim, establishing that he really is a cannibal and that the hero must use his wits to save his own skin. The cannibal's victims may be eaten raw or cooked: the latter circumstance offers an iron roasting spit; the former requires the sharpening of a wooden stake.[7] There are several optional extras: Homer allows Odysseus to give the false name Noman *(Outis)*. This Noman subtheme is so rarely found in later versions of this story as to point to contamination with a completely separate tale, usually transmitted independently. It is only necessary if the one-eyed giant has help that can be summoned and has to be put off by a trick line such as "Noman is hurting me."[8] The Cyclops may offer the hero a ring, which tells the giant where he is, and he must cut off his finger to lose the ring. This is clearly inappropriate to the generally realistic tone of the *Odyssey,* even at its most fantastic, and it is duly omitted.

There are clear literary features to the Homeric working: the story has to be integrated to the overall context of the Trojan War and to the theme of hospitality so central to the *Odyssey;* the Cyclops himself is poignantly characterized by his rapport with the ram, whose underside conceals Odysseus. There is also what seems a calculated decision to imply rather than present the terrifying appearance of the cannibal giant: it is the *Arabian Nights* version that opts for what amounts to a children's bogeyman here.[9] On the other hand, some details self-evidently necessary to the logic of the story are observed correctly in the *Odyssey,* but not always so elsewhere: the same version in the *Arabian Nights,* for example, absurdly allows the hero and his crew to escape from the giant's palace, then simply return again, having found nowhere to hide, in time for still more of them to be eaten.[10]

Even here, we could raise problems of classification. In the first instance we might be tempted to associate the tale with myth because Odysseus is involved, and he is a hero, and myths can be about heroes; it is in the closing stages of the Trojan cycle, which again we are accustomed to classify as myth, though from a historical perspective we might be tempted just as readily to think of it as legend. And then again, we might be tempted to argue that Polyphemus himself is really a son of Poseidon and so belongs once more to myth in his own right. But we still have to take into account the fact that the tale as a whole is also part of the repertoire of international folktale and that in a good deal of the folktale versions the hero is an ordinary folk hero and not the heroic character named Odysseus as such. Furthermore, there is no actual divine intervention required at any point in the tale: this is one part of the *Odyssey* where Odysseus' protecting goddess Athene is not in evidence. And the action of the story does not involve heroism of a normal sort (though Odysseus has obviously kept his nerve throughout); rather is it concerned with typical folktale themes of trickery and cunning.

What, then, can we say about the Polyphemus tale as a whole? We might be tempted to conclude that this is indeed a folktale which has been absorbed into the repertoire of myth, but perhaps this begs a question: Is a particular story deemed to be one thing or the other at least partly on account of its environment? Can we suggest that it is perhaps only convention that makes us classify the Trojan War material as myth in the first place, and could we further ask whether materials seem to look increasingly less "mythical" the further we come from the creation of the universe and the founding of customs into some period close to the present? And on the other hand, if we look at the Polyphemus tale in terms of folktale type, it belongs to a larger category of stupid ogre stories, which run into three figures in the Aarne-Thompson index.[11]

Few folklorists nowadays are likely to take the view that the version in the *Odyssey* is the original: if it had been, we should have expected the Noman theme to appear in a majority of the versions based on it and to be readmitted to the tale by self-correction where it had been lost—this does not really seem to be happening. The general distribution of the oral versions seems to imply a long and well-consolidated process of transmission.[12] When we stand back from the tradition, we can see each of the secondary characteristics already suggested: there is trickster and countertrickster in the battle of wits between the Cyclops and Odysseus; there is a magic object in the ring story; and the cultural level of the story is very simple—it might operate at the level of a contrast between nature and culture, but that is about all.

Example: The Ass Tale

In the case of the Homeric version we can be confident that it would have been performed as part of an actual oral epic and hence as an oral tale in its own right. We have a similar claim to orality in the case of a folktale reported from the other end of antiquity, when St. Augustine claims over a millennium later to have heard the following account[13]:

> For I myself, when I was in Italy, used to hear of such goings-on in one part of the country. They said that women who kept inns, skilled in these evil arts, used to give preparations in cheese to any travellers they wished or were able to, to make them change into beasts of burden and carry any sort of merchandise, and that after the work was done, they resumed their own shape. Nor did they have the minds of beasts, but they still kept their human reason.

Augustine then makes a comparison with Lucius' role in Apuleius' *The Golden Ass*, where a similar but differently motivated experience takes place in Thessaly, a noted center for witchcraft, before adding a further variant:

> For a man by the name of Praestantius used to say that his own father had had that experience: he took the drug in cheese in his own home and lay on his bed as if sleeping, but it had been impossible to wake him. But after some days, Praestantius said, his father woke up, and narrated what had happened to him as dreams. He apparently had become a horse and together with other pack animals he had carried the grain ration for the soldiers. . . . It was ascertained that this had happened just as he described; but all this seemed to him to be just a dream.

The two versions are complementary in a useful way, as the second narrates the pattern of events as they would have appeared to the victim of the magic. Once more, we have a sense of lower cultural level: in the first instance

Augustine cites a version that seems concerned with local superstition and hearsay, once more a magical element, and some sort of trickery. And we might note a possible blurring of categories in the second story: it has very much the feel of a wonder tale or even a ghost/horror story. We also note a mannerism in folklore transmission: the experience does not actually happen to oneself, but to a third party (the "friend of a friend" scenario, where a reporter appears to be once removed from events and so not absolutely responsible for their verification). The foregoing tale and its variant find a well-established earlier parallel in the Circe story in book 10 of the *Odyssey*, though it would appear that adaptation to the rather different medium of the Homeric poem itself has caused a deficient form of the story to be transmitted. No adequate motivation is given in that case for the transformations of Odysseus' crew, who seem simply to be wallowing around the swine pen rather than usefully employed or exploited.[14]

These two instances are immediately recognizable as folktales. There are a great many others, some of them familiar favorites. Type AT 766 deals with the case of Epimenides, as reported by Diogenes Laertius 1.109: the subject goes off, falls asleep for 57 years, and returns to find predictable change. This clearly prefigures the Rip van Winkle story: its most elaborate ancient version is reported in the guise of folk legend as *The Seven Sleepers of Ephesus* in the sixth-century Gallo-Roman hagiographer Gregory of Tours[15]: in both cases the main change is political—just as Rip misses the American Revolution, so the Sleepers miss the conversion of the Roman Empire to Christianity. Some folktales will undergo Christianization, but of a superficial kind, as when AT type 753 has Christ or the devil restore an animal, then a human, by heating in a furnace, boiling, or the like; a second person attempts this, but fails. The ancient secular equivalent is the story of Medea and Pelias: Medea magically rejuvenates a dismembered animal and persuades Pelias' daughters to repeat the experiment on their father, who does not revive.[16] Some traditional tales are perhaps already deceptively enshrined in ancient literary texts. We have noted the role of the *Odyssey* as a container of folktale material as well as that of Apuleius' *The Golden Ass*. Again, AT type 899 (wife substitute for husband's death) is already to be found in Euripides' *Alcestis*, which classicists tend to think of in the first instance as the plot of a Euripidean drama. But it readily emerges as a folktale when compared to tale five of the medieval Turkish *Book of Dede Korkut*, where the Thanatos of the Greek tale is now a Muslim version of an archangel. A number of features of the Greek novel are also readily related to AT types: the motif of the dead woman revived by a grave robber (AT 990) is central to the plot mechanism of Chariton's Greek novel

Chaereas and Callirhoe and also provides a motif in Xenophon of Ephesus' *Ephesian Tale.* Likewise, the tale of Meleager's life as long as a candle lasts (AT 1187) figures as an Ovidian metamorphosis story.[17] Others, again, may be genuinely due to literary transmission: AT type 1419D (two lovers pretend to be a murderer and his fugitive) resurfaces in the seventh day of Giovanni Boccaccio's *Decameron,* having already figured as the Barbarus and Murmex story in Apuleius' *The Golden Ass.*

MYTH

The attempts to distinguish myth from folktale in current usage are a methodological nightmare: this has only a limited bearing on the ancient usage of the Greek term *mythos,* which tends to mean simply a tale, without any certain connotation of its truth. Partly, our perspectives have evolved historically, with nineteenth-century notions of folklore and folktale suggesting primitive survival and some twentieth-century notions of myth suggesting an element of genuine belief; this converges, up to a point, with the idea of myth as largely confined to creation and early etiological stories, but it is hardly practical to press such distinctions.[18] In this case, no definition at all is probably less misleading than one so loaded with qualification as to be practically useless.

Just how convergent myth and folktale turn out to be can be illustrated from the story of Oedipus. This figures automatically in handbooks of Greek mythology, and it might be difficult to find one to suggest that it is not either myth, or legend, or both. The context in which most of us have come to know it is in the two Sophocles tragedies where the hero has the title role: *Oedipus the King* and *Oedipus at Colonus.* The idea that it might better be characterized as something other than tragic myth might offend both literary scholars and many other students of the work across other disciplines. Yet the identity of the Oedipus story as a folktale is not only part of the history of the tale; it is also critical to the interpretation of an international tale type (AT type 931), which has fathered the questionable concept of the Oedipus complex.[19] We have seen in chapter 1 the trail of difficulties that this story has presented to those applying one approach or another. It is time to see whether an awareness of the folktale dimension can throw any light on the matter.

The folktale template might be most clearly seen in the following composite, derived from the widespread modern versions assembled by Lowell Edmunds:

> A child receives a prophecy that if he grows up he will kill his father and marry his mother. He is sent away from his homeland, but accidentally returns and

kills his father during an argument with a supposed stranger (often concerned with looking after a field). He marries the widow, again not recognising the relationship. When the truth comes out he is sent away and imprisoned on an island in the middle of the sea (or some other place); only when a black ram turns white (or after some comparable event) is he finally absolved from his sin; and he can then resume his life.[20]

It is clear from this version that the traditional folktale form of the tale makes it a "death and redemption tale": the Oedipus at Colonus element is an inseparable part of the story, despite Sophocles' treatment of it as a quite separate episode. The key element of meaning in the story is not that we all suppress a subconscious desire to supplant our father and marry our mother; it is rather that destiny is inescapable, and no amount of attempt to avert destiny will succeed in avoiding it, and yet that some prospect of redemption of some kind must be available for someone so innocently burdened with an inescapable doom. Can the folktale versions help us to elucidate earlier episodes in the mythological tradition of Oedipus? The relationship between Oedipus and the "Riddle of the Sphinx" still remains enigmatic,[21] but the nature and context of the riddle itself is itself typically folkloric, as will be noted in the next chapter.[22]

A large number of other Greek myths can be seen very readily in folktale terms, many of them already identified as such, though others not yet so. What is of great interest here is the sort of differences that might occur between a folktale version of a story and the way it might occur in the literary tradition of Greek myth. This is equally the case in the following example.

"Six Around the World" (AT 513A)

A man wishes to marry a certain princess in a far country: he needs first to perform tasks that require a series of six experts: he recruits a man of amazing vision, a man with amazing hearing, and a man who can cover vast distances, etc. to help him in the tasks. They succeed in winning him the princess.

"The Argonautic Saga"

A man wishes to retrieve an object in a far country: he needs first to perform tasks that require specialist help: he comes with fifty experts with amazing powers, which are demonstrated at various points; the king's daughter helps him with the three tasks, and he marries her.

The assembly of a group of experts is clearly identical, but major readjustment has happened elsewhere in the action: it is the king's daughter who performs the tasks, not the experts, who are distinctly underutilized, and she is not the primary motivation for the voyage. Yet it is not because it is either Greek or myth that the versions given by Apollonius of Rhodes or Apollodorus are different[23]; rather, it is because the cultural ambiance of the folktale versions is so much less sophisticated than in the Greek literary versions. The *Book of Dede Korkut* shows the tale as a much more primitive, swashbuckling affair than any of the much earlier Greek versions known to us.[24] And since the pattern of the folktale form is logical, and the traditional Greek mythical form is a confused and illogical blend, it makes sound sense to see the latter as a secondary development.

With so much overlap available, are there *any* tales we should traditionally regard as unmistakably mythological? Take the following etiological tale first encountered as early as Hesiod:

> Zeus was in love with Metis, one of the giants or Titans. She turned into a number of shapes to try to escape his amorous attentions, but finally he caught her and made her pregnant. An oracle of the earth mother warned him that if she became pregnant again, she would bear a son who would depose his father. Zeus decided to avoid this: he opened his mouth and swallowed the girl, child and all. The result was that he himself had a headache, and it was relieved when either Hephaestus or Prometheus split open his head and out came Athena, fully armed.

Now, gods pursuing nondivine or mortal women are a commonplace of Greek mythology: many of the myths are set in a period after the creation of the world but when relationships and distinctions between gods and men have not yet settled down. The warning that Metis will bear a son more powerful than his father is similar to the warning given by Prometheus that Zeus should not marry Thetis because her son Achilles is destined to be more powerful than his father. As to Zeus' swallowing Metis and gaining wisdom, one might think of such an analogy as swallowing a dictionary in order to gain knowledge. Giving birth from the head may perhaps be a relic of creation mythology where gods are not yet fully in human form. Here, however, we have an overall situation which we do not normally tend to encounter in folk- or fairy tale, however we might be expected to account for it. It explains the origin of wisdom in the most simplistic and unnatural way, where the unfashionable word "primitive" still seems appropriate. We seem at last to have found material that can most comfortably and conveniently be described as irreducibly mythical.

Not all myths were recited in ancient literature as part of some attempt to make sense of something else. A good many are retold and reworked for their own sakes or for some purely literary purpose. A good example is the myth of Europa, which belongs to the same group of stories as that of Cadmus below. The skeleton of the story seems to have been firmly enough fixed: Europa was kidnapped from Sidon to Crete by the god Zeus in the guise of a white bull. Few ancient sources pause to discuss any meaning of the myth, whatever it might have been, but there is a great deal of retelling of the story for its own sake or for its picturesque qualities and narrative possibilities. Moschus, Lucian, and Achilles Tatius work it as an idyllic, ornamental story, balancing the embarrassment or the risqué appearance of Europa against the detail of a marine marriage procession extemporized by Eros or Poseidon. Not only do some myths show a great deal of opportunity for literary variation, but they will also occur in a number of variants as well, which seem to be the result not of rewriting and elaboration, but of quite radical redevelopment and remodeling. Take stories of Helen of Troy: most of us are familiar with her part as instigator of the Trojan War because of her elopement with Paris while she was married to Menelaus, but there are many other facets of this versatile lady. She was worshipped as a goddess at Sparta with a tree cult: Was she some local vegetation goddess whose sexual prowess was tied to fertility and growth in nature embodied in a tree?[25] Euripides' *Helen,* however, gives a totally different approach. Helen was not kidnapped by Paris to Troy; he took something to Troy, but it was a false image. He only thought he was sleeping with Helen, while the real Helen was transported to Egypt to be picked up by her husband Menelaus on his way back from Troy, still the perfect faithful wife. This might be radical rewriting of myth by Euripides, to stand the story on its head, but it has something of the flavor of a fairy tale mechanism and a fairy tale ending: we should again do well to suspend judgment.

We must now face the task of making sense of myth overall. It is relatively easy to prescribe convenient definitions that will cover a majority of what any given person is likely to understand by it but very difficult to find a formula that will do justice to the range of meanings that the word "myth" currently commands in English or that the term *mythos* enjoyed within the ancient world. There would be general agreement that some kind of narrative element is involved, that in a myth, something must be told as happening, but that in itself falls very far short of defining the nature of myth. We might also agree that, in general, something less than absolutely literal truth is involved; that myths often but not always entail an element of the explanatory about them; that they involve the doings of gods and/or heroes in the distant past; and that they are somehow distinct from history but may shade imperceptibly into it, as into folktale or legend. A more contentious but, to my mind, true observation is that much depends on usage and cultural context: that it is easier to admit Greek material to be mythical because it is carried in a context of myth than it might be to justify the term myth for materials in at least some other cultures. All this might amount to suggesting that myth is as elastic and subjective a concept as, for example, satire or romance often turns out to be, and in the end we might have to acknowledge that a story with two out of three agreed mythological characteristics would qualify to be called one, at least in the eyes of some.

I should have no doubt about excluding traditions about the English folk hero Robin Hood from myth, on the grounds that there is no divine or explanatory element, while elements not true are easily accounted for as folktale, with perhaps a strong trickster element. It would not surprise me, however, to hear Robin Hood referred to very loosely as a myth or as a mythical figure, though "folk hero" would probably be the most satisfactory term. On the other hand, *Jason and the Golden Fleece,* while much of it is arguably historical or quasi-historical as well as strongly imbued with folktale, I should have no difficulty in accepting as myth by association, even if one were to drop the idea of a golden ram actually flying through the air. The Cyclops story we should find much more difficult. Even although the Homeric version is generally acknowledged as the oldest surviving version, we should be strongly influenced by, to my mind, more authentic versions to see it as a folktale in which divine elements are nonexistent, or nearly so, and explanatory elements not present at all. Yet the mere fact of its presence in the *Odyssey* would be enough for some to allow it to qualify. Only in the case of, say, a master craftsman or a giant spider making the world should we be totally confident of seeing a tale as capable of no other classification than the purely mythical.

Here I am tempted to take issue with a recent and deservedly influential treatment by Ken Dowden, who ties up issues of definition with the characterization of the whole mythological repertoire. For Dowden Greek myth is centered on human relationships; the gods are really secondary, and the Trojan War, with its strong human interest, underlines the fact that Greek myth of any significance is really connected with the legendary fringe of history. This is, for Dowden, the chief of his uses of mythology. To my mind, there is a very strongly Procrustean tendency at work here. Because materials connected with the Trojan War loom large in the work of our exceedingly detailed late mythographer Apollodorus, it is somehow assumed that they are the most significant, and myths dealing with talking animals or the creation of the world are of much less consequence. But we must beware of presuming that what we have represents an authentically proportioned surviving corpus of myth, whereas the kind of creation myths we do have suggest very strongly why later rationalizers would most want to get rid of them: one thinks, in particular, of the Hesiodic origin of Aphrodite from the severed genitals of Ouranos. Another view of the evidence would allow us to say that a small corpus of authentic myth is helped out by semihistorical, semilegendary accretions and that careless usage has promoted the fortunes of Thebes or Troy to occupy a mythical plane to which they are not really entitled. There is also a quite considerable question as to how much of the material we ought to regard as myth is actually Greek at all, rather than merely local variation of an ancient Near Eastern common tradition which is only now being appreciated with any degree of perspective.

FAIRY TALE

Fairy tales have often proved no less elusive to define,[26] except by linking them to standard examples such as "Beauty and the Beast," "Cinderella," or "Snow White." We also tend to think of fairy tales as not much older than the term itself, no older, indeed, than Madame d'Aulnoy's *Contes de Fées* of 1798.[27] I have tried to define the genre elsewhere as "short, imaginative, traditional tales with a high moral and magical content," corresponding to the German term *Märchen* associated with the collection of the Grimms.[28] Fairy tale has proved more difficult to establish in Greek and Latin literature than the other three categories discussed here. Hence, for example, the fact that on neither the classical nor the folklore side is there any very widespread awareness of the extent of ancient Snow Whites or Cinderellas, even when fragments of a novel labeled *Chione* ("snow girl") by its editors is widely known to scholars of the ancient novel. Part of the problem lies in the very limited survival of anything we could think of as children's literature in antiquity. With a child market left to nursery and old wives' tales, there is no corpus of material to be studied. Children could certainly be reared directly on an adult corpus of myths, as is clear from Philostratus' *Eikones,* a series of pictures in a gallery described for a child,[29] and otherwise, we seem to find recognizable elements of familiar modern nursery tales hidden away in unusual mythographers' variants, or scholia to literary texts, rather than assembled in a body that can be directly compared with the corpus put together by Perrault or the Grimms.[30] Consequently, a number of examples can be pointed out that have gone unrecognized, for no better reason than that no one expects them to be there at all. Take the following example[31]:

> King Pyrrhus of Epirus thought he looked like Alexander the Great, and his fawn-
> ing courtiers fell in with his delusion and assured him that this was the case. He
> asked an old woman from Larissa whom she most reminded him of, and she said
> "Batrachion, the Cook, of Larissa." When this man was found, the old woman
> was seen to be telling the truth, and the courtiers were shown up as lying toadies.

Here we have the essential structure of "The Emperor's New Clothes": the contrast between the royal personage who must be flattered by those who wish
to keep their position at court, and the truth-teller who has nothing to lose
because they can never go beyond the bottom of the pecking order. Lucian's
version has effigies of Alexander and others to whom Pyrrhus is compared: this
is reminiscent of the picture gallery variants of "The Emperor's New Clothes,"
where a rogue paints an imaginary picture rather than producing a nonexistent
fabric. Altogether, it is clear that nudity is not the central characteristic of the
story, or possibly the group of narrative jokes to which it belongs.[32] It should, of
course, be asked whether this is really a fairy tale at all. I suspect that only the
accident of its having been retold by Hans Christian Andersen in a predominantly fairy tale collection has caused it to be seen as a kind of honorary fairy
tale, when it might better be regarded as a simple moral exemplum or migratory legend. This example raises the question, How many more such ancient
tales are still unidentified, however we choose to classify them? The following is
perhaps a good deal more difficult to recognize until its very last stages:

Apollonius of Tyana at Corinth[33] (*Life of Apollonius* 4.25)

Among [the disciples of Apollonius] there was a Lycian called Menippus,
a man of twenty-five, of sound judgment and physically well endowed so that
he looked like a handsome, noble athlete. Now Menippus, so most people
supposed, was loved by a foreign woman: she had a beautiful appearance and
a very refined look, and claimed to be rich, although she was really none of
these things but only appeared to be. For as he was walking all alone on the
road to Cenchreae, an apparition encountered him in the guise of a woman,
who clasped his hand and claimed that she had long been in love with him.
She was, she said, a Phoenician woman and claimed that she lived in a sub-
urb of Corinth, naming a particular one. "Come there in the evening," she
told him, "and you will hear me singing and drink wine such as you have
never drunk before, and there will be no rival to bother you; and we shall live
together as two beautiful people." The young man agreed to this, for strong

as he was in everything else to do with philosophy, he was a victim when it came to passion, and he went to her in the evening and from then on paid her constant attention as his lover, not yet realising that she was only an apparition. [Apollonius warns him not to go ahead with the wedding, in vain]. So Apollonius waited for the time of the meal and confronted the guests who had just arrived; "Where," he said, "is the lovely girl who invited you?" "There," said Menippus, and with a blush he made to get up. "And which of the two of you has provided the silver and gold and the rest of the adornments for the banqueting suite?" "The lady," he replied, "for I have nothing else but this," pointing to his philosopher's cloak. . . . [Apollonius continues] "It has no substance, but only the appearance of such. And so that you might be aware of what I mean, this fine bride is an empousa, whom most people think of as lamias and bugaboos. These creatures fall in love, and they have sex, but they desire most of all human flesh and they entice with sexual enticement anyone they want to eat in their feasts." But the apparition said "None of your sacrilegious talk! Get out!" And she pretended to be disgusted at what she heard, and no doubt she tried to make fun of philosophers and claimed that they always talked nonsense. But when the gold goblets and what appeared to be silver were proved to be light as air, and all leapt off out of their sight, the wine-pourers and the cooks and whole staff of servants disappeared. When confounded by Apollonius, the phantom appeared to shed tears and begged him not to torture her or force her to confess her true nature, but when he persisted and would not relax his efforts she confessed to being an empousa and to be fattening Menippus with pleasures so that she could devour his body, for she was in the habit of devouring beautiful young bodies since their blood is uncontaminated.

It might take some time to adjust our focus to what is actually going on in this story: it has the décor of a philosophical tale, or indeed, a hagiographical account, and we might be tempted to rationalize it—a philosopher is trying to tell his pupil that he is the victim of a seductress who is out to drain him dry and who is only after him for his body. But as the tale advances, we realize that this is indeed a vampire story and that Menippus only just escapes her sinking her claws into him. The temptations of the illusory banquet take us to the world of an ancient Hansel and Gretel: the banqueting hall at Corinth is no more and no less than an adult gingerbread house, and the audience really believes in the existence of lamias and hobgoblins. This is a document that belongs firmly to ancient demonology and folklore.

At the other extreme, *Cupid and Psyche* has been cited as a fairy tale, often as if it were an isolated freak that required some other explanation: a synthetic Platonic allegory or an oriental religious mystery text.[34] It is appropriately

recited as an *anilis fabula* by the narrator herself, as the centerpiece of Apuleius'
folk novel, *The Golden Ass:*

> Psyche is a princess with two jealous sisters: she is exposed to be the bride
> of a supposed monster, but is whisked away to a magic palace, where she
> enjoys the favours of an invisible lover, who prohibits her from seeing him.
> She breaks the taboo and finds that he is Cupid; but wax from the candle
> burns him, so that he wakens and departs. Venus finds out and is furious: she
> punishes Psyche with tasks, but the persecuted heroine enjoys the help of such
> folktale helpers as a talking reed; her tasks include the search for the waters of
> life, and like Pandora she is curious to open a baneful box. Jupiter eventually
> acts as a reconciler, Cupid returns, and marriage is duly celebrated.

Such a tale is certainly to be seen as a *Kunstmärchen,* an artistically contrived fairy tale, with deliberately literary purple passages, as when Venus
takes a ride in her celestial car or when Psyche experiences the wonderful palace of Cupid, her unseen "husband." The presentation of Psyche's
initial "wedding," where the girl is exposed at the behest of an oracle for
a rendezvous with a "monster bridegroom" who takes his pleasure of the
virgin "bride" in silence, does not suggest our idea of a children's story, but
the magical world of fairy tale, with its fixation on an ideal marriage of the
princess with the prince and the jealous mother-in-law figure as a rival, all
suggest fairy tale credentials clearly enough.

There has been some dispute over the tale's origin in popular narrative:
Swahn's careful presentation of some 1,200 versions of "the search for the lost
husband" (AT type 425A) seems to me to be hypercritically assailed by Detlev
Fehling, who maintains that the modern tale is not originally a popular story
at all, but a reconstitution of Apuleius based on Fulgentius. But just as some
myths have folktale elements, so it seems perfectly clear that here we have
a popular tale with incidental mythical ornamentation. Jupiter could easily
be replaced by a powerful king or demon, Venus by a powerful witch; all the
other characteristics speak loudly enough of a folktale ethos. Yet the story
certainly does work very clearly on a mythical level. Cupid departs, and fertility and sexual activity ceases so that he has to be brought back: this is fertility
myth, pure and simple. It is not surprising, then, to find two components of
Cupid and Psyche in a Hittite mythical text, as parts of the story of the rather
disruptive god Telepinus; this makes more sense than *Cupid and Psyche* since
the tasks later set for Psyche turn out to be parts of the ritual for getting the
god Telepinus back.[35]

Other ancient fairy tales exist in what seems to me more than embryonic
form: Strabo's version of the story of Rhodopis ends with an unmistakable

slipper test; when combined with Herodotus' version of Rhodopis' story from half a millennium earlier, it suggests that the whole tale we know of as Cinderella was already recognizable by the Augustan era in some form or another. But it is interesting that we have no form of the story presented in the same sort of context as we find *Cupid and Psyche;* rather, we find it presented as history or as Jewish-Hellenistic romance in the story of *Joseph and Asenath.* The role of Rhodopis as a courtesan is clearly incompatible with the tale's presentation as a children's story.[36]

That *Cupid and Psyche* is no isolated specimen should be clear enough, and we should suspect that what survives is only the most frustrating fraction of what is lost. Sometimes we do seem to find no more than fleeting allusion to a lost fairy tale, as when the host at a vulgar Roman dinner party boasts that "the man who was once a frog is now king," an allusion that strongly suggests that the story we know as "The Frog Prince" was already in existence; so in all probability was another tale about a man who found a goblin's cap and went on to find the goblin's treasure.[37] Whatever the problems of classification, there may well have been a great deal more to classify.

LEGEND

Legend is normally understood, in contrast to the previous categories, as having, or appearing to have, some trace of historical basis. Other than that, it can be classified as local or migratory; the former will be confined to commemorating or preserving a tradition of a person or event in one area only, while the latter will do so over more than one site.

A clear example preserved within the canon of Greek myth would be the story of Cadmus, founder of Thebes:

> Cadmus prince of Tyre was sent out by his father Agenor to hunt for his missing sister Europa, after the god Zeus disguised as a bull had carried her off to Crete. After many wanderings he consulted the oracle of Apollo at Delphi and was told to stop looking for Europa, and to follow a cow. He was then to found a city where the cow dropped down. This happened at the site of the future city of Thebes. Unfortunately the land was guarded by a dragon; Cadmus was ordered to kill it and sow the teeth. Armed men sprang up, and by throwing stones into the midst of them Cadmus was able to start a battle in which only a handful remained. After a year of expiation for killing the dragon Cadmus settles at Thebes and introduces writing by means of an alphabet.

We can note a number of different features of this story: Cadmus comes from Tyre in Phoenicia to central Greece, credited with bringing an alphabet. In this sense, there is an element of truth about the tale since the early Greek alphabet does bear a strong resemblance to the Phoenician alphabet. Moreover, Cadmus consults Apollo: this is a regular feature of Greek religious life, in general, and part of the mechanism for the regulation of society since men are expected to act in accordance with the will of the gods. But why should the oracle tell Cadmus to follow a cow? Presumably, the cow would settle where it found the best pasture land. Sowing the dragon's teeth is more difficult to explain, and we are left asking what it might mean: it occurs also in the story of Jason and Medea, where the resulting sown men are dealt with in the same way. But who are "sown men"? We might call them in English "sons of the soil"—native inhabitants—and causing an affray by throwing a stone into their midst would amount to fomenting a civil war. What , then, is the story itself meant to account for? How Thebes came into being, by means of foreign immigration and civil war, in Boeotia, "ox country"? Here, then, we seem to have a reasonably coherent mythologizing of local history: the incoming of a superior, literate culture, whose bearer is able to take advantage of local unrest to divide and rule and take the best grazing land.

Not all legends are quite so readily intelligible: Halliday ties down the tradition of Perseus to an association with the Argolid and with Mycenae[38] and argues for the accretion of fantastic and incredible detail, in the nature and properties of the Gorgon, for example, seeing her destroyer as the center of a hero cult radiating outward from the Argolid. Perseus is the founder of Mycenae, which contains his *heroon;* his cult was echoed in Seriphus, associated with his boyhood. Local folklore explained the silent local frogs as silenced by the hero and abstention from eating lobster because they had been his playthings. There was also a cult center at Tarsus, an Argive settlement: Halliday thought the only trace of other historical detail was the bringing of Andromeda from Joppa.[39] He notes Pausanias' observation of a beehive tomb–type structure at Mycenae as the "tower of brass" and the rocky stones of Seriphus as likely to generate the story of Polydectes and his court as turned to stone. Only the otherworldly Graeae and Gorgons are assigned to fairy tale, as are the magic objects supplied by Hermes for the slaying of the Gorgon.[40] We may here be on rather less secure ground than in the case of Cadmus, but there are at least the makings of a plausible reconstruction.

Local legends may also take the form of etiological tales offered to explain some feature in a landscape: an unusual rock, a flooded village, foundation sacrifice before the building of a building, or the like, a precipice associated with a hero's leap, or a sunken town—one thinks of the story of Philemon and Baucis and the Phrygian flood with which we began.[41] Here arrogance rather than biblical or medieval wickedness causes the devastation. Structures left by former inhabitants of a country may also be related to supernatural builders: giants, devils, fairies, or oriental demons.[42]

MIGRATORY LEGEND

The migratory legend has proved more elusive than the other categories studied so far, if only because the materials for study tend to be more widely diffused, and the same wealth of resources does not yet exist as it does for the international folktale.[43] Patterns of diffusion, if anything, are still more controversial than for "ordinary" folktale. A working definition might be "a story that has attached to a specific quasi-historical character and then adapts on migration to some other place." Once more substantial overlap is to be expected with other categories already discussed.

A useful starting point is a recently studied case, where our earliest example is none other than Odysseus but whose modern bearers are in some sense quasi-historical. Tiresias tells him in the Underworld to make a sacrifice to Poseidon at a place inland where an oar is mistaken for a winnowing fan or similar object.[44] Only when more modern examples are adduced does the purpose of this enigmatic injunction become clear: it is because Odysseus, having found himself farthest from the sea, is then able at last to give up his old life and put an end to all his wanderings.

We find the story told, in particular, in medieval legends of St. Elias founding a church, and the story has been wrenched from a specific figure to a more general one in a story, told by Cedric Whitman, of an old sailor who wanted to retire to where a binnacle was mistaken for a signal lamp. Here the connection with seafaring has been maintained, with its technical nautical reference simply updated, and its wide diffusion is, at least in part, accounted for by the association with the sea: sailors are travelers by definition, and international lore of the sea might be expected to maintain itself indefinitely.[45] The following story from Herodotus seems likewise capable of traveling, perhaps just as widely:

> Three brothers Gauanes, Aeropus and Perdiccas take refuge in a foreign king-
> dom, Lebaea in Macedonia. One tends the horses, another the oxen, a third
> the sheep and goats. The king's wife cooks the food. She notices that for the
> youngest, Perdiccas, the loaf always swells to double the normal size. This is
> reported to the king, who takes it as a portent; the three brothers are ordered
> to leave. But the men claim their wages: the king insultingly offers them the

sunlight that streams in through the smokehole in the roof onto the floor. The youngest scratches a line with his knife round the circle formed by the sunlight, and makes as if to collect it in the folds of his tunic. The king pursues them but they escape, and eventually conquer the whole of Macedonia. Young Perdiccas gives his name to the Royal House.

Here we have a fairly standard tale of the elevation of a youngest son, and so underdog, miraculously marked out for high office, with a trickster motif of taking the symbolic wages to attain a kingdom with different kingship symbols: it echoes the story of the origin of the Scythian kingdom at the beginning of Herodotus, book 4. The whole cultural picture, with the king's wife as baker and the smokehole in the roof, is a very simple and unsophisticated one: yet again, we have the ethos of folk narrative. The fact that the place itself is called Lebaea ("Vessel-ville") suggests the rudiments of a Holy Grail legend, underlined by the familiar enough grail knight name Gauanes (Gawain): only the youngest seeker will inherit the kingdom with the magic vessel.

GHOST STORY

Some categories of tale can cross the boundaries between the major genres outlined above. The ghost story is particularly versatile in its ability to assume or discard realistic or historicizing detail at will. Examples can be cited of the story of the revenant who haunts a haunted house until someone realizes what he wants and gives his exhumed corpse a proper burial.[46] Lucian's *Philopseudes* contains an entertaining variant in a whole collection of supernatural tales, whose folkloric origins can be traced: one is attributed to an actual historical figure, whose statue acts as a kind of policeman, hence historical legend; one features an appearance of Hecate and so could be classified as myth; the sorcerer's apprentice, whose first appearance provides the last tale in the collection, is not here pure folktale but features allusion to an identifiable figure (Pancrates/Pachrates), known to have been active in Egypt in the second century A.D.[47] Perhaps the classic instance of what allows a ghost story to operate is the instance from Cicero,[48] in which a murdered corpse appears to the friend who has failed to protect him and indicates his murderer and where his corpse is hidden. Here we have the essential of ghost stories as we ourselves know them: the "chill factor" in which the unreal or unverifiable supernatural force validates itself in a way that is ultimately beyond explanation.

AARNE-THOMPSON VERSUS PROPP: A CONFLICT OF METHODOLOGIES

Here, then, we should leave our four major categories of storytelling and the various ways we can classify them. I have not hesitated to dwell on the difficulties, and to that end, I note the following puzzle, which looks like a very odd version, or even a conflation, of two tales familiar from Greek mythology but surfacing as an oral folktale in Armenia, recorded in 1915 and running as follows:

> A poor boy has a dream about a beautiful princess, with whom he falls in love. He meets an angel who tells him the only way he can meet her: he is to take a golden bridle given by the angel and put it on a magic horse that will come out of the sea. Having captured the horse he rides till he meets a Tepegoez, a one-eyed giant, who is holding the princess prisoner. The princess tells him that the Tepegoez can only be killed if his eye is put out; and this is duly done in the normal way by means of a red-hot stake. He then rides off with the princess, restores her to her father, and marries her.[49]

What has happened here? We seem to have parts of the Bellerophon story framing the old familiar retelling of the story of the Cyclops. In particular, the idea of the angel giving the hero the golden bridle corresponds to Athena's instructions to Bellerophon as to how to capture Pegasus. We might be tempted to assume that the storyteller here is simply muddled and has split the difference between two old favorites, but the "Third Kalendar's Tale" in the *Arabian Nights* has a hero who spends time among one-eyed men before flying off on a flying horse—we cannot afford to take things for granted. It may be that the Cyclops' princess has dropped out of the Cyclops tale when it was refashioned to fit its place in the *Odyssey.* Whatever the explanation, it is the presence of puzzling hybrids, as they seem in folktale tradition, that gives rise to problems of classification in the first place, and it is in this context that we should consider the problem of competing systems as such.

In the past century a major methodological problem has beset the study of the folktale and the fairy tale in particular, and can scarcely be said to have been fully resolved. Scholars have been struck since the late nineteenth century by the basic similarities (and differences) between versions of different tales and have been much concerned, especially before around 1960, with attempting to trace the diffusion patterns of individual tales. When so many examples had been collected orally only in the nineteenth century, it was difficult to assemble the amount of data necessary to establish any historical perspective. The historic-geographic method evolved by Karl Krohn and his successors set the goal of establishing an archetype, a first form of any given tale, which is then repeated and adapted as it diffuses to reach its present pattern of distribution.[50] Early evidence had to rely on written reports before large collections of oral data became available. These were often able to afford distinct regional features to assist with both the chronology and the geographical patterning and gave rise to a series of monograph treatments of individual tales.[51] The method entailed the indexing of major tale types, and in general, national archives of individual countries have conformed their classification of tales to the type-indexing system developed by Antti Aarne and Stith Thompson in *The Types of the Folktale:* tales are numbered between 1 and 2,500 (with blanks for additional types) in a series of thematic blocks (animal tales, religious tales, stupid ogre stories, jokes and anecdotes, and so on).

Folklorists since the 1960s have pursued a rather different agenda, while a rival method has gained some popularity, generally with those not directly involved with indexing itself. In the late 1920s Vladimir Propp expressed his dissatisfaction with the Aarne-Thompson approach and opted instead for a system emphasizing not the motifs of a tale, but its functions. Propp argued for 31 functions as the basic repertoire for his sample of Russian tales and argued that all fairy tales select from these functions, with the individually numbered functions always falling in the same order. This method remained unknown outside Russia, until an English translation of *The Morphology of the Folktale* in the late 1950s, since which time it has figured as one of the strands in postmodern criticism.[52]

In general, classicists who are serious folklorists, such as William Hansen or Alex Scobie, have used the Aarne-Thompson method; others seem to have convinced themselves that Propp's method is more sophisticated and that it somehow dispenses with the tedium and the atomistic effect of dealing with motifs.[53] I suspect few have seriously concerned themselves with either the close study of Proppian functions, which are scarcely satisfactory as they stand, or with attempts to use the quasi-algebraic notations that Propp attempted to evolve in any manner that can be regarded as constructive.[54] The differences of approach are not just a matter of pedantic labeling, but may actually affect the ease with which we can relate variants to one another (the basic point of the exercise) and the whole way we view a popular traditional tale in the first place.

When we read fairy tales as children, we tend to read the stories as if there is only one possible version of each. We live then in a world where we can confidently tell the difference between "Cinderella" and "Snow White" or between "Jack and the Beanstalk" and "Little Red Riding Hood." But the more fairy tales we read, and the more we read fairy tales collected from different parts of the world, the harder we find it to keep track of how stories develop. We find that bizarre or unusual versions begin to crop up of very familiar tales, and yet "deep down" we can still recognize them (for example, the Grimms' "One-eyes-two-eyes-three-eyes" as a "Cinderella" with ocularly challenged ugly sisters). So how do we make sense of a multiplicity of tales and variants? Are all fairy tales reducible to a formula, and if so, can we find it?

Attempts were already being made in the late nineteenth century to relate fairy tales and draw distinctions between them: Marian Cox produced, in 1892, a collection of 345 different versions of "Cinderella," and now we know well over twice that number. And in 1911, two continental scholars, Bolte and Polivka, began the monumental work of trying to put the Grimms' fairy tales into perspective by comparing other known versions of the tales that occur in the collection. But already, the foundation for a systematic index of folktales was taking shape elsewhere: Antti Aarne produced, in *The Types of the Folktale*, a resource for handling over 2,000 different tale patterns. In practice, not all of these are really full-blown tales: the second thousand tend to fragment into mere jokes and anecdotes, and the first few hundred or so take care of relatively simple animal fables. A substantial subgroup deals with romances rather than fairy tales, where no magic helper tends to be involved, and a large grouping is provided for so-called stupid ogre or stupid devil stories, such as that of Odysseus and Polyphemus. The whole ensemble has the feel of a rather esoteric classified telephone directory: allusion is made under each tale to national folk archives, common in continental Europe, and the number of examples is given of each tale available in each national archive. This can be used to show that a tale is extremely rare in India, but particularly common in Iceland or Lappland. Sometimes this kind of distribution simply reflects the nature of a story: one does not expect Snow Whites in countries where there is never any snow or a "shoe Cinderella" where the natives always walk about barefoot. But in general, one has the feeling that this is a provisional working tool, rather than a final definitive work; one looks forward to the index being revised and expanded as new material is recorded from oral informants and new national tale indexes. There has been a notable problem of selective collecting so that relatively few Near Eastern oriental materials have been linked to the system.

Let us look at an Aarne-Thompson classification of an individual tale, in this case, "Cinderella," types 510/11:

I. The persecuted heroine

    (a1) The heroine is abused by her stepmother and stepsisters; she stays on the hearth and ashes; and

    (a2) she is dressed in rough clothing—cap of rushes, wooden cloak, and so on.

(b) She flees in disguise from her father, who wants to marry her; or

(c) is to be killed by a servant.

II. Magic help

While she is acting as servant (at home or among strangers), she is advised, provided for, and fed

(a) by her dead mother; or

(b) by a tree on the mother's grave; or

(c) by a supernatural being; or

(d) by birds; or

(e) by a goat, a sheep, or a cow.

(f) When the goat (or other helpful animal) is killed, there springs up from her remains a magic tree.

III. Meeting the prince

(a) She dances in beautiful clothing several times with a prince who seeks in vain to keep her, or she is seen by him in church.

(b) She gives hints of the abuse she has endured as a servant girl; or

(c) she is seen in beautiful clothing in her room or in the church.

IV. Proof of identity

(a) She is discovered through the slipper test; or

(b) through a ring. which she throws into the prince's drink or bakes in his bread.

(c) She alone is able to pluck the apple desired by the prince.

V. Marriage with the prince

(A sixth movement applies to a relatively small group only.) There is obviously a working system here, if certainly not a perfect one. The more "Cinderellas" we know, the more easily we might find the need to add extra subsections to each of the five essential steps in the tale; for example, the tale of Rhodopis in Strabo is a "Cinderella" in which the prince does not see the heroine at all before he institutes the slipper test. This is not a failure of the system: it underlines the fact that not enough Near Eastern versions have been collected, where such a motif simply reflects social reality. Also, the system is quite clumsy: the major "Cinderella" variants are indexed under two contiguous types with further subdivision, but there is also cross reference needed to type 480, a kind of "Cinderella," but with a different beginning—two girls go down a well in succession. The good girl meets a witch and treats her kindly; the bad girl is punished for her arrogance; the type then tends to shade into "Cinderella" itself.

What are we to do with all the "Cinderellas" once they have been collected and labeled? We must use them to apply the historic-geographic method by looking at all the versions of the tale that exhibit a distinctive motif and noticing their geographical distribution: if there is a group of "Cinderellas" in the Balkans in which she tells the prince that she comes from Ashville or Coalscuttle Town, we can mark them off as a subgroup; if this group appears nowhere else, we can take this to be a specific, local development, not the original form of the tale; otherwise, we should expect it to be more widely distributed. We can continue along these lines until we have a provisional chronology and some clue as to the constituents of an original version.

We can now turn to the system devised and published by Vladimir Propp in the late 1920s. Propp confessed himself dissatisfied with what he felt was the approximate quality of some of Aarne's analyses of tales and proceeded to analyze a large sample of the Russian fairy tales collected by Afanas'ev in the mid-nineteenth century. On the basis of these he presented a checklist of his 31 functions, of which all the tales he analyzed contained a cross section, *always in the same order:* collectively, these were taken to present a kind of anatomy of the fairy tale (hero encounters villain, hero outsmarts villain, and so on). Nothing happened in any of the tales he analyzed which could not be expressed in terms of one or other of the functions, and so collectively, they offer a matrix for "fairy tale," a master formula or periodic table from which every fairy tale is obliged to select a cross section. In some respects, this might be said to work convincingly and comfortably, as when types are actually sequentially related. If we take *Jason and the Golden Fleece* as basically a fairy tale, the first part ("six around the world") will draw on early functions in the sequence, while its sequel ("girl helper in the hero's flight") will draw on later motifs; if the two are taken together, they will display a larger cross section of the functions.

Propp's view is based on the idea that the main components of a fairy tale are actions rather than objects: in this scheme one does not identify "Cinderella" by the glass slipper but as "hero searches for heroine by means of a token" (or the like): it acknowledges, perhaps more clearly than Aarne-Thompson, the notion of deep structures within essentially mythological material, in a manner which seems to anticipate the Lévi-Straussian structuralists, who turned their attention to myth in the 1950s onward. Put more simply, it fixes its attention on the verbs rather than the nouns.

Propp's system has acquired very considerable acclaim, more from outsiders to folklore than from folklorists themselves, not least because the work was not translated into English until 1958 and so fitted into an analytical climate that can be loosely termed postmodern, where it appeared to play the role of one of many sophisticated analytical tools. It has to be said, however, that not all who have praised or paid lip service to the method have struggled to make it work, which it does rather like Cinderella's shoe to the ugly sisters, especially when applied in direct competition to the Aarne-Thompson method. Here, for example, is a paradigm of Strabo's "Cinderella" applying the nearest Proppian functions:

9 Misfortune or lack is made known: the hero is approached with a request or command; he is allowed to go or he is dispatched (heroine is a mere courtesan without social status).

14 The hero acquires the use of a magical agent (a bird conveys her shoe).

19 The initial misfortune or lack is liquidated (she gains higher social status).

27 The hero is recognized (the heroine's slipper is found in the test).

31 The hero is married and ascends the throne (she marries the pharaoh).

In all fairness to Propp, it has to be said that some of the later functions cover Cinderella's rivalry with the sisters quite well, an element that happens to be inconveniently missing from the Strabo version. But some of the functions do not fit the plot very comfortably, while crucially, the functions do *not* really follow in Propp's rigid order. In some respects the effect is simply to substitute one algebraic language for another, with the decided disadvantage that most folklore archives adopt the Aarne-Thompson system for their indexes, and there is no immediately compelling reason for the enormous labor of converting them.

The central weakness of Propp is the implication that there is only one plot for a fairy tale or folktale, that however we insist on surface difference, tales as disparate as "Cinderella" and "Rumpelstiltskin" are somehow potentially part of one and the same tale complex, if not overlapping variants of one and the same tale. Actual experience of handling tales in bulk suggests that whereas there might be half a dozen or a score of such plots, just as there might be for the stories of Greek tragedy or the surviving repertoire of Greek myth, the idea of a single monomyth is as absurd in practice as it is in theory.

If this were the only fault, we might bear with Propp and feel that he had stumbled on something which we still only vaguely comprehend about the themes of tales. But a still more serious weakness in the eyes of this author is the looseness of some of the functions themselves: the demonstration of parallelisms between variations of a function that Propp gives is unexceptionable (Ivan goes to a far country on some kind of magic conveyance), but it is just as parallel when it occurs in the normal course of Aarne-Thompson analysis, where, in fact, it is much more at home. On the other hand, "hero provides a lack" or the like is so elastic as to make it rather too easy to see parts of a tale as more parallel than they really are.

Advocates of Propp tend to lose sight of the fact that many of the actions labeled as movements in Aarne-Thompson analysis perform as functions themselves. Propp has tried to supplant a tentative but reasonably flexible system with a sometimes sensationally rigid one. But he has neither discovered the DNA nor the periodic table of storytelling and should not be credited with having done so.

CONCLUSION

Such, then, is a tentative view of the main genres we should expect to meet in folkloric narrative. The difficulties of separating them are unsurprisingly reflected in the difficulties of analyzing individual tales according to any universally agreed system. One is reminded of the celebrated Indian tale of the six blind men, who set out to describe the elephant: all accurately describe the part they have felt, but none knows the totality of the elephant in the first place, so that we have six apparently incompatible accounts of the animal's anatomy. So it is with traditional narrative: no one can claim to have ranged over enough of it to produce a universally agreed map projection of the whole.

NOTES

1. For an alternative scheme, see Swann Jones (2002), 8.
2. Herodotus 2.134f.; Strabo 17.1.33.
3. On Pausanias' own levels of belief in his material, see Veyne (1988), 95–102.
4. On the trickster in the ancient world, see chapter 6.
5. For the magical object, see Thompson (1946), 253f.
6. For the Polyphemus story, see Page (1955), 1–20; Mundy (1956); Glenn (1971); Calame (1977); Anderson (2000), 123–131.
7. On the significance of the spit, see Page (1955), 9ff.
8. Hackman (1904), 9–106 (the main tale); 107–154 (Noman).
9. In "Sindbad's Third Voyage," Dawood 130.
10. Ibid., 131.
11. AT types 1000–1199: Polyphemus is type 1137.
12. cf. Hackman (1904), 220ff.
13. *City of God* 18.18.
14. For further discussion of the Apuleius/St. Augustine tales, see Scobie (1983), 258–271.
15. "Canobie Dick," Philip (1995), 241.
16. Ovid, *Met.* 7.297–349; AT type 735, "The Blacksmith and the Devil."

17. Hollis ad. Ovid, *Met.* 8.451; Böemer (1957/58), ad loc; Kakridis (Homeric researches Appendix I) gives 13 modern examples, mainly Greek or Turkish.

18. For the semantics of this problem, see von Hendy (2002), passim; Csapo (2005), 1–9.

19. For recent discussions in a folklore context, see Edmunds and Dundes (1995).

20. For the template, cf. the examples collected in Edmunds (1985).

21. For discussion, see Edmunds (1985), 12f.

22. See *ainigmata* in chapter 6.

23. For a brief discussion, see Anderson (2000), 72–80.

24. *Dede Korkut*, tr. Lewis (1974).

25. For the variants, see Clader (1976); on her divine nature, 63–80.

26. Sometimes classicists have been overprescriptive: Bremmer (1987), 6, insists that fairy tales are unspecific as to time or place, a restriction easily refuted in the case of the Rhodopis story, which Strabo sets in Naucratis, or, for example, Basile's tales of Sapia Liccarda, Zipes (2001), 524.

27. For its history in English, see Opie and Opie (1974), 17f.

28. The best general introduction to folk- and fairy tale remains Thompson (1946). The standard starting point for any tale covered by the Grimms' collections are the five volumes by Bolte and Polivka (1913–1932). An *Enkyklopaedie des Märchens* is still in progress, Ranke (1977–). For the history of printed editions of some best-known fairy tales, see Opie and Opie (1974). There is an excellent collection and analysis geared to the AT index in Hansen (2002).

29. Tr. Fairbanks (1931); commentary by Schoenberger (1968); brief discussion in Anderson (1986), 259–268.

30. Differing perspectives in Anderson (2000) and Hansen (2002).

31. Lucian, *Adversus Indoctum* 21.

32. Brief discussion in Anderson (2003).

33. *VA* 4.25; on the incident, see Scobie (1977), 7–10.

34. Positions usefully summarized in Walsh (1970); Kenney (1990).

35. For a detailed discussion, see Anderson (2000), 61–69, against Fehling (1977).

36. See, once more, Anderson (2000), 27–33.

37. *qui fuit rana nunc est rex; incuboni pilleum rapuisset, thesaurum invenit:* Petronius, *Satyrica* 77.6; 38.8, with the comments of Smith (1975).

38. Halliday (1933), 116f.

39. Ibid., 117–142, passim.

40. Ibid.

41. Ovid, *Met.* 8.617–724.

42. e.g., the connection of Stonehenge with an Arthurian past in Geoffrey of Monmouth and similar lore elsewhere in Arthurian folklore, e.g., Cummins (1992).

43. Motif index in Christiansen (1958).

44. *Odyssey* 11.121–134; Hansen in Edmunds (1990), 239–272.

45. Further examples in Hansen in Edmunds (1990), 242ff.

46. Recent discussion in Anderson (2000), 112ff. (AT type 326A).

47. Further discussion in Anderson (2000), 103ff.

48. Cicero, *de Divinatione* 1.57.

49. C. Downing, *Armenian Folk Tales and Fables*, New York (1972), 168-175.

50. Description in Krohn (1926); Thompson (1946), 396ff., 416ff.

51. Survey in *JFR* vol. 34 (1997), a number largely devoted to the problems and evaluation of motif indexing.

52. Propp (1968).

53. e.g., Griffith in *OCD*, 3rd ed., s.v. folktale.

54. For critical reaction to Propp, see, e.g., Taylor (1964), 114–129; for an overall assessment, see Levin (1967), 32–49.

Five

Folk Wit and Wisdom: From Fable to Anecdote

After the more ambitious and complex tales that constitute folktale, myth, fairy tale, or legend, there are a great many others on a less ambitious scale. Alan Dundes included, beside myths, legends, and folktales, forms as diverse as jokes, proverbs, riddles, chants, charms, blessings, curses, oaths, insults, retorts, taunts, teases, toasts, tongue twisters, and greeting and leave-taking forms among the smaller forms of popularly transmitted folklore, and his list extends much further still.[1] We shall not be able, within the scope of this book, to attempt the collection or even illustration of all of these, but we can offer a sufficient cross section of recognizable forms to note at least their existence in antiquity.

FABLES

Fables and proverbs, in particular, present two overlapping categories of folk wisdom which persisted well beyond the end of antiquity: we might also add riddles into the melting pot of popular culture, and all three forms can acquire value as entertainment as well as wisdom. Fables are perhaps the most familiar kind of popular storytelling in antiquity to us. Yet definition remains elusive.[2] We could suggest that the fable is a short, simple narrative, often with an animal context, containing a lesson for life. We must add "often" because it is easy enough to find materials in the standard fable collections that have neither animal speakers nor even any explicit lesson or moral, and yet their material seems somehow to be in the right place. We also need to underline the expression "lesson for life"; it is not so very often a moral in our sense, like "adultery is morally questionable" or "crime does not pay." It tends, instead, to be a pearl of popular wisdom, often to do with social hierarchy, such as "don't have thoughts above your station," "keep your head below the parapet," or "know how to survive, and you won't get hurt." This sort of wisdom might remind us of materials in the *Book of Proverbs* in the Old Testament and in related literature. It tends to be the common property of a fairly rudimentary community. Sometimes this is reflected in the very coarseness of the subject matter: one thinks of the Sumerian fable of the fox, who relieves himself in the ocean, then proclaims what a great expanse he has filled with his piddle.[3] The Greco-Roman equivalent is more tasteful: the fly riding on the chariot wheel exclaims, "What a great cloud of dust I am stirring up!"[4] We are left with the suspicion that this fable may already have traveled far, even if it has lost some of its crude spontaneity along the way.

We tend to associate fables with a supposed "author" (Aesop) and with a specific type of subject matter (stories of talking animals). All we can really say on this score is that we have fallen heir to a very miscellaneous collection of popular materials and that these are generally associated with Aesop.[5] The fable was early incorporated into literature in some way or other, and more or less literary workings of it persist from Hesiod around 700 B.C. through to the versifying fabulists of late antiquity. Both in elementary rhetorical practice and in poetry, fable was seen to have a literary place and literary possibilities that extended beyond its humble origins.[6] Thanks to many decades of discovery in Asiatic literature, we also have a much clearer notion than was once the case that Aesop does indeed have a long history of predecessors in the literature (and art)[7] of the ancient Near East, and we have also a much clearer notion of the scope of wisdom literature, which is quite clearly not classical in origin.

THE ANIMAL WISDOM FABLE

It is probably in the field of "animal wisdom" that we find our most familiar contact with ancient folklore: in AT 6, "open your mouth and lose your meal" is illustrated by the fox who obtains the cheese from the crow by flattering the latter into singing; one thinks of an elaborate variant in Chaucer's "Nun's Priest's Tale" (once again presented as an orally told tale) or in a more clearly folktale context in Afanas'ev's "The Raven and the Lobster." No less familiar as an ancient animal fable is AT 112, "The Town Mouse and the Country Mouse" (Horace, *Sat.* 2.6; Babrius 108). Some others are indeed so familiar, in both ancient and modern contexts, that they are virtually indistinguishable from proverbs: these would include AT 119B* ("united we stand, divided we fall")[8] (of bulls facing a lion), 123B ("wolf in sheep's clothing"),[9] and the fable of the snail's only trick.[10]

The subject matter of fable may often give some clue as to its age as well. Many of the tales are already living archaisms but keep their place in the repertoire by still remaining intelligible. A substantial proportion are not about an agricultural society at all, but about a society of nomadic hunters, whose preoccupation is the division of spoil (the lion, the fox, and the donkey), though a good many others feature domestic animals, such as sheep and donkeys, and often, their relationship to man (the horse and the soldier). The fable featured by Aulus Gellius about the farmer and the reapers is thus unusual: fields of wheat or barley will normally leave little room for animal dialogue.[11] Simple trades are also featured, as are, occasionally, basic institutions of civilization, such as cities or assemblies, but the canon of fable is virtually closed by the time Socrates is said to be turning Aesopic fable into verse in the *Phaedo* (61B). We rarely, if ever, have fables of schoolmasters or situations which employ literacy: asses may wish to dance, but not to read.[12] Only occasionally do we meet a cultural oddity like the flute-playing fisherman or the smart reply of a camel "not without the muse."[13]

Most Aesopic fables are concerned, then, with a society that still endorses "might is right" or "survival of the fittest." It follows that such a version as "the fox and the cheese" is in that form likely to be much more recent than a version involving fox and meat: the cheese is a man-made product and presupposes a settled pastoral society, where meat can also belong to a world of hunter-gatherers.[14] Many fables, however, do involve the use by animals of relatively advanced human institutions: where animals attend an assembly, we are likely to be looking at a direct metaphor of human activity.

The convention of enabling animals to talk goes far toward defining the genre. It is much older than the Greek world, as testified by a range of Sumerian examples, already arranged in collections in this earliest of documented civilizations. It may owe its existence to an ethos where all of nature is considered animate and equally wise or to a realization, amply confirmed by Greek observation, that animals have both self-preservation instincts and social skills. Animal participants are not the only typical ingredient, however: the fable will expect to impart, either explicitly or implicitly, an element of wisdom, however defined. Sometimes the analogy to men will be quite explicit: Babrius 5 refers to Tanagran cocks "whose valour, they say, is like that of men."

OTHER FABLE TYPES

Sometimes the simple fable collections are stretched to include much more elaborate material than talking animals: take the story presented in Phaedrus Appendix 15, the "Widow of Ephesus." We can justify the inclusion of this merry tale as a fable, in the sense that the basic point is about quick-witted self-preservation: the widow needs to be able to save her lover, the soldier, from execution, and the only way is to offer her husband's body as a substitute corpse. No less appropriate is the tale of the quack doctor, a *bon mot* to a fool.[15] Moreover, men are used, often stereotyped like the animals and often cast in trades as opposed to species, but mythical scenarios can also be introduced, as can plants or even abstracts: the north wind and the sun are combatants to steal the man's coat.[16] But there are many other categories of fable. Most obvious would be stories, whether or not involving animals, that are mythological (and often etiological) in character ("how X came to be Y"). Many such stories are either myths or quasi-myths about origins and often involve Prometheus or Hermes so that they can have a trickster basis. Most prominent of the latter is Babrius' version of the etiological tale of why Arabs are liars (because they hijacked the wagon on which Hermes was delivering lies to all nations).[17]

PREOCCUPATIONS OF THE FABULIST

There is a telling range of preoccupations in the fables: in Babrius 14 the fox tells the bear, "I'd rather you tore the corpse than touch the living": there is always the potential for criticizing the powerful. There is also an emphasis on being fooled and not being fooled—a cock is not deceived by the cat suspended from a peg (Babrius 16): "I have seen many bags before this, but none had the teeth of a live cat"; compare fox and lion, fly and spider, or mice and weasel (Phaedrus 4.2). A further theme is the survival of the little fish captured (small ones slip through) (Babrius 4, cf. Babrius 5: defeated cock doesn't get taken by eagle). Or again, foolish creatures imitate others whose endowments are different: fox and crow, kite imitating a horse (Babrius 73). Many are concerned with learning by bitter experience (the victim of foolishness repents at the last moment with "fool that I was". . . as when the lion learns a lesson from man's "stinging messenger" (the arrow in Babrius 1)). Allegories and etiologies also have free rein at this simplest of levels, as in the confrontation between Truth and Falsehood or War and his bride: the only bride for the god War to marry is Insolence, to whom he is devoted.

Sometimes the moral is quite unambiguous, as in Babrius 13: a farmer kills a crane caught with the storks spoiling his crop (a clear implication of "shun evil companions"). But often enough, the *epimythion,* or added moral, is either editorial, or at least suspected of being so ("the mythos says" in Phaedrus fable 8). Sometimes, again, the moral is not easy to establish: when the fisherman in Babrius 9 pipes the fish and they don't come up to the net, he taunts them that it would be better had they danced when he piped the music. But why? Would they have escaped the net by dancing? Sometimes, too, a quite genuine moral does not really work. Phaedrus tells the story of the ass and the priest of Cybele (4.1) to indicate that ill-fated people are dogged by misery after their deaths. This is obviously untrue, since they cannot feel it. The story only really makes sense as a *bon mot,* or even a sick joke: the ass expected peace in death, but now he receives new blows (when his flayed skin is used to cover a drum).

THEME AND VARIATION

On the whole, fabulists go about their business without further ado. But rhetorical variation and elaboration is not excluded from the genre. Sometimes embellishment is actually a necessary part of the story, as when the ugly slave girl is decked in elaborate clothes (Babrius 11). Sometimes the fable represents a developed mythological dialogue: Babrius (12.7ff.) has the swallow in conversation with the nightingale in the aftermath of the myth of Tereus and Procne: and said the swallow, "Dearest, are you still alive? This is the first I have seen of you since our tragedy in Thrace. Some cruel fate has always intervened to separate us. . . ."

In length the fable represents almost the minimum narrative material and shades almost imperceptibly into the proverb. The expression "dog in the manger" as it stands is not a tale; even in basic narrative form, "a dog refused to allow a horse to eat its fodder from the manger," it still does not have the force of a fable. It needs "so that the horse grew thin and died" before one feels that this is a story rather than a mere statement.[18]

Sometimes, on the other hand, considerable narrative development is possible, as in the story of the frogs who ask for a king. The simple subject only requires the frogs and their two embassies to Zeus, with the consequences of both. But Phaedrus adds inter alia the details that Aesop told the story during the tyranny of Peisistratus to cure unrest that might lead to worse. Still more elaborately, they persuade Mercury to intercede with Jupiter.[19] Sometimes, on the other hand, a tale told in a good deal of detail turns out to be antirhetorical (Babrius 15): the Theban praises Heracles, the Athenian more glibly praises Theseus; the punch line is "Let Theseus be angry with us the Boeotians, and let Heracles be angry with you Athenians" (a variant on the lion and the hare: "a fine speech, but it hasn't got claws and teeth like us").[20]

Each fabulist we are able to study has his own personality. Both Babrius and more especially Phaedrus will add comments in his own person, the latter in somewhat tendentious prefaces; if Babrius is talking in an *epimythion* about the evils of anger, we will be told, "There is some kind of nemesis for anger—may I take care to avoid it!" (Babrius 11.11). Or in Phaedrus the fable of the weasel and the mice is appended to illustrate what usefulness you will find among the petty minded ("the mind knows what care has hidden deep within. . . ."). Indeed, in their interventions the fabulists often reveal a kind of naive moralism that has something in common with that of Aelian. A mention of Socrates in a *bon mot* at Phaedrus 3.10 triggers off: "By the way I am not unwilling to die Socrates' death if only I may attain his fame, and like him, I will endure malice provided my ashes are vindicated"—the two lines clumsily break the flow of the sentence. It is as if the naïve writer feels that spontaneous reverence is called for. The fabulist never strays too far from humble origins and a humble outlook.

There may also be a certain taste for odd detail. In Babrius we find the foolish farmer who sets fire to the fox's tail or the man with the ugly slave mistress.[21] But there is also the possibility of setting fable on a royal road of rhetorical entertainment, as in the following example from Apuleius' *Florida*[22]:

A crow and a fox caught sight of a morsel of food at the same moment and hurried to seize it. Their greed was equal, but their speed was not. Reynard ran, but the crow flew, with the result that the bird was too quick for the quadruped, slid down the wind on extended pinions, outstripped and forestalled him. Then rejoicing at this victory in the race for the booty, the crow flew into a neighbouring oak and sat out of reach on the topmost bough. The fox, being unable to hurl a stone, launched a trick at him and reached him. For coming up to the foot of the tree, he stopped there, and seeing the robber high above him exulting in his booty, began to praise him with cunning words. "Fool that I was thus vainly to contend with Apollo's bird! For his body is exquisitely proportioned, neither exceeding small nor yet too large, but just of the size demanded by use and beauty; his plumage is soft, his head sharp and fine, his beak strong. Nay more, he has wings with which to follow, keen eyes with which to see, and claws with which to seize his prey. As for his colour, what can I say? There are two transcendent hues, the blackness of pitch and the whiteness of snow, the colours that distinguish night and day. Both of these hues Apollo has given to the birds he loves, white to the swan and black to the crow. Would he had given the latter a voice like the sweet song he has conferred upon the swan, that so fair a bird, so far excelling all the fowls of the air, might not live, as now he lives, voiceless, the darling of the god of eloquence, but he himself mute and tongueless." [The crow opens his mouth] and thus lost by his song what his wings had won him, while the fox recovered by craft what his feet had lost him.(tr. H.E. Butler)

The tale culminates in a well-polished *sententia,* after an uninhibited parade of verbal smartness and a display of rhetorical figures, but the actual moral as the basic purpose of the story has now fallen out of sight.

Rarely do we have an opportunity to make close comparison between two examples of *Kunstfabel.* But "The Town Mouse and the Country Mouse" is presented at roughly the same length by both Horace and Babrius, with enough divergence to allow us to see where difference is possible. The basic outline leaves little room for alteration. The main opportunities are in describing the contrasting diets of the two mice. Thereafter Horace manages considerably more of a scare (door banging, mastiffs on the prowl, as opposed to the two routine human interruptions offered by Phaedrus) to send the mice into panic. But the main difference is the considerate nature of the country mouse, giving the best of its humble board to the town mouse, while the latter, as seems implied, takes first taste of all the town produce himself, even if under pretext of being the slave "taster." The town mouse is also notably a philosopher, encouraging its friend to a *carpe diem* attitude. There are a few minor divergences—a more extravagant touch of the evening in Horace and attribution to one of the poet's Sabine neighbors Cestius, so that this is presented as a countryman's tale.

A considerable development is offered by the pair of fables in Achilles Tatius 2.20ff. These are used unusually as an actual prefiguration of an incident in the plot. The name of a surly servitor Conops (Gnat) prompts a telling of "the lion, the elephant, and the gnat" (why should the lion be afraid of the cock when the elephant is afraid of the gnat?), which is not told out of scale to normal fables, but hints that Gnat will be a formidable opponent to Satyrus and his master's amorous intrigue. Satyrus replies with the fable of "the lion, the gnat, and the spider," this time developed to much more ambitious length, casting Gnat, in effect, as a boastful sophist about to fall victim to the spider (Satyrus):

I fear it would be laughable to go through the whole catalogue of my prowess. I am the ultimate war machine; at the trumpet-call I am ready for action: my mouth is both trumpet and missile, so that I am both bandsman and bowman. I am both bow and arrow, for my wings fire me through the air, and when I fall upon the enemy I make a wound like an arrow.

By the second sophistic period, even gnats have learned to talk like sophists, but the tellers of even the most sophisticated fables are still marked out as servants.

A mythology grows up over the origins of fable itself—Babrius attributes animal fable to the Golden Age:

Praef. 5ff.

In the Golden Age not just humans but the rest of the animals were able to speak, and knew such words as we humans speak to one another. They held assemblies in the middle of the forest; the pine spoke, and so did the leaves of the laurel. The fish would chat with a friendly sailor as it swam, and the sparrows exchanged wise words with the farmer.

Philostratus goes one better, with a typical charter-type creation myth for the genre: once upon a time, Zeus, the king of the gods, told the god Hermes to give out the different kinds of literary talent to all the great authors. Homer was given epic poetry, Aeschylus was given tragedy, and so on down the line. When all the different kinds of literature had been given out, Aesop was still there, and there was nothing left for him—until Hermes remembered the kind of stories he had heard at his mother's knee. And so Aesop was given fables, and he has them to this day.[23] But the inclusion of literary genres in a story of this simple type suggests how far the world of fable has moved on.

In spite of the self-contained and generally miniature scale of most of the stories, the fable has considerable potential for larger development well beyond the immediate rhetorical development of individual examples. We have a parodic beast epic of probably Hellenistic date in the *Batrachomuiomachia,* the *Battle of the Frogs and the Mice,* whose initial incident overlaps with a fable of the frog and the water snake.[24] A recent papyrus publication of the *War of the Mice and the Weasels* appears to be treated along the same lines; we should bear in mind the closeness of weasels in antiquity to the role we more naturally assign to the cat. One notes several fables in the standard collections with such a potential, as when dog ambassadors are sent to the court of Jupiter in a tale of scatological misadventure.[25] The obvious opportunities are illustrated by the *Batrachomuiomachia* itself—extended boastful speeches by the tiny warriors, especially comic in their application of Homeric epithets and genealogies to the combatants ("Slicesnatcher, dear son of Gnawer, son of blameless Breadfilcher") and by the imposition of divine machinery, already once more a commonplace in the fables themselves ("the frogs petition Zeus. . . .').

PROVERBS[26]

Proverbs are traditional sayings which tend to dispense anonymous folk wisdom or common sense: they exist and spread orally, but they are capable of literary appearance and subliterary collection; otherwise, we should be unaware of their attested existence altogether. A good many seem to have traveled well: one thinks of "it won't always be the Saturnalia" (an ancient version of "the party's over"[27]), "to call a spade a spade," or "dancing in the dark."[28]

The contexts in which we expect proverbs to be transmitted will reflect their careers as popular wisdom: elementary didactic literature in the New Testament preserves for us "Thou canst see the mote in thy brother's eye, but not the beam in thine own"[29]—as a popular teacher, Jesus Christ can draw upon easily accessible folk wisdom. It is unsurprising to encounter variants in both Horace's *sermones* ("conversation pieces," "chats") and in freedmen's conversation in Petronius, where proverbial wisdom is part of a stream-of-consciousness texture ("you can see the louse on someone else, but not the flea on yourself"—with typically impolite earthiness[30]). This raises the question, indeed, of the vocabulary and subject matter of proverbs, based firmly in the world of the everyday ("knocking one nail out with another"), but the odd exotic item is not ruled out, such as Lucian's "scrubbing an Aethiop white" (*Adversus Indoctum* 28).

Often, but not always, a proverb will turn out to be an abbreviated narrative: for example, "dog in the manger" reflects directly the brief Aesopic story that a dog guards the horse's provender so well that the horse dies while the dog is unable to eat it himself and so does no good to anyone. (The reverse development cannot be true: the story makes perfect sense and so cannot be argued as an inept attempt to explain an unintelligible proverb whose meaning is now lost.) So, too, AT 776 (killing the goose that laid the golden egg, available in its full fable form as Babrius 123).

In Petronius' *Satyrica* we have a unique resource: a long stretch of chitchat among low-life characters that emphasizes how easily the speakers resort to popular cliché. Some are straightforward enough: *serva me, servabo te* ("you be nice to me, and I'll be nice to you"). Similar jingles from inscriptions on ancient rings are also to be found: *ama me, amabo te; memini tui, memento mei*,[31] in each case with a conspicuous element of wordplay to add to the quotability. Our own equivalent would be "you scratch my back, and I'll scratch yours." Similarly, *Sat.* 45.13 *manus manum lavat,* literally, "hand washes hand" or "one good turn deserves another."[32]

Others have a decided liveliness. Take *tamquam copo compilatus* ("like the innkeeper that was robbed"). Here we have a humorous paradox, given the predatory reputation of ancient innkeepers; in this case, there is additional alliteration. There is also a further hint of the same subject in Aesop: an innkeeper is cheated of fine clothes by a guest who claims to be a werewolf so that the innkeeper runs away.[33] Sometimes Petronius' proverbial expressions are more difficult to explain: the host tells a ghost story that is *asina in tegulis* ("an ass on the tiles")—an amazing sight? *Mus in matella* ("the mouse in the piss pot") seems, from its context, to suggest that the mouse is trapped and that the unsavory image is meant to underline the low level of politeness of a freedman. Others again, such as *Sed tace lingua, dabo panem* ("silence, tongue, I will give you bread to eat") are fairly self-evident in meaning ("let's drop the subject"), even without any parallels being available.[34]

Short samplings of Petronius suggest how easy it is for informal popular speech to slip into a proverbial texture: in Petronius 45 alone we have embellished commonplaces like "'now this way, now that,' as the rustic said when he'd lost the spotted pig," "what we don't have today, we'll have tomorrow," or "if you were somewhere else, you'd be saying the pigs walk about ready-cooked back here."[35] One notes the recurrence of domestic animals in proverbial material: Trimalchio and his friends are never too far from the farmyard.

JOKES AND CONUNDRUMS

A large proportion of jokes, ancient and modern, are minimalist narratives about comic situations, very often involving naïve or foolish behavior and often without specific reference. Take the following versions:

> A numskull was about to suffer shipwreck. So he requested some writing tablets in order that he might make out his will.
>
> While a numskull was voyaging, a powerful storm raged and his slaves were wailing. "Don't cry," he said, "I have set all of you free in my will."
>
> A bad poet Eumolpus tried to continue writing a turgid poem while the vessel he was travelling in was sinking in a storm.[36]

The first pair come from a late antique subliterary joke book, the *Philogelos:* the point lies in the completion of a task which circumstances have rendered futile. The third is woven along with much other popular material into the fabric of

Petronius' novel (*Sat.* 115.1–5). Once more, we are reminded of the fluidity of the most commonplace material. The modern equivalent is tied to a historical disaster: we ourselves talk of "shifting the deck chairs on the Titanic."

There were a number of collections of jokes in antiquity and an extant discussion in Macrobius *Saturnalia* 2.1.8–15, appropriately enough in the setting of a dinner party, while Suetonius credited the Augustan Melissus with assembling 150 books of jokes.[37] These examples might lead us to ask what makes a joke, or better still, what makes a good one? Those of the *Philogelos* seem on the whole rather labored and often artificial, and the naïvety of their characters more or less unbelievable. The interesting thing about the book from a folklorist's point of view is the thought world and the standpoint of the teller. Much is made, for example, of the idiocies of the *scholastikos* ("egghead"): intellectuals are treated with suspicion[38] and are notoriously clumsy about practical matters obvious enough to everyone else. Prejudice is also carried against proverbial communities of idiots: Abderites, Sidonians, Cumaeans.[39] We have the potential for jokes against the Scots or the Welsh. Some of the examples deal with bodily functions, occasionally stretching to the highly improbable in search of a *bon mot,* as when a tragic actor has two lovers, one with bad breath, the other with body odor: when the first demands a kiss and the second a hug, he is reduced to tragic exclamation.

The *Philogelos* treats the jokes partly thematically, as if for the convenience of a jester making professional use of a collection. We certainly hear in Plautus of parasites using joke books,[40] as indeed Shakespearian jesters were later to do. But we have a much more illuminating illustration of the circumstances of joke transmission in Petronius' *Satyrica,* where such jokes emerge as part of the realistic portrayal of the speech mannerisms and thought processes of the uneducated freedman at Trimalchio's dinner, and so the "folk." We also hear of Horace taking pleasure in rustic banter, though once again, his versions of this banter seem distinctly labored.[41]

Closely allied to jokes are (particularly verbal) puzzles (*ainigmata,* "conundrums"). Here a joke is often involved as well, this time directly at the expense of the person asked, but not expected to find, the answer. One of the most persistently recurrent units of popular material is the riddle: among the simplest examples are "I do X and not Y. What am I?" As with ordinary jokes, we can see the form surfacing once more in realistic fiction: one of the guests at Trimalchio's party asks a young boy,[42]

> I come from us long, I come from us broad. Tell me what I am. I'll tell you: something that runs away from us and doesn't move from its place: something that grows from us and gets smaller.

Both "shadow" and "penis" would be plausible answers: if the interlocutor offers one alternative, then the propounder can always claim the other answer to be the correct one. In Petronius, too, we see the association of riddles with children: "Big mouth, big mouth, how many fingers am I holding up?"[43] The recurrence of such riddles in a context like the *Life of Aesop* underlines the popular character of both: here there is the familiar challenge of "drinking the sea" (escape: it can't be done until all the rivers are dammed). A further category of riddle featured in Petronius is the collection of rebus riddles at *Sat.* 56: objects of food are given alternative and less immediately intelligible names, for example, flies and a flytrap, raisins and attic honey; compare our "fly cemetery" (a raisin confection sandwiched between layers of pastry). Here, too, the feeble puns suggest fairly closely the standard of our own Christmas cracker jokes in a similar "party-time" context: the hapless and bored narrator Encolpius clearly implies that they were eminently forgettable.

A good deal more clever, and more profitable, is the polysemic oracle used by the priests of Atargatis in Apuleius, *Met.* 9.8 ("Why do the harnessed oxen plough the field?/To make the seeds luxuriant harvest yield"). The words appear to have no inherent meaning other than the literal one but can be interpreted to suit the hopes of any optimistic enquirer, whether someone wishing to marry, or go on a commercial undertaking, or any other enterprise requiring an oracle.

As in the case of fable, a special category of riddle seems to have developed in antiquity in which an often rudimentary puzzle is set in a rather more ambitious story: one thinks of the questions put by Alexander the Great to the gymnosophists ("Which is bigger, the sea or the land?") in the *Alexander Romance* or of similar kinds of questions put by the Emperor Hadrian to "Secundus, the silent philosopher."[44] These cases do not represent a learned tradition so much as a popular taste for the *bons mots* and responses of the Great and the Good. A celebrated example of wide diffusion is one Homer was said to have been unable to solve: two boys come back from fishing and, asked if they had caught anything, reply,

What we caught we left behind, what we did not catch we carry off (lice?)[45]

Here once again the undignified and trivial answer tells us something about the social and cultural level of the transmission. A no less celebrated example is the trick riddle set by Samson for the Philistines ("out of the strong came forth sweetness") because he had been able to observe the carcass of a lion in which bees had made their hive.[46] The same riddle experienced an unexpected renaissance in popular culture in the last century on the label of

Tate and Lyle syrup tins. Further examples would be those set in the *Aesop Romance* in the riddle contest that Aesop solves between the King of Egypt and the King of Babylon, the ingredients of which eventually give rise to the medieval tradition of King John and the Abbot *(Kaiser und Abt):* the frame story is that a man in authority is unable to solve a riddle or riddles, but a much humbler man in disguise is able to stand in for him with the answers.[47] Indeed, this type of story underlines the very nature of folk wisdom: someone lower down the social scale is likely to pick up simple wisdom at a level which the more socially elevated will be unable to reach.

The so-called riddle of Oedipus remains one of the most puzzling of riddles embedded in celebrated tales: "What walks on four legs in the morning, on two at noon, and on three in the evening?" It seems, as it stands, to have no relevance to the rest of the Oedipus story. What is rarely taken into account is that this may have been only one of the riddles of the sphinx, and that others, one of which at least is ancient, seem to allude to the rest of the story. Our problem is that much of the folklore aspect of Oedipus has become submerged or dropped out and that Sophocles' celebrated version ignores it altogether.[48]

CHILDREN'S SONGS

The Greco-Roman tendency to treat children as miniature adults, or to consign their care in the upper classes to the nursery, has meant that there has been no systematic account to survive antiquity.[49] The Complaisant Man is ridiculed for engaging with his host's children and playing games with them, one of which is actually mentioned as "wineskin, hatchet" *(askos, pelekus)*. With even less dignity Agesilaus of Sparta rides on a walkingstick to amuse children.[50] Once more, Trimalchio, too, behaves with no more dignity when he has a convenient child to play with.

The lexicographer Julius Pollux[51] collects a number of examples, including prisoner's base, tug of war, hide and seek, blind man's buff, ducks and drakes, I-spy, chuckies, and king of the castle; a few more are preserved in lyric[52] as *carmina popularia*. Blind man's buff was played with the hunter as the brazen fly,[53] a wasp-colored gadfly *(tabanus)* lurching around apparently blind and stinging the cattle. The other contestants beat the fly with strips of leather and shout, "You'll hunt, but you won't catch." There were two apparently rather similar games, one for girls, the other for boys, featuring one child in the middle. In the latter a boy with a pot on his head is surrounded by others shouting, "Who holds the pot?" with the answer, "I, Midas." If Midas touches one of the others with his foot, he takes his place in the middle. Presumably there is some allusion to the Midas touch here, but the significance of the pot escapes us. So does the background of some others, just as that of the English nursery rhyme "Ride a Cock Horse to Banbury Cross" might do. Such is the girls' game, Torty Tortoise, with its reduplication *(cheli chelone)*, but the allusions are not clear beyond that:

> Torty Tortoise, what are you doing in the middle?
> I am weaving wool and Milesian cloth.
> But what was your child doing, when he was lost?
> He jumped from his white horses into the sea.

Halliday conjectures that the last line implies some action such as catching the lost child, but we do not know enough.[54]

Some further songs may have had a horror background: there was "fly beetles, a savage wolf is chasing you" or "send away the *strix,* the night-crier, from the land, the bird without name, upon the swift ships." The *strix* here is the vampire, who sucks children's blood in the form of a screech owl. Halliday compares "Ladybird, Ladybird, fly away home/your house is on fire, your children all gone."[55] At least two such apparently ominous songs feature a crow: in one it seems to be an ill-omened bird in the context of a wedding; in the other, which may or may not be connected, it seems to be the recipient of some sort of collection, as a guarantee of good outcome for a bride.[56] Otherwise, this song has almost a flavor of "penny for the Guy,"[57] and might well have been sung by children going from house to house and singing the song for a reward.

ANECDOTE

An anecdote is literally anything "not given out," that is not published, a narrative that still has to be told and is presumed to be as yet only in limited oral circulation, if at all. But it is a convenient category in our own thinking to cover trivial stories about the famous or not so famous, whether involving a definite punch line, or *bon mot,* or not, and whether or not dealing with the past or with present experience.

What ingredients are necessary to make a good anecdote? We need something memorable, unusual, tellable, paradoxical, and perhaps also appealing to a particular cultural interest group. We might ask why this or that example appealed to a collector like Aelian, or why did any collector select *this* story about Alexander? The collections of ancient miscellanists, in particular, abound in examples, and it is from them that we can most readily gauge the possibilities and limitations of this small change of narrative.

Take the following episode, chosen almost at random from Aelian's *Varia Historia* (8.16):

> Peisistratus obtained power and ruled as a tyrant. Solon sat in front of his house with shield and spear and said that he had taken up arms in defence of his country to the best of his ability, being unable to command a force on grounds of age, but loyal in spirit. However, Peisistratus did Solon no harm, whether out of respect for the man and his wisdom—or because of recollections of youth—he is said to have been Solon's favourite boy.

In our parlance this would amount to little more than "Solon staged a one-man peaceful protest against Peisistratus, who chose to ignore it." It is clearly a historical anecdote, whether true or false. And it is its very anecdotal quality which might render the latter issue of no importance. Solon did not bring about any revolution by his action: had he done so, it would have ranked as part of a larger historical process. The anecdotal nature of the story resides partly in the fact that it did not matter: had Peisistratus taken it seriously and prepared to execute Solon, we should have had the act of a political martyr, and again, a different kind of story.

Instead, we have the sense of a one-off curiosity here, and that is why the incident should have been told at all. But it does accord with a broader type of tale, which makes a certain kind of point: it embodies the contrast between a wise man and a ruler, where some incidental or paradoxical gesture (a one-man army) serves to register a moral point. Solon cannot overthrow the tyrant, but at least he has made his protest. A similar kind of story would be that in which Diogenes asks Alexander the Great to get out of his light, or where Diogenes once more engages in rolling a crock up the hill because all the rest of the Corinthians are preparing for war (against Philip of Macedon). This kind of situation is not too far a cry from Sir Francis Drake and the Game of Bowls: the great man can operate at a trivial level.

Such a formula is capable of elaboration into a full-blown narrative stretch, if not an actual tale:

Aelian, *VH* I.16

When the ship had arrived from Delos and Socrates was due to be executed, Apollodorus, Socrates' companion came to the prison, bringing him an expensive *chiton* finely woven in wool, and a cloak of the same sort. And he wanted Socrates to wear the *chiton* and put on the cloak, then drink the hemlock. For he said that he would not be without the fineries for an elegant funeral if he died in them—for his body would lie awaiting burial with its adornment, and not suffer any loss of dignity. That was what Apollodorus requested of Socrates. But Socrates would not have it, but said to Crito, Simmias and Phaedo: "how can Apollodorus see fit to think of me like this, if he really believes that he will see Socrates like this after he has drunk this poisoned loving cup of the Athenians? If he imagines the person who will soon lie collapsed at his feet is me, he obviously does not know me."

A more concentrated form of the story, as a *chreia* or *bon mot,* might have run like this: Socrates was about to be executed. When Apollodorus offered him a woolen tunic, he replied, "It will neither lengthen my life nor sweeten the taste of the hemlock." Why *this* particular treatment? We might argue that Aelian has a special affection for Socratic anecdote, and therefore "famous last words" of Socrates demand a flourish. The story is made more formal and elaborate by the additional cast of Crito, Simmias, and Phaedo; on the other hand, the tunic and the cloak are trivial items, again belonging to the normal world of "what Socrates/Alexander had for breakfast." The philosophic cliché illustrated in the example is, of course, the variety of luxury and the deceptiveness of appearances.

The anecdote, like the fable, reveals a world with a sense of cultural values and at least a measure of predictability. Take a further random sample from Aelian's *Varia Historia* (13.32):

> Xenocrates of Chalcedon, Plato's friend, was caring and not just kind to men but showed compassion for many brute beasts. And so one day when he was sitting in the open air, a sparrow being hunted down by a hawk flew down into his lap. He welcomed and concealed it, keeping it safe until the pursuer flew off. And when he had dispelled its fear he opened the cloak and let go the bird, saying that he had not betrayed a suppliant.

Here there is virtually nothing to the story but the application of a banal metaphor: the bird seen as a suppliant gives us a *bon mot* of sorts, and the attribution to a friend of Plato provides it with a prestigious and cultural context. We should perhaps add that the story probably appealed to Aelian because of its rapport between human and animal: the author of 17 books of *Natural History* might expect to have a general interest in the whole area.

Perhaps the most significant contrast between the anecdote and the fable is that the natural milieu of the latter tends to be the educated world, hence Aelian, *VH* 14.13:

> Agathon used many antitheses in a number of his works, and when someone by way of correcting his plays wanted to remove them from his text, he said,

"But you, my friend, have not noticed that you are destroying the good
(*agathon*) in Agathon."

There is a passable pun here: you are destroying the "good in Agathon," and
"the agathon in Agathon" is itself a quotable phrase. The matter belongs not
only to a literary milieu, but to that of the Athenian Golden Age. There is
also another characteristic motif here: the reverence for great literary or artistic names, who generally emerge as knowing better than their small-minded
critics.

As a matter of course, anecdotes are subject to variation, on the whole, one
suspects, rather more so than fables. In the case of historical anecdotes this
may be because unimportant details are difficult to verify and hence subject
to more or less random change through lapses of memory. When Aelian tells
the unusual story of the Ptolemy who executed orders while playing dice or
draughts, he finds a way of avoiding the precise identity of his subject (actually Ptolemy III, identified by the name of his wife Berenike). There are more
obvious blunders, as when Hippomachus is a wrestling master in Aelian, *VH*
2.6, but a music master in 14.8.

The Chreia

One particular development within ancient anecdote is the *chreia* or *bon
mot,* the "quotable quote." The standard form for what became an elementary
rhetorical exercise might be put like this: "The famous X had the habit of
doing Y; asked by Z why he did this, he replied, 'I should prefer to be laughed
at by A than to be criticized by B.'" Some examples are even shorter. But the
basic structure tends to be the setting of circumstances that require resolution
by a punch line and the providing of a straight man who can ask the right
question to elicit it. Here is an actual example:

Aelian, *VH* 2.36

Isocrates too, in extreme old age, fell ill, and when someone asked him how he
was keeping he said: "I am well, either way: if I live, I shall have more people
to admire me, if I die, I shall have more people to praise me."

A considerable amount of variation is possible, however. For example,
laconic replies from Sparta not attributed to any individual can be sent to
another city and amount to a *chreia* form, as indeed can those published
in Sparta itself, such as the decree that "men from Clazomenae should be
allowed to behave badly" or that "Alexander be considered a god because

he wants to be." Often, doublets of the same basic anecdote will produce significant differences according to context,[58] given the different ethos of gossip mongering and serious biography. Aelian (*VH* 2.18) even quotes two different punch lines for what the luxury-loving general Timotheus says after a simple dinner with Plato: to his family, "People who have dinner with Plato are in good form the next day"; and to Plato directly, "Plato, you dine well, but you have tomorrow in view rather than today." One might argue that a *chreia* can be effected in actions done as opposed to words, as when Xenophon hears of his son's death in battle and removes a garland from his head; having been told that his son died victorious, he restores the garland (Aelian, *VH* 3.1).

The World of Anecdote: People and Themes

Certain people and themes tend to recur in the world of the *chreia* with some regularity. Socrates and Alexander the Great can probably lay claim to be the all-time favorites (and in some sense, popular idols in their own right), but any intellectual, artist, or political celebrity might qualify. The favorite situation, the scene between Alexander and Diogenes, is also quite typical, offering an encounter in which the wise layman gets the better of the naïve ruler. (Compare also Aelian, *VH* 2.2, the case of Alexander's horse.) A typical pair might be Aelian, *VH* 3.27 (Socrates stops Plato buying weapons to go and fight as a mercenary and converts him to philosophy instead) and 3.28, where he shows Alcibiades a map of Attica ("Are you then conceited about properties which are not even a fraction of the earth?")).

A special application of the anecdote in rhetorical use is as material for a rhetorician's prologues or introductions, often with considerable shaping en route: once again, the kind of subject matter selected will accord special priority to tales of performers—Lucian features Herodotus, while Apuleius chooses the flute player Antigenidas (*Florida* 4). A notable subcategory of stories concerns the confrontation of laypeople (or powerful Philistines) to artists or similarly cultural experts:

Aelian, *VH* 14.8

The sculptor Polyclitus made two versions of the same subject, one to please the masses, the other to satisfy the canons of his art. He indulged popular taste in the following way: he chopped and changed the one according to the opinion of those who came in, in deference to their suggestions. So he showed both pieces: the one was praised by everyone, and the other was laughed at.

Polyclitus' reaction was this: "But you created the one you are criticising, I created the one you are admiring."[59]

A typical working of this paradox is between artist or musician and ruler: we have the anecdote told of a cithara player and Philip of Macedon (Plutarch, *Mor.* 67F) or Antigonus (Aelian, *VH* 9.36), in which, in response to criticism, the artist wishes that the ruler will not attain such misfortune as to give him more expertise than the cithara player himself. The *bon mot* relies on a social hierarchy, where musicians are accorded a great deal less prestige than is now the case. A further typical scenario is between philosopher or layman and tyrant, the former usually acquitting himself more convincingly.

A Specialty: The Great Man Eats the Wrong Diet

Some anecdotes rely for their effect and popularity on the very triviality of their subject matter—one notes, in particular, the formula "how can you eat X and do Y?".

> Antisthenes, the Cynic philosopher, when he was washing green vegetables and had noticed Aristippus, the Cyrenaic, walking in the company of Dionysius, the Sicilian tyrant, said: "Aristippus, if you were content with these vegetables, you would not be following the footsteps of a king"; Aristippus replied: "But if you could speak profitably with a king, you would not be content with the vegetables either."[60]

Compare the anecdote about Lysander (*VH* 3.20), given an ox and a cake. After he asks the ingredients of the cake—honey, cheese, and so on—he dismisses it as not food for free men, while giving orders to cook the ox.[61] This kind of *chreia* is driven, like many similar anecdotes, by the assumption that great men are not supposed to do trivial things; the *chreia* usually makes the point that these are essential, or even preferable, in some way.

Anecdotes of Firsthand Experience

Whatever a writer's actual talent, there should be no misunderstanding of the firsthand reporting of actual incidents of which a writer has just heard or in which he has actually taken part:

Pliny, *Ep.* 2.20

> Verania, Piso's wife, was lying gravely ill—the Piso Galba adopted. Regulus went to her. First the cheek of the man, to go to the wife when she was ill, when he had

been her husband's bitterest enemy, and she absolutely loathed him! Bad enough, if he had only gone there; but he actually sat next to the bed and asked her what day and hour she had been born. When he hears, he gives a look of concentration, focuses his eyes and moves his lips, waves his fingers and does his computation. Then silence. When he had kept her on tenterhooks with anticipation, he said "You are going through a danger period but you will come through it. To make matters clearer for you, I will consult a soothsayer I have often used." Without delay he performs a sacrifice, and confirms that the entrails agree with her horoscope. In her anxiety she believes him, calls for a codicil to her will and gives Regulus a legacy. Then she gets worse, and with her dying breath calls him worthless, treacherous and worse, for perjuring himself to her on the life of his son.

Here the string of present tenses, the personal aside from Pliny himself, and the whole atmosphere of immediacy guarantee the authenticity of the tale, but he has also introduced it with what sounds like the cry of an itinerant storyteller (*Assem para et accipe auream fabulam:* "have your money ready, and listen to a priceless story"). We are in the world of the street-corner anecdote-monger ("You've never heard the latest. . . .").

The Lives of Poets

A special category within which the anecdote flourishes is the subgenre of "lives of poets." Some lives are set fairly and squarely in a "grammatical" tradition, but these and their more imaginative products are alike vulnerable to spurious inference from a writer's own works. The whole industry was no doubt fueled by the status acquired by Homer, Aeschylus, Sophocles, and Stesichorus as the focus of actual hero cults in specific localities.[62] Such lives are where to find information relating to the avenged deaths of Hesiod or Stesichorus, poets being seen as under divine protection, or their survival in miraculous circumstances. (Simonides is even assigned an early instance of the "grateful dead" folktale.) There are also fanciful childhood miracles surrounding their cultivation by bees (as associates of the Muses) and generally remarkable tales surrounding them: the ultimate in these is the tale tradition about the lyric poet Arion of Lesbos, which finds its way into formal historiography and mythography as well. There are no set ingredients for a poet's tale, though public scandal and special cases offer a potent combination: one thinks in particular of the story in Heraclides Ponticus (fr. 170) about Aeschylus, accused of profaning the Eleusinian mysteries and acquitted because of the war services of his brother Cynegirus, celebrated for the loss of a hand at Marathon. This sort of material is ripe for development in declamation themes, as the part of it relating to Cynegirus actually was.[63]

Arion of Lesbos: "The Tale That Has Everything"?

Herodotus' own narrative skill and economy in handling the story is considerable. It is introduced with some historical matter-of-factness, a note on the tradition and the achievement of Arion himself:

> The Corinthians and Lesbians are agreed that a great wonder took place during the lifetime of Periander, that Arion of Methymna arrived in Taenarus, after being carried there on the back of a dolphin. This Arion was the most eminent lyre-player of his age, and invented and named the dithyramb, which he then taught in Corinth.

In giving this detail at the outset Herodotus is acting as reporter rather than storyteller. He then gives, in due order, Arion's stay at Corinth, the move to Italy and Sicily, where he becomes wealthy, and his return, entrusted to a Corinthian crew; realization that they are plotting and unavailing efforts to save his life; the request to give a final "concert performance"; then the final leap into the sea, where he is carried to Taenarum by the dolphin, and in turn is able to betray the unjust crew to Periander. The story is commemorated at Taenarum with a bronze statue of the dolphin.

It is not hard to appreciate the tale's appeal, especially at a school level: it is clearly told, it presents an animal miracle and a simple business of right triumphing over wrong, and it presents a virtuoso performance under bizarre but memorable circumstances.

In the imitators of Herodotus' version all seem concerned to emulate the master, yet none, in fact, seems to include all the details or cite them completely accurately. We have three workings from the early Roman Empire: those by Gellius (16.19) and by Fronto are fairly close paraphrases but have quite clearly treated Herodotus as a literary model. The version that ends Plutarch's *Banquet of the Seven Sages* ingeniously contrives the story as an immediate event reported to Periander of Corinth as breaking news (*Mor.* 160Dff.): the action is presented through the eyes of one of the participants at Periander's feast—Gorgus was among a number of people celebrating a festival at the shore when the dolphins actually landed Arion. Only at the end does Periander actually proceed with the arrest of the sailors; the tale is concentrated on an *ecphrasis,* a formal rhetorical description, as Arion arrives at the shore:

Plutarch, *Mor.* 160F–161A

The moon was shining on the sea; there was no wind, but calm and tranquillity; from a distance there could be seen a ripple close to the promontory, coming to land, with foam and a great roar from the surge, so that everyone ran in amazement to where it was reaching the shore. Before they were able to guess what was hurtling towards them so quickly, dolphins were sighted, some thronging in a circle, others leading the way towards the smoothest part of the shore, others again behind, as if serving as a rearguard. And in the midst, raised above the water, was an indistinct mass, difficult to make out, but like a body: until the dolphins drew close together and put in to shore and laid on dry land a man still breathing and able to move. Then they moved off towards the promontory, jumping higher than before, playing as if for joy and gambolling.

In this demonstration of *enargeia* (vividness), rhetorical artifice comes back full circle into spontaneous storytelling.

Mixing Categories: A Jocular Ghost Story

Sometimes anecdote types can be effectively merged, as in the following *chreia* at the expense of the impossible Herodes:

Demonax 24

When the superlative Herodes was in mourning for Pollux, who had died before his time, and saw fit to have a chariot yoked for him and horses yoked to it as if the youth was about to mount it, and have dinner prepared for the boy, Demonax went up to him and said: "I am bringing you a message from Pollux." Herodes was delighted and supposed that Demonax too, like all the rest, was playing along with his grief, and said: "What does Pollux want then, Demonax?" "He is criticising you for not going off to join him at once."

The circumstances of the story are well confirmed by the testimony of Philostratus in his life of Herodes, who dwells on this magnate's extremes of grief over several bereavements; the *bons mots* of Demonax, while sometimes stereotypical, are probably genuine enough. Here we have, then, a jocular ghost story in the form of a *chreia* or *apomnemoneuma* ("reminiscence"): a put-down on the subject of current superstition and in the form of hot gossip.

A similar story in a less than jocular form is offered by Plutarch:

Consolatio ad Apollonium 14.109

They tell the following tale about the Italian Euthynous. He was the son of Elysius from Terina, foremost among the men of his day in virtue, wealth and reputation; [the young man] died suddenly from an unknown cause. Now Elysius suspected, as might anyone else, that he had been poisoned; for he was the sole heir to his father's great patrimony and wealth. At a loss to test this, he approached a site for the conjuring up of the dead; he made the preliminary sacrifice prescribed by custom, lay down, and saw the following vision. His father appeared to him, and on seeing him he explained the misfortune that had befallen his son, and begged and pleaded for him to help in finding who had killed his son. And he replied: "that is why I have come. But take from this man what he brings you, for from that you will know about everything you are grieving about." Now there was a young man following him, resembling his son and close to him in age and appearance. He asked who he was, and the young man replied, "I am the spirit *(daimon)* of your son," and with this handed him a message. When Elysius opened it he saw the following three lines:

> In truth the minds of men wander in foolishness;
> Euthynous lies dead by appointed destiny.
> It was not right for him to live, nor for his parents.

The story tends, in this instance, to defeat the expectation of the ghost story type just as clearly as the jocular reply of the alleged ghost in Demonax's story: death is natural, and there is no need of extraordinary or exceptional treatment of the fact.

CONCLUSION

We might choose to spend much longer in the world of day-to-day gossip and banter, though sadly, we lack the kind of spread of evidence that would enable us to produce an equivalent of the Opies' *The Lore and Language of Schoolchildren* for antiquity. What is worth emphasizing on a very limited sample is the difficulty of containing material that is naturally lively and spontaneous, and above all transmissible, within any one genre: fable and proverb shade into one another, and both can readily invade the domain of the numskull story, while many of the materials find their own way of climbing the social ladder into more formal literature somehow or other, whether in increasingly sophisticated rhetorical fables or in the polite or impolite symposia of the educated.

NOTES

1. Dundes (1965), 3; for a useful anthology of the smaller popular forms, see Hansen (1998), 249–340.

2. On the history of the fable, see van Dijk (1997); Adrados rev. (with van Dijk) (1999) I; for a bibliography of fable scholarship, see Carnes (1985); there is a useful, short overview in Holzberg (1993).

3. On Sumerian fables, see Kramer (1981), 124–131; West (1997), 502–505.

4. cf. Perry (1965), xxxi (citing *Aesopica* 724).

5. On the problems of the formation of the Aesopic corpus, see Perry (1965), xi–xix.

6. For example, see Plato, *Phaedo* 61B (Socrates turning Aesop into verse).

7. Excellent range of examples in Houlihan (2001).

8. Babrius 44; Perry (1965), 372; Halm 386.

9. Perry (1965), 451, from Nikephoros Basilakis; Walz 427; Halm 376.

10. 105; Grimm and Grimm (1922), 75, BP; Perry (1965), 605 (cat).

11. Babrius 128, 76; Gellius 2.29.

12. But *Aesopica* 264, on an ass able to read.

13. Babrius 9, 8.3.

14. For the latter version, Apuleius, *Florida* 25 van der Vliet, tr. Butler (1909), 215f.

15. Chambry 133.

16. Babrius 18; Aesop 46; Avianus 4.

17. Babrius 57; sometimes the latter category does occur in animal stories (Babrius 81: the fox points out to the ape that there is no way of checking his boasts about an ancestral tomb).

18. Lucian, *adversus indoctum* 30 (dog in the manger), (*LCL* 2.210f.).

19. Phaedrus 1.2.

20. Perry (1965), 450.

21. Babrius 10, 11.

22. *Florida* 25 van der Vliet, tr. Butler (1909).

23. Philostratus, *Life of Apollonius* 5.15.

24. For the fable, see Babrius 141; Phaedrus 4.1.

25. Phaedrus 4.19.

26. On the ethos of proverbial wisdom, see 27ff. above.

27. Seneca, *Apoc.* 12, *dicebam vobis, non semper Saturnalia erunt;* cf. Lucian, *Merc. Cond.* 16: "Do you think you'll always be celebrating the Dionysia?"

28. Lucian, *Juppiter Tragoedus* 32; *Hermotimus* 49.

29. Luke 6:41.

30. Horace, *Sat.* 1.3.25ff.; Petronius 57.7.

31. *Sat.* 44.3; Heraeus 122.

32. See also Seneca, *Apoc.* 9.6, where the texture of satire allows a good many proverbial expressions.

33. *Sat.* 62.12; Aesop 197 Halm.

34. *Sat.* 63.2, 58.9, 69.3.

35. Further descriptions of a Cockayne-like land in Athenaeus 268f.

36. *Philogelos* 30, 25, tr. Hansen (1998), 279; Petronius 115.1–5.

37. For a brief résumé, see Baldwin (1983), ixff.

38. cf. Aristophanes's joke about Socrates, Aristophanes, *Clouds* 168–174.

39. On the Abderites, see Demosthenes 17.23.

40. Plautus, *Persa* 392–395; *Stichus* 400.

41. Horace, *Sat.* 1.5.51–50, 1.7.

42. Ibid., 58.8f.

43. Ibid., 64.12; in the case of *bucca bucca*, there are, indeed, modern versions; see Brewster in Dundes (1965), 338–368; chapter 3.

44. *Alexander Romance* 3.6 (which is bigger, the sea or the land?); similar material in the legend of Secundus.

45. "Contest of Homer and Hesiod," from *Homeric Hymns and Apocrypha*, West (2003), 326.

46. Judges 14:8–14.

47. *Life of Aesop* 105–123; for *King John and the Abbott*, see Anderson (1923).

48. For Theodectes' contribution, fr. 4 Nauck; for the overall context, see Edmunds (1995), 147–173, esp. 151–155; Edmunds cites a modern folktale version containing a riddle similar to that preserved in Theodectes.

49. Halliday (1924), 70f.

50. *Characters* 5.5; *Agesilaus* 25.

51. Pollux, *Onomasticon* 9.113, 123.

52. *Carmina popularia* nos. 847–883 in Greek Lyric, *LCL* 5, 232–269.

53. With Halliday's, emendation, nom. for accusative of *chalke muia* (1923), 112.

54. Halliday (1924), 112; see further Erinna fr. 1 in the *Supplementum Hellenisticum* for a possible reference to the game, but the papyrus is too damaged to allow certainty.

55. Halliday (1924), 115 (his translation).

56. cf. Athenaeus 8.359D–360A.

57. Halliday (1924), 117.

58. What Themistocles enjoyed most (Plutarch, *Themistocles* 17/Aelian, *VH* 13.43); Cicero and Aelian on the execution of Leon by Dionysius (Aelian, *VH* 13.34/ Cicero, *Tusculans* 5.60); Themistocles and the necklace (Plutarch, *Them.* 18, *Mor,.* 808F; Aelian, *VH* 13.40); Themistocles and Eurybiades (Plutarch, *Them.* 11, *Mor.* 185B; Aelian, *VH* 13.40).

59. cf. *VH* 2.2, between Zeuxis and Megabyzus (even the slaves laugh at the latter when he masquerades as an art critic); or the story of Apelles and Alexander's horse, cf. Pliny, *NH* 35.95.

60. Hock and O'Neil (1986), 305f., from *Vat. Gram.* 15–22; they list at least six other versions.

61. There is a doublet about Agesilaus in Athenaeus 657 B.C. Other variations: when Polemo of Laodicea ran into a sophist buying sausages and sprats and cheap delicacies, he said, "I say sir! It is not possible to give a fine performance of the thought of Darius and Xerxes by feeding on sprats" (*VS* 541). Or again: Antigonus Gonatas rebukes the epic poet Antagoras for cooking a dish of conger eels in the camp in the dress of a cook. Asked if he thought Homer had recorded Agamemnon's exploits when cooking eels, Antagoras asked whether Agamemnon had performed his exploits while investigating who was cooking a conger eel in his camp (Athenaeus 8.340f).

62. cf. Lefkowitz (1981), 87.

63. Further discussion in Lefkowitz (1981), 173.

Six

The Personnel of Folklore: From Nymphs to Bogeymen

In this chapter we shall be looking at some of the personnel of folklore: not the Olympian gods, though they may do folkloric things from time to time, but the minor supernaturals, most likely to operate at a popular level, very often, if not predominantly, in rural contexts, and offering overlapping frameworks of belief about the workings of some sort of other world, however it might be understood. We shall be concerned, from time to time, with the problem of continuities between ancient and subsequent folk belief, but often inconclusively, given the nature of the evidence.

NYMPHS

Nymphs are typically portrayed as beautiful but supernatural young women inhabiting country places, be they woods, streams, mountains, or caves.[1] Men are attracted to them and may form often dangerous or ambiguous relationships with them. Unlike the cases of gods consorting with mortal women, where the outcome is usually a pregnancy and the founding of a divinely sanctioned house, human male relationships with nymphs may take a variety of forms: Larson may not be far off the mark when she suggests that "the nymph is also an idealized mythopoetic version of the village girl at the peak of her sexual desirability, so that her interactions with mortal men can hardly avoid connotations of sexual attraction."[2] The nymph, unlike the mortal victim of a god, may take the initiative and may also take revenge on an unfaithful mortal. To cut down a nymph's tree or boast of having slept with one can be costly. The prospects for Hylas, dragged down by nymphs (Theocritus) or married to a nymph (Apollonius of Rhodes), spells the end of his mortal identity. More obviously folkloric is the plain prose report in Nymphis:

FGrH 432 F 5b

> In the same way one might note some of the songs which they sing at one of their local festivals, invoking one of their ancient heroes by the name of Bormos. . . . This figure they say was the son of a prominent wealthy man, and that in his handsome appearance and the prime of his youth he exceeded all others. As he was supervising work on his estate and wanted to give his reapers some water, he went to fetch it and disappeared.

To this bald local tradition among the Mariandynoi, Hesychius adds the detail that Bormos was *nympholeptos,* "snatched by the nymphs."[3] According to Nymphis, they searched the countryside "accompanied by the singing of a dirge, which they all still use to this day"; similarly, the inhabitants of Chios have a periodic sacrifice and search for Hylas, with the priest continuing to call out the lost youth's name. Nor are such tales confined to the traditional subject matter and treatment characteristic of Hellenistic poetry, as in the case of Echo, Salmacis, and others. We have an epitaph of the second century A.D.: "it was not death, but the naiads who snatched the excellent child to be their playmate" (possibly a reference to a childhood drowning accident, but the phenomenon of *nympholepsis* can occur in literature anywhere from Homer onward).[4]

These kinds of tales are indeed echoed in modern Greek folklore: Larson cites a case from Kos, where a young man is seized by *neraides,* detained under magic in a cave, and forced to dance with the nymphs every night till dawn; he escapes with the help of a talisman, a cloth marked with crosses. Stories of a girl rescued from desire to join the nymphs in the woods has echoes of the story of Melampus, where a professional exorcist is needed to restore victims to their right minds.[5]

A reverse of initiative by a nymph has the overpowering of the nymph herself, as in the celebrated case of Thetis, where her mortal husband Peleus has to take her in a cave by capture: Larson relates this to the swan maiden motif in Indo-European folklore, where the swan's costume is hidden by the hero to maintain the loyalty of the supernatural maiden, to be recovered and allow her departure.[6] A further situation has a hero who rescues the nymph's tree from falling and so saves the nymph's life: this appears to entitle the rescuer to sexual favors, as in the case of Arcas of Arcadia and several variants. In one of the variants the rescuer, Rhoicus, somehow transgresses afterward, to his cost.[7] There are also tales of the nymph's revenge if a hubristic mortal cuts down her tree: Apollonius of Rhodes cites the case of Paraibios' father, and his son has to sacrifice to the offended nymph to avoid a family curse, while Erysichthon is inflicted with unquenchable hunger for a similar impiety and is driven to the extreme of self-cannibalism.[8]

Local distribution of shrines and traditions of nymphs throw further light on their activities, and the novel by Longus, *Daphnis and Chloe,* suggests a fairly convincing picture of how an educated imperial Greek author could imagine the activities of a still living cult of nymphs. Much of the point of the story hinges on the fact that the country foundlings Daphnis and Chloe, with their rustic foster parents, are too provincial and naïve to take any interest in the traditional Olympian deities, but they are consistently pious toward the nymphs and (on their prompting) will recognize Pan as well. The nymphs have a shrine in the cave where Chloe herself was found as an exposed infant: not only do they act as guardian spirits, but they tip off Daphnis by appearing to him in a dream as to where he can find a dowry which will secure him marriage to Chloe. When the latter is kidnapped, they tell Daphnis to pray to Pan, who scares her captors and secures her release.[9] In such actions they function in effect as a trio of fairy godmothers, objects of genuine pastoral worship. Both Pyrrha and Mytilene show the head of eponymous nymphs already in their fifth- and fourth-century coinage,[10] and Larson's research testifies to a spread of local worship of local nymph figures throughout the Greek world, most particularly in Boeotia, but notably, too, in Arcadia, the "natural" home of their frequent associate, Pan. It is this local aspect of nymphs which naturally ties them to the folklore of the countryside: we even note the presence of nymphs beside the Ilyssos when Socrates takes his celebrated stroll outside the city walls.[11]

The association between nymphs and water accounts for their frequent association with healing springs, sometimes in association with Heracles, who likewise has an interest in thermal springs: the Pythiades of Phthia Therma in Bithynais became a cult of three virgin martyrs, Menodora, Metrodora, and Nymphodora, killed under the emperor Galerius and, of course, still capable of taking over the roles of the nymphs at the baths.[12] Nymphs may be the natural target of Pan, who does not, however, always succeed in making conquests: one thinks of the tales of Pan and Syrinx, Echo or Pitys; Bithynia preserved a tradition that Nikaia was raped by Dionysus after he had changed the water of her local spring into wine[13]; and very often, local heroes are described as the offspring of one divine parent and a nymph.[14]

Some nymphs had cults capable of long and complex historical development. Cyrene starts as a Thessalian nymph beloved of Apollo; she ends with queenly status in Egypt, fostered by the Battiad dynasty and celebrated as the mother of the culture hero Aristaeus, and especially associated with a spring of Apollo there. Both sites were part of Argonautic history, and chance similarity of name may have associated the Thessalian story with the Libyan city.[15] A plurality of nymphs may also reflect local indigenous Libyan tradition. In Crete the picture is different again, where a nymph such as Amaltheia, the nurturer of the infant Zeus, can be pictured as a goat, a nymph, or a pairing of both; a similar ambiguity attaches to whether the daughters of Melisseus feed Zeus as bees or nymphs; some of Zeus' nymphs even end up as constellations (Cynosoura, Helike). Crete also produces siblings of the nymphs not only as satyrs but as Kouretes, embodiments of growth in nature, in multiples of three, like some of the nymphs themselves.[16]

Greek nymph cults could be exported: we hear in imperial times of a rite in which Egyptian children were "given to the nymphs" of the Nile, to be returned to their parents at adolescence. A tomb of one Isidora commemorates her being snatched away by the nymphs and their construction of a shrine for her, where she is now commemorated with offerings proper to nymphs, or milk, oil, wine, and flowers. Again, she may simply have died by drowning, or she may have died while "given to the nymphs."[17]

Are nymphs fairies? Strictly speaking, the latter are related etymologically to the *fata*, the all-wise spinning women who attend the newborn child and make predictions for the future (from Fr. *fée*). But in some respects they seem certainly the closest thing and are, in many respects, at least analogous.[18] The modern Greek *neraides* certainly seem to preserve much of the manner we expect of modern fairy lore: beauty, fondness for human offspring and affairs with mortals, and vindictive and whimsical behavior. Rose cites the story of a midwife who was called out to attend on a *neraid*[19] birth and was paid in fairy gold in the form of onion peel which turned into Turkish gold coins on her reaching home. A priest allows a *neraid* baby to ride his mule at his mother's request—the mule bolts, and the priest makes the sign of the cross and takes refuge in the church. He returns the baby to the mother on condition that she digs a well and plants a vineyard, and the bargain is duly kept, according to a local tradition from Mesta in Chios. Most of the activities of *neraides* can be paralleled for either *neraids* themselves or other nymphs in antiquity: the version of the story of Daphnis preserved by Aelian has him falling in love with and then innocently betraying his nymph lover[20]; both can be closely connected with wells or receive honey cakes or similar offerings.

PAN, FAUNS

Male supernatural creatures which are the counterparts of the nymphs take the form of Pan,[21] singular or plural, *silenoi,* and satyrs, where distinctions are possible: these came to be equated with Italian *fauni.* While nymphs are depicted as desirable young women, Pans and the rest are masculine, not permanently erect like Priapus, but shaggy and sexually predatory, with goat-like (or horse-like) hinderparts and sexual energy to match. As in the case of the nymphs, their association is rural—mountains, woods, and solitary places. Pan himself has a persistent association with Arcadia, itself a wild, isolated, and mountainous region, with an unusual place in the history of Greek culture, and the whole crew have also an association with the ecstatic deity Dionysus, not originally Olympian and given to wild and sexually nuanced celebration, again in the wilds.[22] Pan can be a warrior, as when he appears to inspire the Athenians at Marathon and is rewarded with a cave on the Acropolis itself.[23] The phenomenon of "panic" itself, like Bacchic *ekstasis,* has an eerie otherness and a sense of possession about it; one thinks of the *nympholepsis* of the nymphs. Eusebius quotes from Porphyry a case where nine woodcutters are found close to death after being terrorized by a manifestation of Pan, to be fortunately saved only on the intervention of Artemis,[24] as was later explained by an oracle. It appears that he not only has the syrinx, as expected, but wields a *rhabdos* (staff), which Borgeaud guesses functions here as a magic wand, sending the woodcutters into a stupor; in Nonnus he can similarly charm Typhon into a daydream and illusion.[25] One notes that Pan is not just a symbolic herdsman: he can even copulate with goats and so be still closer to the animal world,[26] and he can be depicted with goat head and ithyphallic human body with a short tail, as when depicted pursuing a goatherd on the Pan Painter Crater.[27]

One notes an ambiguity in the actions of Pan-related personnel: Silenus, in particular, doubles as the dissolute, comic drunkard on the one hand and the epitome of ancient wisdom on the other. We know a great deal less than we should like about the encounter of Silenus with Midas, with whom he engages in conversation for days on end after being captured by the drugging of his well; we hear of a fantastic disquisition about life on another continent, where things are topsy-turvy, as well as of the misery of the human condition.[28] A no less puzzling picture emerges from the early and often gruesome mythological repertoire that Silenus tells his captors in Virgil's Sixth Eclogue.[29] The whole repertoire of the still elusive dramatic genre satyric drama has a range close to both myth and folklore: delight at the finding of amazing inventions (fire or music), attempts at freedom from ogres, and the like.[30]

DEMONS

Of all the terms that refer to supernatural figures in ancient folklore, the most troublesome is the Greek term *daimon,* used for any supernatural creature but traditionally much less for deities than for "lower" supernatural beings. Demons are attributed with any number of supernatural operations[31]:

> All the air is full of souls; and these are regarded as *daimones* and heroes; and by these men are sent dreams and signs of disease and health, and not only to men but to sheep and other livestock. To these demons we perform purifications and apotropaic rites, all manner of divination, interpretation of random remarks, and the like.

The problem for the folklorist is the intellectual additions and accretions the term has taken on.[32] Sometimes *daimones* seem to be conceived as helpful and well disposed to humans, in other contexts the reverse (and invariably so in Christian polemic in late antiquity). The term can mean things as various as "inner voice," "conscience," "supernatural prompting," or "guardian angel." It occurs as early as Homer, where it can represent a divinity proper, and figures also in relation to heroes in Pindar, whether for the hero's good or ill. Here is a picture of a kind typically presented by the late antique magical papyri:

> If you give him a command, straightway he performs the task: he sends dreams, brings women or men without the use of magic material, he kills, he destroys, he stirs up winds from the earth, he carries gold, silver, bronze, and he gives them to you whenever the need arises; and he frees from bonds a person chained in prison, he opens doors, he causes invisibility so that no-one can see you at will ... and he will tell you about the illness of a man, whether he will live or die, even on what day and at what hour of night. And he will also give you both wild herbs and the power to cure, and you will be worshipped as a god since you have a god as a friend.[33]

The complication is the career of the term in Greek philosophical language from Plato onward. Socrates talks about his *daimon,* and the Socratic *daimon* was to figure in philosophical discussion and speculation to the end of antiquity on the strength of it. As early as the *Symposium,* the term *daimonion* is said to be between god and mortal, and potentially ambiguous sacred functions are being attributed to the *daimones.*[34] Plutarch embraced a Middle Platonism which both formally invested *daimones* with intermediate status between gods and men and developed their maleficent side:

They say that these demigods have a nature far more powerful than ours, but that they have divine nature not unmixed and unadulterated, but partaking in the nature of the soul and the perceptions of the body. They experience pleasure and pain, and all the feelings that are inherent in these changes disturb some more than others. For in daimones, as in humans, there are different degrees of virtue and vice.[35]

It is unsurprising that the activities of *daimones* in obscene rites have the flavor of a witches' Sabbath, entailing impropriety, self-mutilation, and obscene language and behavior to satisfy the evil demons. Philo Judaeus had already presented them as chastisers under God's control, while Plotinus has them in Neoplatonist debates over the status of theurgy, with its claims to be able to purify through ritual and to control supernatural forces by the same means.[36]

In the more popular Jewish and subsequently Judeo-Christian world a similar picture might be said to have intensified: there are good *daemones* in the angels, bad ones in the fallen angels, and there is a markedly greater stress on the wickedness of evil demons, with a more blatantly sexual and lustful character (rather than concerned simply with disease, for example). Intertestamentary Jewish writings furnish the necessary proof texts. A key association now becomes that between magic and evil demons: this was still further extended in the Apocrypha to the New Testament, with Simon Magus associated with wicked demons, and as predominantly in the New Testament itself, demons are felt to be wicked.[37] Satan and Christ are polarized, but at least in the Apocryphal writings, there is, again, a folkloric flavor. The second-to third-century Apocryphal material has an air of competition in miraclem-ongering about it: Simon has a repertoire of cheap, sensational illusions, at least in the view of his enemies.[38]

With such a range of nuances the trouble with demons is that they can be just about anything, as in the following exposition by Pythagoras of Rhodes[39]:

First, what the proper term for them ("spectral apparitions") is, whether they are gods or *daimones* or emanations *(aporrhoai)* of these, and whether there is only one who appears now in this form, now in that; or whether they are many all different from each other, some well-disposed, others malign, some who sometimes speak the truth and others who are utterly fraudulent. (tr. R. Gordon)

He also describes the disagreements of older and more recent writers and finally reaches the conclusion that spectral appearances are an emanation from (a single) demon. This amounts to the ultimate in "now you see them, now you don't."

HEROES AND SAINTS

It is one thing to describe or commemorate the deeds of heroes, another to make them objects of cult. If the former is the more prominent in literature, it is much more obviously the latter that strikes us outside it. Cults of heroes appear to gather momentum from the Homeric age onward and to take a variety of forms, close to the cults of chthonic deities at the upper end of the spectrum or to that of the dead at large at the other; the same could be said of heroes' shrines themselves, varying in size from whole sanctuary complexes, like that of Hippolytus at Troezen, to distinctly scaled down structures around a tomb. Like the nymphs, heroes and their cults tended to be localized. Perhaps our most detailed literary evocation of a hero cult is that pertaining to Achilles in the Troad: the hero lingers in the view of a local vinedresser around where he fell at Troy; the vinedresser himself claims the ghost of the first fallen hero at Troy, Protesilaos, as his patron;[40] the scenario can be archaeologically matched with evidence from the Black Sea coast.[41]

Nor was heroicization confined to the heroes of the Bronze Age: Lucian sarcastically foresees the institution of a cult to his own contemporary, the self-martyred Peregrinus, complete with relics:

Lucian, *Peregrinus* 41

Just picture what is likely to happen in his honour in the future—all the bees that will settle on the site, all the cicadas singing on it, all the crows settling on it like the tomb of Hesiod, and all that sort of thing. As for the statues, both from the Eleans and the rest of the Greeks, to whom he said he had sent missives, I know that many will be set up right away. And they say he sent letters to almost all the cities of repute, testaments and exhortations and regulations. And he appointed to this end certain envoys from among his friends, entitling them messengers of the dead and envoys from the Underworld.

Indeed, Lucian does not hesitate to accuse Peregrinus of having orchestrated his hero cult fully in advance:

Lucian, *Peregrinus* 27

But also he makes up myths and repeats certain prophecies, ancient ones of course, that he is to be a nocturnal guardian spirit; it is clear also that he already wants altars and expects a golden image of himself. And by Zeus, it would not be surprising among so many idiots to find some ready to claim that they were cured by him of quartan fevers, and that they themselves had personally encountered this spirit of the night. And these confounded disciples will, I imagine, arrange for an oracle and a sacred site at the place of the pyre, because the famous Proteus the son of Zeus, the one who gave him his title, was inclined to soothsaying. I give you my word too, that priests will be designated with whips or brands or some such displays of wonder, or my goodness some nocturnal mystery will be set up in his honour, with a torchlight festival at the place of the pyre.

For all Lucian's skepticism his fears testify to a religious climate where cults are by no means confined to the heroes of the past. Pagan saints can present themselves at any time.

GHOSTS

At the lower end of the scale, hero cults could be said to entail the "powerful dead." But there is an active role in folklore, also, for the ordinary dead, or at least such of them as are specially enough categorized to be still active in the life of humans.[42] There was a peculiar status occupied by the prematurely dead, victims of death by violence, those not yet married, and those without tombs. It might be taken for granted that ghosts are popularly believed to hang around graves and tombs, as having still a corporeal element around them, according to Plato.[43] Several efforts are made to offer other subdivisions of ghosts, as in their celebrated throng in *Aeneid* 6.[44] Apuleius[45] gives an unusual classification, where lemurs are naturally equated with a kind of demon who looks after descendants, further divided into lares; exiled ghosts becoming *larvae* (more often, lemurs are seen as malign ghosts). Tertullian points out the susceptibility of ghosts to the magical manipulation of practitioners.[46] Apuleius illustrates precisely this,[47] where a woman compels the ghost of another woman killed by violence to kill her husband, whereupon he, as a member of the undead, appears, in turn, to his daughter to reveal her stepmother's crime. A similar tale is reported earlier by Cicero[48] in relation to two companions staying in Megara, one about to be murdered by an innkeeper and in a dream. imploring the other, staying elsewhere, to help him, then once again, when murdered, divulging the whereabouts of his own already murdered corpse.

SOME MORE "LITTLE PEOPLE": THE DEMONS OF THE NURSERY

In addition to such major forces as Pans, demons, and the like, there is also a no doubt even larger cast of rather more trivial characters, whose natural place is as bogeymen in the nursery.[49] Sometimes more major players can be used in this way, as when the Cyclopes or even Hermes plays the part of a bogeyman[50]:

> When any girl should chance to disobey her mother, she calls the Cyclopes to the child, Arges or Steropes; and from within the house Hermes comes, stained with burnt ashes. And immediately he plays the bogey man *(mormussetai)* to the child and she runs off to her mother's lap, hands over her eyes.

But there are more specialized players: Lamia, Akko, Alphito, Baubo, Gorgo, Mormo, and their friends, for whom such actions are still more routine. A number of what might most naturally be called gremlins make regular appearances as bogeymen used to scare naughty children: the origins and (minimal) tradition attached to each of these testifies to their being drawn from a wide background. Lamia, the beautiful Libyan daughter of Belus and Libya,[51] lost her own children by Zeus through the vengeance of Hera. Mormo is variously a Laestrygonian queen who lost her own children and now eats those of others[52] or a Corinthian who ate her own children.[53] Empousa appears most celebratedly in Aristophanes, *Frogs* 285–295, where she is a shape-shifting inhabitant of the Underworld who takes on the appearance of a cow, mule, beautiful woman, and god.[54] Gello first appears in Sappho fr. 178 and continues into the Middle Ages and even into modern times[55] as Ghellou: she was a death-causing spirit out to avenge her own premature death; the modern version gains entrance to households and attacks young mothers. Moires[56] offer a modern counterpart to the Moira of classical myth and folklore: their function in antiquity is to decide the fate of newly born children; there may be a natural overlap with the function of Fortune (Tyche), who may, like the Moires,[57] appear also in the plural.

Others are more enigmatic, such as the Cabeiri or Cronos-Saturn in his persona of a child-eating ogre. We have tantalizing information, also, on the *daktuloi* (fingers, hence dwarves) associated with the nursing of Zeus and perhaps owing their distinctiveness to an early native Cretan cult: they are presented as born from the soil that fell from the hands of a nymph, either Ida herself or Anchiale in the cave at Dikte. Sophocles gives their number as 10, 5 male and 5 female, elsewhere separated into male right hand, female left. They have associations, like the *kabeiroi* themselves, with both a mother goddess and craft skills, metalworking and magic.[58] We are as close to the world of the seven dwarfs here as we are likely to come.

SOME LATE TEXTS

It will be clear enough that the foregoing supernatural figures of folklore are not quite the Puck and fairy ring of English folk- and fakelore, though they are scarcely any further removed from modern Greek folklore than we should expect, given the cultural gulf between ancient polytheism and the Orthodox church. But they do have an equivalent function: they are the ancient and unchanging forces of the countryside, or the survivals of rural superstition, to use the language of a now very dated approach. A number of late antique texts can be used to illustrate aspects of these phenomena: Plutarch's account of the death of Pan[59]; the version of the Daphnis legend embodied in Longus' pastoral novel *Daphnis and Chloe;* and the following encounter with a strange man of the woods in Philostratus' life of Herodes Atticus:

Philostratus, *Lives of the Sophists* 552ff.

This was a youth on the threshold of manhood, as tall as a towering Celt (he was actually about eight feet tall) . . . his hair grew long on both sides, he had bushy eyebrows that met as if into one, and his eyes gave forth a bright flash which gave a hint of his impulsive nature; he had a hooked nose and a sturdy neck, the result of hard work rather than diet. His chest too was well-shaped and youthfully slim, and his legs bent slightly outwards, which made for a firm stance. He was draped in a garment sewn out of wolf-skins, and he used to take on wild boars, jackals, wolves and bulls in heat, and would display the scars from these contests. Some say that this Heracles was a "son of the soil, sprung from among the people of Boeotia," but Herodes says that he heard him say that his mother was a woman of such strength that she served as a cowherd, while his father was the farmer-hero Marathon whose statue stands at Marathon itself. Herodes asked this Heracles whether he was immortal as well. But he replied "I live only longer than a mortal." He asked him also what he lived on and "Heracles" said "I live on milk most of the time, and am fed by goats and herds of cows and breeding mares, and the she-ass too offers a good light milk. But when I come across barley meal, I consume ten quarts, and farmers in Marathon and Boeotia supply me with this banquet; and they give me the nickname 'Agathion' ['little goodfellow'] because they think I actually bring them good luck."

We can see why such an image would have appealed to Herodes Atticus: the stranger has the credentials of noble savage and primitive survival, and he well illustrates the notion, one way or another, of the *agathos daimon*. Except in size and lack of mischief, he well fits the rural English notion of a Robin Goodfellow figure. Lucian alluded briefly (*Demonax* 1) to "his great size and extraordinary strength, his open-air lifestyle on Parnassus, his uncomfortable bed, his living off the mountain and his achievements in taking out robbers, making roads in inaccessible country and bridging places difficult to cross." As in the case of Robin Goodfellow, he is the offspring of divine and human liaison, and Robin Goodfellow will similarly perform tasks in exchange for bread and milk.[60]

THE TRICKSTER

One figure stands out from the rest of this motley crew, many of them local to a Greek cultural context in the form we have them. We find that a number of quite crucial operations in the relationship between gods and men have been brought about by means of treachery or trickery, and indeed, we can become aware that some gods or heroes, and indeed antiheroes, are perhaps best seen as professional tricksters.[61] This brings us face to face with one of the most international of folkloric figures, the trickster,[62] who turns out, unsurprisingly, to be also one of the most chameleonic and resourceful, transcending most categories of classification. He may be anything from a clever god to a clever slave, who easily crosses boundaries between creation-mythology and local village pranks. The general stereotype in nonliterate societies, well studied by anthropologists and Jungian psychologists alike, can be characterized along the following lines:

> The trickster is a subversive but also creative figure (Prometheus functions as a creator figure, but disobeys Zeus).
> He may come from a whole generation of tricksters (Odysseus is grandson of Autolycus, Sisyphus is the son of Prometheus).
> He is as much likely to be the victim of tricks as their perpetrator (Sisyphus seduces Autolycus' daughter in revenge for the latter's theft of his cattle).
> The counter-trick is a constantly recurring theme.
> He can be a seducer of extraordinary powers (Hermes in popular representation with simply a head and genitals, as a symbol of good luck).
> He can come to a sticky end when he overplays his hand . . . (Sisyphus offends the gods by escaping death, but reckoning in the Underworld awaits

when he finally dies of old age; Prometheus is strung up in the Caucasus, though finally does a deal and is rescued).

He is not too far from animal connexions (Autolycus might be translated "self-wolf").

He is an underdog.

Not every trickster figure is likely to show all of these characteristics at any one showing, but taken together, they form a pattern which most tricksters will sooner or later draw on.

Hermes

We can now trace aspects of these features over several familiar Greek figures. The god most clearly connected with cunning, trickery, and culture is Hermes; in Homer he is already fully grown and a herald of Zeus, escorter of the souls to the Underworld. But the *Homeric Hymn to Hermes* preserves a very different picture, where he is practicing thievery even from the cradle, including the rustling of Apollo's cattle. This development continues: he invents the lyre and exchanges it for Apollo's cattle, and he occasions great amusement on the part of Zeus at this baby prank.[63] We should notice the connection here already between thieving and invention and resourcefulness: it is as if the idea of theft and entrepreneurship are somehow linked or indeed indivisible. It is no surprise that the patron god of thieves should also be that of commerce.

But Hermes is not the first to show traits or traces of the trickster. It is rather Prometheus who immediately springs to mind, not least because he is of an older generation and a different line from Zeus himself. He is a Titan, and there is perhaps here a suggestion that cunning, wisdom, and experience is a trait of an older and wiser generation, not to be despised or underestimated. And trickery and resourcefulness are associated with charter mythology, helping mankind to attain his present destiny in the face of arbitrary decisions of his fellow gods. He gives mankind fire and cheats Zeus of the better portion of sacrifices on mankind's behalf. But this stimulates a countertrickery by the gods, so that man is no better off.[64]

We see a similar role already in the case of the Sumerian Enki, Babylonian Ea. He acts to save mankind from the flood by a trick, by tipping off Utnapishtim, the Noah figure of the Babylonian flood story. And yet in the Adapa story, when man has antagonized him, Ea tells Adapa to go up to heaven and not eat food, causing him to lose the prospect of immortality.[65] We should note that Enki-Ea and Prometheus are both involved in flood myths in the same way: Ea tips off Utnapishtim, where Prometheus warns his own son Deucalion in one version to build an ark. The biblical Noah invents wine, and his sons found the different races of the world; we have a similar wine myth attached to the family of Deucalion himself, whose son Orestheus discovers the first vinestock (though this myth is generally supplanted in Greek tradition by that of Dionysus).

It seems a pity that we know next to nothing about the most acknowledged trickster in Greek literature, namely Sisyphus. He is presented as a king of Corinth, and he has a contest of wits with the other master of trickery, Autolycus. The latter's father, Hermes, gives him the power always to escape capture when he commits his robberies and also enables him to disguise whatever he has stolen so that he can turn a black animal into a white one. Sisyphus accordingly notices that his own flocks are getting smaller, while those of Autolycus are getting larger, and he is able to detect the trick by marking his cattle on the undersides of their hooves.[66] Most subversive among Sisyphus' own tricks is that he outwits Death. Zeus had sent Death to fetch him for betraying Zeus' affair with Aigina; Sisyphus hoodwinked Death and bound him; Death was freed by Ares and came back to get Sisyphus, but the hero told his wife Merope not to bury his body, which meant that he could not be admitted to the Underworld. He was allowed by Hades to go back to earth to punish his wife Merope for impiety. Back to life, he made a point of not doing so and lived until he died of old age (but he still had to face punishment in the Underworld).[67] One notes the strong resemblance between Sisyphus and the Xisouthros, the Sumerian Noah/Deucalion figure: we might notice that the biblical Noah, too, lives to an unnaturally long age.

Odysseus himself exhibits comparable traits: we find him already in the *Odyssey* with a record of trickery at Troy, as a resourceful liar, as he has to be to survive Penelope's suitors, and as a liar even for pleasure, when he deceives his aged father, Laertes. He makes love to a goddess and a witch figure in Calypso and Circe and is a taker of risks that do not always pay off, as when he is trapped by the Cyclops. Later tradition makes him the enemy and murderer of Palamedes, a rival in resourcefulness, and he is a synonym for treachery in the treatment of Philoctetes, whose magic bow he must obtain if Troy is to fall. For all the dignity of Sophocles' version in the *Philoctetes*, the simple trickster of folklore is built into the plot itself.

Some Native American Tricksters

But comparison further afield suggests that Greek trickster material has been toned down and overlaid with civilized and civilizing treatment. It is perhaps in North American Indian oral mythology that we can now effectively catch a glimpse of a full-functioning trickster cycle in its most uninhibited and archaic form. Paul Radin's study, *The Trickster*, presents a whole sequence of similar cycles, of which the most elaborate is that of the Winnebago trickster, from the borders of Wisconsin and Nebraska. In this case the trickster is not given any precise animal form, though it is clear that he inhabits an animal society none too far removed from that of Aesopic fable: he has a rivalry with the mink, the coyote, and the bear (whom he kills).[68] In a good many cases it has to be said that his resourceful pranks are as often as not turned against the trickster himself. He kills a buffalo by surrounding it with straw men and sending it into mud. But why? Because he left his weapons behind in a fit of temper because they could not do anything on their own. Or his right hand has arguments with his left hand about the division of the carcass, and the left hand is injured in the struggle; or he burns his own backside without quite realizing it; or his genitals are sent off to have intercourse with a chief's daughter by remote control but get substantially bitten off by a vindictive chipmunk when he uses them to trap it inside a hole in a tree. This kind of escapade goes hand in hand with stories that involve laxatives: he gives a mink one such laxative and arranges for him to sleep with a chief's daughter—with imaginable results.[69]

The Ultimate Ancient Trickster?

Extant ancient literature has not quite matched the crude directness of the North American tricksters. It is perhaps in a human and folktale context that we find the most clearly articulated materials in antiquity: Herodotus tells several episodes of a story that survives in modern versions in Georgia and elsewhere about a resourceful Egyptian rogue who robs a king[70] and manages to sleep with the latter's daughter, sent to a brothel as a honey trap. He escapes by giving her a dead man's arm, only to marry her as a reward for his resourcefulness. We have a Greek doublet of the robbery at least in a tradition about Agamedes and Trophonius (Pausanias 9.37.3). But the most thorough and sustained portrait of an ancient trickster figure to survive is probably the Aesop of the *Life of Aesop*, an anonymous and popular work of indefinite date.[71] Here we have a single trickster figure endowed with the full set of traits suggested above: he is a natural underdog, being misshapen and initially dumb, and he has to cope time and time again with the treachery of his fellow slaves or his master; he is not too far removed from animal connections since he is sufficiently misshapen to pass for some sort of animal and excite frequent ridicule on that account. He is adept at countertrickery, as when he turns the tables on the fellows slaves who try to frame him for eating the figs they have stolen. He persuades his master to administer an enema, and they throw up the figs, while he does not. He is sexually well endowed, as his master's wife lusts after his enormous member, and he can service her nine times in apparently quick succession (and think of a smart way to deceive his master into allowing him to do so a 10th time). He is subversive toward his stupid and conceited master, Xanthias of Samos, and amazingly ingenious when he solves the riddles the king of Babylon has received from the king of Egypt. He, too, comes to a sticky end when he insults Apollo and the Delphians and is thrown over a cliff in revenge. Of the standard prescription, only one is missing here: the genealogical connection with other tricksters. Above all, Aesop is quite securely a figure of folklore, and the so-called *Aesop Romance* is the nearest thing antiquity produced to the manner and matter of Renaissance and post-Renaissance chapbooks. The riddle context occurs early in the oriental tale of Ahiquar; it would be no surprise to find doublets of more of such a text.

CONCLUSION

It is scarcely possible to construct a system or hierarchy in which our various operatives can function in relation to one another. We naturally expect the personnel of folklore to be varied, especially given the wide chronological span of Greco-Roman civilization and its geographical spread. Pans and nymphs may be in an often ambiguous relationship to one another: a Pan figure might well function as a trickster, as the satyrs seem routinely to have done in satyric drama, and there is a natural overlap between Pans and demons. But however much intellectuals might try, there is no realistic way of putting child-eating monsters and demons invoked in curses into the same thought world as the local nymphs, other than by saying that in the popular imagination, there is room for any number of such creatures and that all may be necessary to keep the supernatural world in operation.

NOTES

1. See Larson (2001), esp. 61–90.
2. Ibid., 65.
3. s.v. Bormon.
4. *IG* 14.2040.
5. Larson (2001), 70f.
6. Ibid., 71ff.

7. For the special case of Arkas, see Anderson (2004), 18; Pausanias 8.41–5.

8. Apollonius, 2.456–89; Callimachus, *Hymn* 6; Ovid, *Met.* 8.738–878.

9. *Daphnis and Chloe* 1.4ff., 3.27, 2.21–28.

10. Larson (2001), 197.

11. Plato, *Phaedrus* 230B.

12. Larson (2001), 196f.

13. Memnon of Heracleia, *FGrH* 434 F 1.28.9; Larson (2001), 196.

14. On nymphs and "limenality/initiation," cf. Dowden (1989), 126–129.

15. Larson (2001), 188–191.

16. References in Larson (2001), 185.

17. Texts and discussion in Larson (2001), 191ff.

18. cf. also Purkiss (2000).

19. For the folklore of *neraides,* see Lawson (1910), 130–146.

20. Aelian, *Varia Historia* 10.18.

21. On Pan and Arcadia, see Borgeaud (1988), 47–73.

22. On the association, see Borgeaud (1988), 100.

23. Herodotus 6.105ff.; Borgeaud (1988), 133ff.

24. Eusebius, *PE* 5.5f.; Borgeaud (1988), 117.

25. Nonnus 1.409–534; Borgeaud (1988), 121.

26. Borgeaud (1988), 125; Johns (1982), facing p. 16 (Herculaneum).

27. Borgeaud (1988), plate 4 (Pan Painter Crater, James Fund and Special Contribution 10.185).

28. Theopompus, *FGrH* 115F, 75c.

29. For interpretation, see Coleman (1977), 203–206.

30. e.g., Seaford (1984), 33–44.

31. Alexander Polyhistor, cited by Diogenes Laertius 8.32, *FGrH* 273 F93, para. 32.

32. Flint et al. (1999), 281ff.

33. *PGM* 1.97–103, 187–191, tr. O'Neil in Betz (1986), 5–8.

34. Plato, *Sym.* 202E–203A.

35. Plutarch, *Mor.* 360E.

36. Good exposition of classical demonology in Flint et al. (1999), 282–292.

37. References in Flint et al. (1999), 292–309.

38. Flint et al. (1999), 301.

39. Pythagoras of Rhodes, ap. Aeneas of Gaza, *Theophrastus*, p. 54 Colonna.

40. Philostratus, *Heroicus* 4ff.

41. Hedreen (1991), 313–330.

42. Texts in Ogden (2002), 146–178, and esp. (2001), on necromancy.

43. Plato, *Phaedo* 81Cf.

44. *Aeneid* 6.325–30, 426–443.

45. *De Deo Socratis* 15.

46. Tertullian, *de Anima* 56f., with Ogden (2002), 151.

47. Apuleius, *Met.* 9.29ff.

48. Cicero, *de Divinatione* 1.57.

49. On the concept of the bogeyman, see Warner (1999).

50. Callimachus, *Hymn to Artemis* 66–71.

51. Schol.Aristophenes, *Pax.* 758, *LIMC* 6.189; Fontenrose (1959), 100–104, 115 no. 7.

52. Schol. Theocritus 15.40; *Schol. Aristides 42 Dindorff; also Xen., *Hell.* 4.4.17; Tambornino, *RE* 16.1, 309–311; Rohde, *Psyche* Appendix 6.

53. For child-killing demons in general, see Johnston (1995).

54. See also *RE* 5 (1905), 2540–2543; cf. Philostratus, *VA* 4.25; cf. Hecate, Lamia.

55. Lawson (1910), 176–179; Lobel and Page; Burkert (1992) sees as a Gallu-Demon in Sumero-Akkadian (cf. Rohde, *Psyche* Appendix 6); again, a woman who died an untimely death, Suda; see also Rose (1959), 143.

56. Rose (1959), 143f.

57. Ibid., 144. This evidence is taken that "a philosophical theory (of *daimones*) has made its way into fairly general belief in ancient times, has arrived by two different routes, one official, the other popular, into the minds of the peasants of today." But it should be clear enough that Plato is drawing for his Socratic *daimon* on a simple and popular notion.

58. On these, see Burkert (1985), 281–285.

59. Plutarch, *De Defectu Oraculorum* 17, *Mor.* 419B–E, on which see Hansen (2002), 133–136.

60. Further discussion in Anderson (1994), 128ff.

61. For the trickster in relation to Greek mythology, see Kerenyi in Radin (1956), 173–191; and in general, Hynes and Doty (1993). Doty's treatment is inclined to treat testimony in, e.g., Lucian and Plato as more or less of equal value with standard early literary sources; in the latter case, in particular, this is treacherous, at least for attempting to establish a basic folkloric picture of Hermes.

62. For the type, see Hynes and Doty (1993).

63. *Homeric Hymn to Hermes* 12–520, passim.

64. For analysis of the two Hesiodic treatments, see Vernant (1980), 183–201.

65. For Enki, see Kramer and Maier (1989).

66. Gantz (1993), 173–176 (Sisyphus in general); trick with the hooves, Hyginus, *Fabulae* 201, scholiast on Lycophron 344.

67. References in Gantz (1993), 174.

68. Text of the Winnebago cycle in Radin (1972), 3–53.

69. Ibid., sections 4, 3, 5, 14, 16, 38, 45.

70. Herodotus 2.121 (tale of Rhampsinitus's treasury).

71. For characterization, see Hansen (1998), 106–111.

Seven
Folk Customs, Luck, Superstition

Apart from the world of nymphs, demons, and diverse bogeymen stands the ordinary day-to-day world of humans, governed as they are, according to Lucian,[1] by hope and fear. That state of affairs will account for many of the observances and behavior patterns we can see embodied in popular custom. Among the practices in antiquity that might be puzzling, unintelligible, or otherwise unfamiliar, one stands out from the pages of Plutarch's *Roman Questions* as instantly recognizable and familiar: Why are brides carried over the threshold and do not go of their own accord?[2] We still maintain the custom (or have revived it) with no more unanimity of explanation than had the Roman world itself. It serves as a useful introduction to the world of customs—traditions that are "done because they're done" but which would doubtless have had *some* original reason to account for them. This particular custom embraces notions of liminality, a favorite preoccupation of the anthropologist: it marks out marriage as a turning point or rite of passage that must be accompanied by ritual in order to ensure good luck. Plutarch offers no fewer than three explanations: that it is a survival of an old Roman tradition of marriage by capture, instituted by the founder Romulus in person, or that it represents the ritual unwillingness of the bride to enter the place where she will lose her virginity (which, on reflection, is little more than a variant on the previous explanation since Romulus himself was said to have initiated the practice). The third explanation is perhaps more ominous: the bride is brought to the house under constraint and may not leave of her own free will. Plutarch adds a parallel to this last reason from his native Boeotia—the custom of burning the axles of the bride's conveyance so that she is symbolically prevented from leaving.[3] The avoidance of bad luck is not suggested by Plutarch but is certainly the point of an allusion in a wedding poem of Catullus; it is also a common explanation in subsequent accounts of the custom, either because contact with the earth will drain the bride or because spirits congregate at the threshold—presumably, a bride who stumbled over the threshold would quite literally "get off on the wrong footing."[4]

Before we puzzle over individual practices, the label "folk customs" itself should be seen as a deliberately flexible one: it will include religious rituals and ceremonies where these are of popular origin and will exclude religious festivals inspired by a single-named historic individuals, like the Roman Imperial Cult conceived as propaganda for individual emperors. It will include acts that mark phases of the month or year and the basic life cycle of birth, marriage, and death and rites to delineate and protect home and family.

FESTIVALS

General descriptions of ancient festivals are readily available and perhaps too easily tail off into collections of curiosities, in much the same way as they obviously did in the eyes of ancient antiquarian scholars like Plutarch in the two sets of *Greek Questions* and *Roman Questions*.[5] But it is useful first to pose a folklorist's or anthropologist's question as to why we celebrate festivals at all and what might be the typical ingredients of a traditional celebration or observance in the first place.[6] We must face the fact that festivals frequently survive with a momentum of their own when their original meaning has been forgotten, a fact deplored often enough in relation to "the commercialization of Christmas" in a largely secular society. Very often, the incidental aspects of festivals such as holidays (games, pranks, drinking, or other licentious behavior) are likely to perpetuate themselves, even when formally ceremonial aspects of a festival are subject to change: people simply need a break, and such breaks may align themselves with natural lulls in the work cycles of an agricultural community and involve a whole local population at fixed points in the calendar. Others are more restricted, such as those confined to occupational or family groups, with the latter, in particular, concerned with rites of passage, including birth, puberty, marriage, and death. Secondary celebrations may readily engage around them, such as christening customs and birthday parties, the bachelor party and show of presents before a wedding, wedding anniversaries thereafter, or funeral wakes after a death. The notion of "excuse for a celebration" may seldom be too far away, even in the last of these instances. Festivals may be also seen as promoting communal cohesion, often with a secondary economic or political stimulus; in the special case of rites of passage, there will be the acceptance of a new role in life. They may include some traditional validation, such as a legendary foundation and its commemoration, the cultivation of some symbol, feasting and drinking (formal or informal), traditional singing, dancing, and recitation. And further tradition is likely to become attracted to an existing core, in ways which later generations may find difficult to explain.

THE FARMER'S YEAR

A substantial number of Greek cults fall back on the conservative countryside and underline the continuing importance of agriculture and stock rearing: these will have dictated diet in large measure for the population as a whole[7] and so the whole rhythm of the year itself. Such a highly educated writer as Maximus of Tyre in the second century A.D. acknowledges the rural base of festivals:

> It seems to me that only the farmers seem to have instituted festivals and initiations. They are the first to have established dancing choruses in honour of Dionysus at the wine press and rites in honour of Demeter at the threshing floor.[8]

There is a very strong relationship in both Greek and Roman practice between agricultural practicality and divinely sanctioned custom: at the beginning of his treatise *On Farm Management (de agri cultura)* Varro emphasizes his invocation to Father Jupiter and Mother Earth, then the Sun and Moon, as marking the season for sowing and reaping; then Ceres and Bacchus as the providers of grain and wine; and perhaps more surprisingly, Robigus (Mildew) as the deity who keeps away blight, thanks to the observance of the Robigalia. The list continues, and ends with Bonus Eventus, the god of good fortune: *sine successu ac bono eventu frustratio est, non cultura* (without good order and good luck, there is failure, not cultivation).[9] Accordingly, a high proportion of major cults have agricultural origins, and rites may reflect basic agricultural tasks: sowing, reaping, threshing, gardening, and fruit watering, all of them needing divine protection at an ancient and quasi-magical level. Hence Demeter and Kore (the Maiden) appear in relation to cereals more often in the farming instructor Hesiod than in the aristocratic subject matter of Homer. For Hesiod, basic agricultural tasks belong to Demeter: sowing and plowing to the Proerosia, seeding to the Thesmophoria, harvesting to the Anthesteria, and so on; and there is a prayer to Demeter and Zeus that the fruit of Demeter is to be full and heavy when the handle of the plow is to be grasped to begin sowing.[10] Hence the Thesmophoria in autumn for sowing; in winter, sacrifice to Demeter *chloe* for corn threshing. The Thesmophoria was a woman's festival, in which female fertility was prayed for as well as that of the crops; putrefied remains of previously sacrificed pigs were mixed with seed corn and laid on altars, as fertility magic, the swine being sacred to Demeter. The Thargelia was seen in antiquity itself as a festival of first fruits, after the pot containing the first harvested cereals in May. It also entailed the use of a *pharmakos* ("scapegoat") to act as a purification agent: this marginal figure was sumptuously fed, paraded, then ejected from the city or even thrown over a cliff, thus cleansing the land before the next agricultural year.[11]

The festivals of Dionysus are best known in Athens through their connections with Attic drama, but again, their basic credentials are related to the rhythms of viticulture. The Rural Dionysia was celebrated at deme or village level in December, and our earliest surviving Old Comedy, Aristophanes' *Acharnians,* has a presentation of it: the head of the household sings an obscene song in honor of Phales, two slaves carry a phallus in procession, and the master's daughter acts as a basket carrier. The City Dionysia in March also entailed procession (again including a phallus) and was celebrated in honor of Dionysus in relation to Eleuthera, where he had driven mad the daughters of Eleuther and appeared at a dispute between Xanthus and Melanthus.

The Anthesteria, in February, is more puzzling: it entailed the sampling of the new vintage, a drinking competition to empty a five-liter measure *(chytra),* slave participation, and presents of little *chytra* to children, but this is curiously joined to a third day's celebration placating the dead or evil spirits. We may be dealing with arbitrary conflation, or it may be that a precise and rational connection still eludes us. Of the third dramatic festival, the Lenaea, we know little (January/early February): Eleusinian officials participated, and there may accordingly have been connection with the mysteries.

As to festivals in general, many seem to go back to Neolithic origins, such as the Bouphonia (ox slaying), and many would have originated in communities of village status, to be taken over eventually by a *polis,* or city-state. Many of the fertility festivals were performed by women and also enjoyed the status of mysteries. A mythological origin might underlie the civic identity of a festival, as in the case of the Athenian Oschophoria and Deipnophoria, associated with the events of Theseus' expedition to Crete:[12] the former, indeed, entailed the telling of tales, in commemoration of those told to the youthful victims en route to Crete as a sacrifice to the Minotaur.

We have a great deal of scattered information about cults elsewhere in Greece, often casually distributed among the sources described in chapter 2. Such, for example, is the ritual described by Pausanias around the hero cult of Aristomenes among the Messenians.[13] The author gives an account of how the Thebans claimed to have retrieved Aristomenes' body from Rhodes and that even after his death, he had been present at the battle of Leuctra (compare the Athenian claim of the presence of Pan at Marathon) and that in an alternative tradition the oracle of Trophonius had instructed that his shield had been used by the Thebans as a talisman. The variation in the tradition appears to point to popular propaganda on the part of the Thebans: a major historical turning point has still to be validated by divine intervention.

The same primarily rural inflexion of ancient religious festival is to be found among Roman celebrations[14] such as the Compitalia[15]: even the name derives from the intersection point of four farms, where a four-directional shrine was set up to enable the lar, or household spirit, to travel freely. The festival marked the end of the agricultural year: the farmers would hang up a plow on the shrine itself, together with a woolen doll for each free member of the household, with a woolen ball for each of the slaves; the next day, there would be a sacrifice at the altar and a holiday—the workforce had to be renewed for the work of the months ahead. The festival was urbanized around apartment blocks under a president, with street intersections serving as the central point for improvised festivities: the equivalent of a modern street party, in other words.

As in Greece, too, the rhythm of some festivals is self-determined by the nature of ancient agriculture. Where it was impossible to ensure that all cattle were supplied with sufficient winter fodder and when few agricultural tasks could be undertaken, circumstances favored the occurrence of a festival like the Saturnalia (December 17), the Compitalia (January), and the Kalends of January itself, near enough to the winter solstice to act as a natural beginning of the year. For similar reason the Consualia is set as the festival of a Roman granary deity Conus (*condere*, "store"), with festivals on August 21 and December 15, marking the gathering of the harvest and the onset of winter, also associated with two festivals of Ops: Opconsivia (August 25) and Opalia (December 19).[16]

Cato the Elder offers some rituals and prayers for specific agricultural operations: to Jupiter before sowing or at the harvest or for expiation when cutting down a tree or at the borders of a field.[17] The author's marked conservatism and aversion to foreign (especially Greek) imported customs guarantees the native nature of such rituals, at least as he regarded them. Such is the prayer and offerings to Jupiter Dapalis accompanying a rest day for oxen and their drivers as well as for the participants in the rite: the libation and sacrifice itself is followed by the planting of millet, panic grass, garlic, and lentils. A complex routine of offerings and prayers to Ceres, Janus, Jupiter, and Juno is prescribed for the offering of *proca praecidianea* before the harvesting of spelt, wheat, barely, beans, and rape seed. For the clearing of a grove the formula has to be wider and less specific ("whether thou be god or goddess to whom this grove is sacred") and the *piaculum* of a pig has to be offered, with additional rites for every day (inclusive of rest days) that the corresponding land is being worked. Field borders are particularly critical to the farmer, and a *suoveturilia* (sacrifice of pig, lamb, and calf) is required: "that thou mayest keep away, avert, and remove sickness, both visible and invisible, barrenness and destruction, ruin [of crops] and foul weather; and that thou mayest allow my harvest, my grain vineyards, and my bushes to flourish, and to bring forth abundantly; protect my shepherds and my flocks, and grant vigour to me, my house and my household. . . ." (the elaborately inclusive grammar of sacrificial routine continues, in order to leave no contingency to chance).[18]

SOME PUZZLING FESTIVALS

The festivals of the Parilia and Lupercalia illustrate different folk-based customs again, but rather less intelligibly. Ovid presents the former in his versified calendar, the *Fasti,* as follows:

> Kindly Pales, may you grant me your favour as I sing the rites of the shepherd, if I offer my respects to your festival. Indeed I have often borne the ashes of a calf and the bean straws in my full hands to provide purification. Indeed I have leapt over the three flames laid in order, and the wet laurel has sprinkled its water on me. The goddess is moved and looks favourably on my work. My ship slides from its dock, already my sails have the winds they need. Go, people, gather material for fumigation from the virgin's altar: Vesta will give it; by her gift you will be pure: the blood of a horse and the ashes of a calf will grant you purification, the third ingredient the empty stalks of hard beans.[19]

He then continues with specific instructions to the country shepherd: he is to purify the sheep at the onset of dusk, sprinkling the ground with water and sweeping it with a broom; he has to decorate the pen with leaves and branches and garland the door. He has to make smoke from pure sulfur, which has to touch the sheep. The wood is specified as male olive, pine, juniper, and laurel; there is to be millet in a basket with millet cakes as an offering to the country goddess: she has to have her favorite meats and milk in a pail, as an offering to Pales.

Ovid then offers a great variety of explanations for the origin of the festival: the fire is purificatory, and the body is to be touched by both this and the other basic element water. He offers reference to Phaethon and Deucalion and to the elements of fire and water as life-forces: was the discovery of fire the origins of the Parilia, or Aeneas' escape from the flames of Troy, or the burning of the old houses at the transition to the new dwellings of Rome? Plutarch also connects it with early Rome, but as a secondary development from a pre-Roman rural festival.[20] Once more, the sheer diversity of explanation underlines how little was certainly known in the Augustan period. Whatever the actual explanation, the details are now preserved in their own terms and for their own sake.

Like the Parilia, the Lupercalia was seen as a festival of purification, and although he offers explanations, Plutarch does not pretend to be able to explain the enactments precisely:

> And moreover we see that the Luperci begin their circuit from the place where Romulus is held to have been exposed. But the ceremonies make it difficult to make conjectures about their origin. For the priests sacrifice goats, and when two young lads of noble ancestry have been brought before them, some touch the lads' foreheads with a blood-stained knife, while others at once wipe away the stains by applying wool dipped in milk. And the lads have to laugh when their foreheads have been wiped. And after this they cut the goatskins into strips and run back and forth wearing nothing but a loincloth, and using the thongs to strike anyone they meet. And the young wives do not avoid these blows, but consider that they help with conception and childbirth. It is a peculiar feature of the festival that the Luperci also sacrifice a dog.[21]

The details are so specific and eccentric as to suggest that some mythical story is being reenacted that was already lost by Plutarch's time and that is still safely beyond reconstruction.[22] Plutarch cites an antiquarian Butas as suggesting that it reenacted the victory race of Romulus and Remus themselves after the defeat of Amulius: the sword is advanced as a symbol of their original danger, the milk of their nourishment; Caius Acilius had suggested that before the city was founded, Romulus' followers had lost their flocks, and this reenacts a search for them, naked, so that they should not be troubled by sweat, and that the sacrifice of the dog is purificatory—the dog would then be a sacrifice to the original she-wolf. Some combination of the various explanations might also be plausible: the fact that the youths are two in number and aristocratic would indeed suggest Romulus and Remus, while the laughter still remains beyond explanation.

The explanation advanced by H. J. Rose, however, remains convincing. No god is mentioned as having been honored, and so the ceremony may well have been an ancient magical one, of a "beating of the bounds" character, to ward off evils from the ancient historical pomerium of the earliest territory of Rome (extending only a little beyond the Palatine), including the evil for a very small community of infertility. The etymology of Luperci (from *lupus* + *arceo* = wolf-averter?) is consistent with identifying the young men as "goat-men" rather than as the wolves themselves.[23] But other explanations are possible, including a context in February where a commemoration of the dead is taking place.

In some instances we cannot always afford to trust even sources whom we might have expected to be reliable reporters, as in the case of Ovid's account of the Robigalia:

Ovid, *Fasti* 4.905–942

On that day [April 25], as I was coming back to Rome from Nomentum, a crowd in white robes stood blocking the middle of the road. A priest was making his way to the grove of ancient Mildew, to offer the entrails of a dog and sheep to the flames. At once I approached so as not to be unaware of the rite. Your priest, Romulus, pronounced these words: "Scaly Mildew, spare the corn of Ceres, and let its smooth top tremble on the surface of the soil. Allow the crops, nurtured by the favouring stars of the heavens, to grow until they are ready for the sickle. Your power is no light one: the corn you have marked down, the miserable farmers count as lost. Nor do the winds harm the corn as much as you, nor the rains, nor does it pale like this when consumed by the white frost, so much as when the sun warms the damp stalks. Then is the time for anger, dread goddess: spare it I pray and keep your scabrous hands from the harvest: do not harm the crops: it is enough for you to be able to harm them. . . ." The incense, the wine, the sheep's gut and the disgusting entrails of a filthy hound, we saw him offer it on the hearth. Then he said: "Why, you ask, is a strange victim offered in these rites?" [as I had asked]: "listen to the reason," said the priest. "The dog is the one they call the Icarian, and when the earth is parched dry at the rise of that constellation, the corn ripens too early. This dog is laid on the altar in place of the starry dog, and he is killed only because of his name."

Explanation, or alleged explanation, connects the sacrifice of the dog with the rise of the Dog star. This was not until August 2: there must be at least confusion, if not misinformation, here: a dog was indeed sacrificed at the point where the crops were deemed to be at risk from mildew, but this may well have been a movable feast, which the Robigalia was not, and so a matter of coincidence. Nor is this the only difficulty, as Ovid should be coming from the east and not the north. We might ask whether a clearly official festival should be labeled as folkloric, but the presiding by the priest of Romulus and the attribution of the festival to Numa by Pliny both underline that this was regarded as an early festival. The oddity of Mildew as a deity itself being asked not to infect the crops has an air, certainly, of prerational religion about it.[24] All this might lead us to believe that either the priest himself is ill informed or the details of the connection between the dog and the rite were genuinely lost and Ovid himself genuinely misinformed, but the vividness of the occasion may be suspect in itself. All in all, it is difficult to imagine why either Ovid or anyone else should have chosen to invent the curious blend of details offered.

From suspicion of the authenticity of rites we can move to the prospect of fakelore itself. We have a useful notice in Lucian of an invented festival, but one drawing very heavily on traditional elements and operating at what was, in effect, village level. Although we have the name of the inventor, and so this festival is neither completely traditional nor anonymous, it gives us an insight into how potential traditions could be activated in the first place. The false prophet Alexander, as Lucian sees him, is seeking to extend the publicity and prestige of his oracle:[25]

> For Alexander set up mysteries and torchlight ceremonies and priesthoods, lasting three days in succession, to be held every year. And on the first day there was a proclamation, as at Athens, as follows: "If any atheist or Christian or Epicurean has arrived to spy on these rites, let him depart at once; but let those who believe in the gods celebrate the mysteries with heaven's blessing." Then right at the beginning there was a "driving out": Alexander began with "Christians Out!," and the whole mob would respond with "Epicureans Out!" Then there was Leto in childbirth and the birth of Apollo, his marriage to Coronis, and the birth of Asclepius. On the second day there was the epiphany of Glycon and the birth of the god. On the third there was the wedding of Podalirius and the mother of Alexander: it was named the day of torches and torches were burned. And lastly there was the love of Selene and Alexander, and the birth of Rutilianus' wife. Our Endymion Alexander bore the torch and served as hierophant . . . a short time later he came in again dressed as a priest, in utter silence, and he himself would say in a loud voice "Hail Glycon!"; and his acolytes, some sort of Eumolpids and Kerukes no doubt from Paphlagonia, with brogans on their feet and a good deal of garlic on their breath, would respond "Hail Alexander!" And often in the torchlight and the mystery frolics his thigh would be deliberately exposed and show itself golden, of course covered around with gilded leather and gleaming in the lamplight.

Lucian's ironic language points to the cultural contrast with the mysteries of Eleusis, of which the ceremonies at Abonouteichos are a poor man's caricature, and in a sense we are dealing with a kind of folk-kitsch. The Eleusinian

Mysteries were indeed a three-day festival, like this one, but Alexander has cut corners by skipping the long period of run-up and eliding the *xenelasia,* the expulsion of outsiders, into the three-day period itself: it may well be that the native Cappadocians, gullible as they are, simply cannot afford too much time off. There is also a sense that Alexander himself is something of a one-man band in the way that Lucian makes him keep himself the center of attention. But from another perspective we have a useful description of evolving cult and the potent combination of myth, healing, spectacle, and the rest.

Nor are the mysteries invented by Alexander our only known picture of vigorous local tradition. Likewise, in the later second century A.D. Apuleius reports, albeit in a fictional context, the operation of an annual Risus festival, a festival of laughter, celebrated at Hypata in Thessaly, of which his antihero Lucius is the butt—actually accused of three murders that have not taken place (*Met.* 3.11). We have no particular reason to question the plausibility (as opposed to the authenticity) of such a carnavalesque procedure: we can compare the Roman Saturnalia, with its role reversals and generally anarchic atmosphere, and indeed our own April Fool's day, which may owe something to the latter. But the fact that a single outsider is made the victim for the whole town has once more the air of a *pharmakos* about it: Lucius may be pressed into service as, in some sense, a scapegoat.

LUCKY AND UNLUCKY DAYS

Perhaps the most obvious material of any to classify as folklore is the complex of superstitions relating to lucky and unlucky days. This author's childhood was exposed to little beyond avoiding Friday the 13th or the weather lore that rain on St. Swithin's day would last for 40 days. But Greco-Roman tradition was much richer. Hesiod's *Works and Days* devotes its "days" section to a mixture of materials: days that are generally lucky, sometimes distinction between even degrees of lucky day (the 12th luckier than the 11th), and on sometimes arbitrary grounds—the spider spins its web and the ant hoards its pile on the 12th. There is a clear analogy with advice to a woman to set up her loom and get on with work on the same day. Some days are good for one thing, but bad for another.

Comparison with other ancient cultures affords only limited explanation of these oddities. The information does not always accord, though there is more Babylonian than Egyptian about Hesiod's material. Some of the thinking there must have been might have begun by associating a particular day with a god and then transferring the god's attributes to the day: this seems an obvious procedure to explain why the "first sixth" of the month (in a tripartite subdivision) is favorable for the birth of a boy[26] but that he will be "fond of sharp speech, lies and cursing words, and stealthy converse," echoing attributes of Hermes. Other divine associations give rise to a fear of fifth days: the Erinyes assisted at the birth of personified Oath and Strife on a fifth day.[27]

Some days are once again tied to specifically agricultural operations: it might come as a surprise that Hesiod enjoins the eighth of the month for gelding the boar and the bull, the 12th for the mule.[28] It may also be ominous that some of the lore is said to be known only to few.[29] This is as much as to suggest that such associations are no longer fully observed and that Hesiod is either exceptionally purist or superstitiously conservative. At any rate, the key is in the conclusion: "That man is prosperous and blessed in them who knows all these things and performs his work faultless in the eyes of the deathless gods"—again, a reminder of the divine associations of at least some of the operations.

Such "day" superstitions continue with variation throughout antiquity, as in the *apophrades* (impure days) in the Athenian calendar: they could have an association with inauspicious rites, such as those of the Plynteria, the ritual washing of the statue of Athena, or with homicide trials in the Areopagus, or (possibly) with the moonless period at the end of the month. The result was temple closure and the avoidance of business enterprise. It is no surprise to find Trimalchio with his own personal calendar of lucky and unlucky days, and Roman practice had official lists of *dies nefasti* on which no official business could be transacted.[30] But the interest in Hesiod's information lies in its uniqueness: it engages with topics different from and more detailed than those in more recent hemerological literature, and it is clearly from an echelon that is quite different from anything else that has survived.[31] One notes that Virgil did not include a "days" section as such in the *Georgics,* where so much else of Hesiod is echoed.

Nor were only days as such connected with ill luck,[32] as noted in an unusual aside in Lucian:

And we give a wide berth to people who are lame in the right foot, especially if we see them in the early hours. And if anyone should spot a castrato or a eunuch or a monkey just after leaving home, he turns back and goes home, guessing in advance that his business for the day will not be good, on account of the initial difficult and unfortunate portent. But at the outset of the whole year, its first doorway and stepping forth, and very dawning, if someone should see a shameful person who does and endures forbidden things, is notorious on that account, a physical wreck, and all but bearing the name of the deeds themselves, a cheat, a conman, a perjurer, a disaster, a pillory, an abyss, would one not avoid him and compare him to a day of infamy?

Ill luck is not a matter on which one can afford to take chances.

BIRTH, PUBERTY, MARRIAGE, DEATH

Beyond the rhythm of fixed days and annual festivals stand the more widely spaced occasions in the lives of individuals, which we can review briefly in their natural chronological order. These are readily identifiable rites of passage, though here, again, we can be left with curious amalgams of explicable symbolism and arbitrary survival not always capable of immediate explanation.

Childbirth

Greek practice at birth entailed the fixing of an olive branch to the door of the *oikos* on the birth of a boy, a fillet of wool on that of a girl. Then the *amphidromia* ("running round") was performed on the fifth or seventh day after birth. The infant was carried around the hearth of the home and then placed on the ground, centering the life of the child within the *oikos* and the hearth. Acceptance by the father was at this point as well as, in some cases, the naming of the infant (who would be exposed if rejected). The decision in Sparta rested with the tribal elders rather than the father, symbolizing the community, and the exposure was more brutal, the throwing down of the rejected infant into a chasm *apothetai,* "the throwaway place." The mother had to be purified after the birth, whether by lustration, bathing in the sea, or by the blood of a piglet, with the burning of incense and sulphur. The apparatus of birthing was dedicated to the appropriate deities: Artemis, Eileithyia, and Demeter Kourotrophos. The 10th day after birth was used for a family celebration and sacrifice and might also entail gifts for the child.[33]

In Rome the presiding deity, Juno Lucina, corresponding to Greek Eilythuia, was required in childbirth. Evil spirits had to be duly expelled from the house following the birth itself. The child could not be raised until the father had lifted it up from the ground: the birth of a girl required the spreading of a couch for Juno; for a boy a table had to be laid for Hercules. The offering would have lasted until the mother herself was purified and the child itself formally named, a period of eight or nine still vulnerable days.

Puberty

Coming of age ceremonies were also observed in both cultures: we are familiar with St. Paul's "but when I became a man, I put away childish things."[34] The Apatouria in Ionian cities serves as an illustration: much of the ceremony centered on the young boy's admission to a clan or phratry of supposed blood relations; the *koureion* sacrifice on the third day of the festival coincided with the dedication of a lock of the boy's hair to Artemis and with it his departure from childhood. The former represented separation from childhood, the latter integration into adulthood.[35] For girls, puberty rites were less systematic because the girl did not attain full adult citizenship: there were religious functions[36] (to act as Arrephoros at the Arrhephoria in honor of Athena, or to act as a bear in honor of Artemis at Brauron), but these were confined to a select few.

In a Roman context, coming of age would have meant, for a boy, the dedication of the *bulla*, the amulet worn as a protective charm through childhood. This would coincide with the adoption of the *toga virilis*, a plain white toga replacing the purple-bordered one worn by male children. Then began *tirocinium fori*, enrollment in the list of citizens, and thank offerings for his reaching manhood. The oldest day set aside for this was the festival of the Liberalia (March 17), but other days later came to be used. As in Greece, it was the next stage, marriage, that entailed significant customary celebration.

Marriage

Greek marriage celebrations entailed a change of status for both parties, with the woman in effect exchanging one master for another when she moved away from the father's home and hearth to that of the husband. Sacrifices were offered on the eve of marriage to appropriate deities, and the bride would dedicate toys and other symbols of childhood, normally to Artemis; ceremonial bathing was done by both parties. (The Kallirhoe spring of the Ilissos supplied the water in the case of Athens.) Most significantly, a child, both of whose parents were still living, would wear a wreath of thorns and acorns, hand around bread to guests, and give the formula "I have banished evil and found good": this was held to symbolize the transition from savagery to agricultural domesticity, reinforced by the symbolism of the bride's bringing a frying pan to cook barley and the hanging of a pestle and mortar before the bridal chamber; sesame cakes were included in the wedding meal, to promote fecundity. A torch-lit procession in the evening conveyed the bride to the new husband's house. She could be brought in a wagon drawn by mules or oxen, with the singing of wedding songs in honor of Hymen, the god of marriage; she was greeted at the door by the groom's parents, given fertility symbols of sesame and honey cake and quince or date, and would tour her new household.[37] *Katachusmata* at weddings (throwing of rice, small coins, sweetmeats) are perhaps too general to indicate continuity to modern custom; it is, in any case, difficult to determine the ancient ceremonies themselves in sufficient detail. There was a curious custom of a young boy on Chios sleeping with the bride the night before the wedding and whose parents had to be still alive.[38] There was also the custom of sowing and plowing, an obvious sexual metaphor; the bride was required to weep on her wedding day (hence "weeping like a bride") and to be unveiled to the husband, who has not yet seen her face.

Roman marriage ceremonies, though simply requiring technical eligibility and consent, also tended to seek divine approval through sacrifice and through the symbolism of escorting the bride to the husband's house: nuts were thrown, and there was *fescennina iocatio*—ribald jokes—not to mention our own familiar carrying of the bride across the threshold (already discussed above). There was also decoration of the doorposts with wool and anointing to appease the spirits of the threshold. Plutarch's *Roman Questions*[39] (1f.) adds curious and not clearly explained customs: the bride must touch fire and water; the torches to be lit must be neither fewer nor more than five.[40]

Death

Greek custom required the laying out of the body *(prothesis),* the funeral procession itself *(ekphora),* and the actual disposal. Mostly, this was a family matter, rather than requiring an undertaker *(nekrophoros, nekrothaptos)* and other professional operators, and there was no actual burial service. Burials and cremations could coexist, without any difference in conceived effect. Offerings were, however, made to the grave, including cakes and libations, *choae,* mainly of water. Victims of murder were held to be bent on vengeance, hence the *maschalismos,* the cutting off of extremities. Hero cults to the heroic dead persisted into the empire and entailed blood sacrifice. Popular belief tends to persist in the concept of undifferentiated dead; more exotic fates were exceptional, such as *katasterismos,* the metamorphosis of eminent individuals into stars, the belief in the presence of souls in the ether, the doctrine of Pythagorean transmigration, or the idea of a blessed afterlife offered by the mysteries.[41]

Roman usage required washing, anointing, and formal dressing of the corpse, the aversion of the face by a relative in the presence of the gods before lighting the torch for inhumation, and the deposition of the ashes in due course for deposit of the urn in a family vault as well as the gathering of any necessities for the afterlife; eight days of mourning culminated in a sacrifice to the household gods, the lares; formal commemoration was not confined to anniversaries.[42] There was a strong sense of separation of living and dead: the house of bereavement was marked by cypress branches, and sanctuaries were closed on days of sacrifice for the dead. The Manes, the spirits of the dead (often plural even for the one individual), existed outside the towns: there was regular cult worship during the Parentalia (February 13–21) and at other times. Only the funerary cult guaranteed survival after death, whether celebrated by living descendants, by the owner of the land containing the tomb, or by a funerary association *(collegium)*. Unburied dead haunted inhabited places and the living as lemures, to be appeased at Lemuria in May. Actual deification was exceptional, as was Greek *katasterismos*.[43]

Plutarch's *Roman Questions* contains a problem about the explanation of ceremony for receiving into society someone who has mistakenly been given funeral rites on the erroneous assumption that he has died: he cites the case of one Aristinos, who consulted the Delphic oracle and received advice amounting to "being born again" (that is, being treated by women like a newborn child, as a form of protection). Plutarch pursues the explanation that such persons are not allowed directly into an enclosed space because they are deemed to be ceremonially impure but must let themselves down from the roof through an open area.[44]

A number of funerary customs seem to survive in some form: the threefold judges of the dead, no longer Minos, Aeacus, and Rhadamanthus, might be felt as God, the Virgin Mary, and the Holy Apostles. Other survivals include the ceremonial closing of the eyes of the deceased by a female relative, shrouding of the deceased in white, and carrying the corpse to the grave with the face exposed; Rose also compares the mourning of Hector in the *Iliad* to the modern practice (extempore laments and eulogies) and regards it as unbroken.[45] There is also the use of water (variously) to purify the corpse; commemoration of death on the 3rd, 6th, 9th, and 40th days after death (modern 30th) and on the last days of the 3rd, 6th, and 9th months as well as anniversaries; or the use of frumenty (boiled grain) at funeral meals and the use of the *panaghia* (the Virgin) as an object of prayer (together with other healing saints).[46]

In the end, however, we might well be tempted to ask the obvious enough question, What are folk customs for? We might answer broadly and without reference to any individual acts, "to promote the continued welfare of the community and the individual," in respect of the maintenance of sustenance and fertility, avoidance of supernatural vengeance, ritual impurity, or bad luck. We might, of course, add "to have a rest or some fun, especially in winter, when agricultural operations may be limited," and to mark significant points in the calendar and life-cycle of the community and the individual.

SUPERSTITION

Many of the ceremonial details summarized above are directly or indirectly connected with the ensuring of good luck for the individual and the community and, more particularly, the aversion of bad. The whole notion of good and bad luck and their acquisition and avoidance naturally lead us into the discussion of superstition itself. The Latin root *superstitio* suggests no more than "survival." It has attracted the notion of surviving but outdated belief: the ancient notion was communicated in Greek by the term *deisidaimonia,* which we might translate rather as "fear of supernatural forces." Each of the two terms tends to have its own slightly different emphasis on available evidence. *Deisidaimonia* starts off with a positive sense of "religious scrupulousness," "god-fearing," but takes on the connotations made famous by Theophrastus' celebrated caricature of the *Deisidaimon*[47] (*Char.* 16): here we find an obsessiveness for (trivial) ritual, a timorousness toward the gods (Theophrastus' *deilia pros to daimonion,* an exaggerated regard for dreams and portents), and a determination to protect oneself against malign influences by repeated purification. Plutarch, in his *de Superstitione,* reinforces Theophrastus' picture. Latin writers from Plautus onward employ *superstitio* in a similarly negative sense: one thinks of Pliny's characterization of Christianity as a *prava et immodica superstitio* ("a degenerate superstition carried to excessive lengths," *Ep.* 10.96.8). This indeed illustrates the Latin tendency to use *superstitio* as a term of disrespect for the religious beliefs of outsiders, as, for example, on Egyptian or Jewish rites,[48] a usage reciprocated in Christian polemical writing in turn. The Roman concept indicates from the end of the first century B.C. onward a deviation from piety into unrestrained observance—excessive ritual, addiction to prophecy, and gullibility at the hand of charlatans. It could affect all classes: Cicero's *de Divinatione* and *de Natura Deorum* aim at the elite.

Some practices we can at least recognize as our own: wishing others a prosperous New Year hardly seems to require explanation, while another familiar custom requires very little: it is even generally admitted that absent people feel by the buzzing of the ears that they are being spoken about.[49] But in any given area the cumulative effect of such small details can offer a minefield to the overscrupulous and overwary. Some sense of the sheer diversity of superstitions that might concern one small but important area of daily life can be suggested by the following cavalcade from the Elder Pliny:[50]

> We ward off the evil omen caused by mentioning fire at a meal by the pouring of water under the table. It is thought to be the most unfavourable of omens if someone leaves the meal while the floor is being swept, or when a table or

dumb-waiter is removed while a guest is drinking. There is a dissertation by
Servius Sulpicius, a man of standing, on reasons for not bringing a table.

Fear of fire was a serious matter in so combustible a city as ancient Rome,
and the offering may have been a simple matter of analogical thinking or
the placating of an original fire demon, or of spirits of the dead attracted to
the prospect of light. Trimalchio answers the mere possibility of a cockcrow
prefiguring a fire with wine under the table (*Sat.* 74.1f.), the latter probably
a hint of his excessive extravagance rather than a genuine variation. Sweeping
the floor might have had associations with a death rite, as it has in comparative material elsewhere. Servius Sulpicius (consul, 51 B.C.) was a considerable
and prolific antiquarian, but a whole scroll on such a topic once more underlines the relevance of what we might see as pedantic irrationality.

At the other extreme the observation of unusual weather signs could por-
tend disaster on a national or cosmic scale (observations of "bloody" grain,
extreme atmospheric conditions, unusual appearances or behavior of animals
and the like). When taken in a political context, these could not be lightly
dismissed, as in the context of Rome's failures in the Second Punic War;[51]
indeed, the psychological effect might be of self-fulfilling prophecy, as when
Aristodemus, King of the Messenians against Sparta, committed suicide when
seers gave adverse interpretations to the howling of wolves or the growth of
quitch around his ancestral hearth.

A more or less random cross section of Plutarch's *Greek Questions* and
Roman Questions will leave us with some notion of the ceremonial and not-
so-ceremonial taboos that had accumulated by the early Empire: often, the
variety of solutions suggested underlines the loss of any decisively convincing
explanation. A number of taboos relate to gender distinction when covering
or uncovering the head: people cover their heads when adoring the gods, but
uncover them when greeting honorable men). Why is the head uncovered
when sacrificing to Saturn and to Honour? Why do daughters have uncovered heads and flowing hair when carrying fathers to burial, while sons have
their heads covered? One thinks of the conventions in this writer's own childhood relating to women covering heads in church, while men did not, still
in accordance with first-century Pauline teaching and for apparently no other
reason. Some of Plutarch's other "problems" concern bridal taboos: Why do
men not take wives during the month of May? Why does the bridegroom
approach the bride for the first time in the dark without any light? Why do
they part the hair of brides with the point of a javelin? Some figures seem
positively to have attracted taboos: the *Flamen Dialis* was hedged around by a
great battery of them, and life for this individual must have been pure to the

point of great inconvenience and discomfort; or again, a god such as Saturn or an animal such as the dog seems to attract repeated speculation to explain the anomalies surrounding them.[52]

The ultimate distaste for *deisidaimonia* comes in Plutarch's short essay *de Superstitione 165F–166A:*

> While awake [superstitious people] deceive themselves and expend their energies and trouble themselves, falling into the hands of mountebanks and charlatans who tell them "If you are afraid of a vision in your sleep, and you have entertained the rout of Hecate below, summon the old hag who does purificatory rites and bathe in the sea and spend the whole day sitting on the ground."

Spending the rest of the day may tell us much: it is the leisured few who have the time to nurse their neuroses who will fall victim to this sort of advice, dispensed by the many classes of charlatan attuned to the market for it. Plutarch (166A) deplores the derivation from barbarian custom of

> mud-baths, wallowing in dung, immersions, falling flat on the ground, shameful prostrations before the gods, and bizarre grovellings.

One thinks, too, of the performance (for such it is) of the priest in Apuleius who confesses his sins while self-flagellating (*Met.* 8.28): this act and the latter half of Plutarch's list certainly have an oriental flavor. The victim in Plutarch's view has changed little since the days of Theophrastus half a millennium before, though interestingly, there is a much sharper notion of what we ourselves might call a guilt trip[53]:

> But if he falls victim to the slightest mischance, in his anxiety he sits down and makes up other severe, serious and inescapable toils, and imposes on himself fears and terrors and suspicions and worries, applying every kind of hysteria and howling. For he blames heaven for them all—not man or chance or bad timing or himself, and alleges that from that source a divine cascade of mischief has befallen him, not because he has had bad luck, but because the gods hate him, and he is being punished and paying the price and suffering everything deservedly through his own faults. But to the superstitious man every physical weakness, loss of property, loss of children, and misfortunes and failures in his public life are "Blows from heaven" or "attacks of an evil spirit" . . . he sits outside in sackcloth and in filthy rags, often rolling naked in the mud, while he confesses to lapses and errors of his own—that he ate or drank this or that, or walked a path forbidden by the gods; but if he is especially lucky and is only mildly inflicted with superstition, he sits at home and fumigates himself, and

smearing himself all over with mud, and the old hags, in the words of Bion "bring whatever comes to hand and put it on him and bind it fast to him."

There is, accordingly, the sense of superstition as what we might term an obsessional neurosis:[54]

> But the laughable things done and suffered through superstition, its words and actions, its charms and magic spells, its scurryings and drumbeats and filthy purifications, and impure cleansings, barbarous and unlawful afflictions and mortifications in shrines, these all cause some to say that it would be better that the gods should not exist than that they should, if they welcome such actions and act so arrogantly and pettily, and take offence so easily.

There is something approaching a rhetoric of rationality on Plutarch's part throughout the treatise *de Superstitione,* but Lucian's Alexander had a celebrated dupe, the eminent consular Rutilianus,[55] whose conduct suggests how close to the truth it may have been. Lucian himself has been suspected of drawing on Theophrastus' caricature, but there was plenty of superstition coupled with vanity in the second-century Greek world: we have only to look at the so-called *Sacred Tales* of Aelius Aristides to see almost a diary of superstition in action.

CONCLUSION

It is difficult to generalize on our existing evidence on folk customs: the sheer weight and diversity of data on the one hand, and the unfortunate distribution of evidence on the other, does not give us a very complete understanding of what it was like to experience the traditional lore of archaic Greece, say, or Imperial Rome, or of second-century A.D. Asia Minor. We should bear in mind, too, that the best-attested calendar festivals of classical Athens or the Roman Republic represent only a tiny fraction of the admittedly very patchy information we have on the Greco-Roman world as a whole. The encounters of Paul in *The Acts of the Apostles* testify to the diversity of cult practice and religious reflex to be encountered in Asia Minor and around the Aegean alone. What we can be clear about, however, is that there was not just stultification of custom: we have a sense, also, of development and renewal as well.

NOTES

1. Lucian, *Alexander* 8.
2. Plutarch, *Roman Questions* 29.

3. Ibid.
4. Catullus 61.159ff.; Opie and Tatem (1989), 40.
5. On Greek festivals, see, e.g., Parke (1977) (Athens); on Roman festivals, see Scullard (1981).
6. For discussion, see Smith in Dorson (1972), 159–171, unfortunately focusing largely on Christian festivals.
7. e.g., Nilsson (1940), 22–41.
8. Maximus of Tyre, *Or.* 24.5; for the relation of sacred origins to an earlier hunter-gatherer context, see Burkert (1983).
9. Varro, *de Re Rustica* 1.1.6.
10. *Works and Days* 465–469.
11. For details of individual Attic festivals, see Parke (1977).
12. For example, Plutarch, *Theseus* 23.2f.
13. Pausanias 4.32.3ff. On the whole subject of Aristomenes, see the stimulating recent study by Ogden (2004).
14. Ogilvie (1969), 70–99.
15. Dionysius of Halicarnassus, *Roman Antiquities* 4.14.
16. Ovid, *Fasti* 3.199f.
17. Cato, *de Agri Cultura* 139f., 141.
18. Cato 141.
19. *Fasti* 4.723–729.
20. Plutarch, *Romulus* 21.7 (citing C. Acilius).
21. Ibid., 21.4f.
22. On the Lupercalia, cf. Wiseman (1995), 77–88.
23. Rose (1959), 205f; for other etymologies, see Wiseman (1995), 87.
24. See, further, Frazer's *LCL* Appendix; Scullard (1981), 108f.
25. Lucian, *Alexander* 39f.
26. Hesiod, *Works and Days* 785–789.
27. Ibid., 802ff.
28. Ibid., 790f.
29. Ibid., 814, 820, 824.
30. Petronius 30.4; on the *dies nefasti,* see Scullard (1981), 44f.
31. See further West (1978), 346–350, on the general character of this section.
32. Lucian, *Pseudologista* 17, *LCL* 5.392f.
33. Zaidman and Pantel (1992), 64f.
34. I Corinthians 13:11.
35. On the *Apatouria,* see Parke (1977), 88–92.
36. Aristophanes, *Lysistrata* 642–647.
37. Further details in Rose (1959), 145.
38. Rose (1959), 145f.
39. *Roman Questions* 1f.
40. See further Treggiari (1991), 161–170.
41. On Greek death in general, see Sourvinou-Inwood (1995).

42. Ogilvie (1969), 75.
43. On Roman burial customs in general, see Toynbee (1971).
44. *Roman Questions* 5.
45. Rose, *GR* 148.
46. Rose, *GR* 150f.
47. *Characters* 16.
48. On Jews, *Juvenal.* 6.314ff., 511., 14.96.
49. *NH* 28.22, 28.24.
50. Pliny 28.26f.
51. Livy 22.1.8–20.
52. On the *Flamines,* see Vanggaard (1988).
53. Plutarch, *Mor.* 168Aff.
54. Ibid., 171Af.
55. *Alexander* 30, with Caster's commentary.

Eight

Animal, Vegetable, Mineral: The Natural World in Popular Perception

Just as there are customs, beliefs, and practices relating to the life of man, so there are others relating to the natural world, both where it is familiar to humans in their daily lives and can be drawn upon for folk remedies, and where it is exotic and far enough removed from ordinary experience to be the material for "wonders." A number of animals, plants, and minerals have acquired a folkloric identity of their own, both in the ancient world and beyond, sometimes at odds with scientific observation, sometimes overlapping or coinciding with it. Outside these well-defined categories, there are many more that we could construct less exclusively, such as superstitions attaching to places or whole localities. It is worthwhile to note and illustrate the kinds of themes we have pursued hitherto: blurred characterizations, mixtures of rational and irrational, arbitrary survivals, and the sense of striving after a wider picture that is somehow beyond us. All these will be familiar, again, in dealing with the natural world. We could have drawn all our examples from the Elder Pliny alone, such is the wealth of lore of varying quality on so much. A wider but no less random range of examples must suffice.

ANIMALS

Animals, and particularly animals from amphibians to mammals, invite analogy to humans by the possession of roughly similar facial features and limbs. Observations of animals, as from a hunting context, tend to reinforce the analogies and to give rise to speculations of metamorphosis in one direction or the other, both into and out of human form.[1] The problems naturally begin with the anthropocentric notion of animals fundamental to a popular, prescientific viewpoint, through which they are endowed with human attributes such as cunning, valor, and the like. We might note especially the Elder Pliny's description of men and dolphins in a cooperative hunt for fish.[2] Sometimes he can see nature as whimsical, as when it appears to devise and enjoy the spectacle of the snake ambushing the elephant, only for the two animals to die together after their resourceful battle.[3] Pliny is also much given to thinking in terms of sympathies or antipathies between species: sometimes these are rational, if, for example, certain species are competing for food, as when the raven and the golden oriole search at night for each other's eggs.[4] Snakes can be viewed as having an antipathy for the ash tree because the ash is an antidote for snakebite: Pliny actually claims to have seen a snake prefer to escape through fire than through ash leaves when surrounded by both.[5] Much of such lore derives from insufficient observation: one does not stay too long to observe tigers or porcupines—traditions have accordingly produced a "tiger-porcupine," the *martichoras*.[6] The experience of imitative birds easily gives rise to the idea of talking animals and reinforces the notion of an animate world. We should also note some differences in animal folklore due to local perceptions: some folklore areas will adopt the fox as the cunning animal, others the cat, while even a single animal, such as the snake, may be viewed in completely different ways, as benign and connected with good luck or as the cunning tempter of Eve.[7]

It is tempting to produce a mere catalog of animal wonders and curiosities as lore, but it is more illuminating to attempt to establish a few tendencies in animal lore types. Apart from such a celebrated tale as that of the geese on the Capitol warning the Romans of the presence of the Gauls,[8] there is a large dossier of prescient animals in materials that are shared in common between folklore, philosophy, and popular morality, as in much of Plutarch's discussions on animal instinct. We accordingly find the observation that tortoises seek out marjoram after eating snakes, dogs purge themselves by eating grass, the ibis by giving itself a clyster of brine, and the she-bear after hibernation by eating wild arum; goats in Crete eat dittany to remove arrows from themselves, while elephants practice surgery by pulling spears and arrows from wounded men.[9] Sometimes authors will overinterpret the rationality or virtue of animals, as when the traditionally cunning fox judges the water running below the ice to test its firmness and is seen as acting syllogistically.[10] Pliny even seems to try to make elephants into model Romans: he credits them with a natural religion and the ability to venerate the heavenly bodies, to say nothing of the circus tricks he uncritically accepts.[11] The evidence as a whole testifies to a substantial inventory of animals directly helpful or harmful to man and hence of animal powers in medicine and magic.[12] For example, the chthonic habitat and otherworldly appearance of the mole ensured it a special place:

Pliny, *NH* 30.19f.

Of all the animals the magi hold moles in highest regard . . . they give credence to no other entrails as much, and they credit no other creature with more supernatural capacities, so that if someone should swallow the heart of a mole, fresh and still palpitating, they promise the power of divination and foreknowledge of future events. By removing the tooth of a living mole and binding it to the person, they claim that toothache can be cured.

Some proverbial notions of our own are already in place amid the general catalog of animal wonders: Aelian's uncritical compilation on natural history gives us the white elephant and the mystery of the elephants' graveyard.[13] On the swan's song he accepts the popular tradition and accounts for it by suggesting that the swan sings because it has nothing to fear in death. But other positions are possible: his near-contemporary Lucian has a very different approach—boatmen on the Po tell him how awful the swan's voice is, and the swansong itself is passed over in silence.[14]

Beside the animals with which it is possible to become familiar, or supposedly so, there is a hallowed rogues' gallery of mythical beasts, of varying degrees of exoticism, for which it is more difficult to find a basis. As so often, labeling may be a problem here: it is purely arbitrary association that causes us to call the phoenix a creature of myth and the unicorn a creature of folklore. The phoenix, indeed, has been linked with all three, as a "legendary bird that featured in the mythology of the ancient world, common to the folklore of Greece, India, Egypt, China, Japan, and Arabia."[15] Nor is it as perverse as some suppose, to suggest some sort of pastiche of extant birds observed at a distance: I owe to Geoffrey Arnott the suggestion that a constituent of the phoenix is the lammergeier, whose feathers, when molting in sunlight, might be observed as flames; one might add birds that are actually observed to use fire. We might also note the diffusion of the tradition, with an epicenter well to the east of the Greco-Roman world.[16] The cosmic overtones of the phoenix suggest, on the whole, myth rather than folklore, where the distinction can be pressed: a creature representing the sun and with a long span of calendar years between incinerations.[17] There may well be a Zoroastrian input to a bird connected both with fire and reconstitution: one thinks of the role of vultures in recycling the Zoroastrian dead. For other such fabulous creatures the unfolding science of paleozoology has much to offer: Mayor notes the possibility that the traditions of gold-guarding griffins arise from observation of beaked quadruped dinosaur fossils by gold-mining nomads in central Asia.[18]

TRUE AND FALSE IN ANIMAL LORE: TWO CASES

A student of folklore must be alert to the contextual clues offered by different versions of the same information. It is instructive to compare two presentations of a story about one and the same dolphin, related respectively by the two Plinys, uncle and nephew, in the latter part of the first century A.D.:

Pliny the Elder, *NH* 9.26

In like fashion another dolphin within recent years, on the African coast at Hippo Diarrhytus, would be fed by human hand and allow itself to be touched and play with swimmers and give them rides; but when anointed with unguent by the proconsul of Africa Flavianus, it was made drowsy, apparently by the strange odour; it drifted as if lifeless, kept away for several months from human contact as if repelled by the injury; afterwards it came back and was a source of wonder as before.

Thus far Pliny the Elder acts as the encyclopedist, for whom the matter is an observable fact, but still a wonder nonetheless, balancing as it were between contemporary legend and lore. But the more illuminating context belongs to the nephew:

I have hit on information that is true but very like fiction, and worthy of your most thoroughly felicitous and clearly poetic talent. I came across it while various amazing tales were doing the rounds over dinner. My source was very reliable. . . . In [a swimmers'] race one boy, more adventurous than the rest, ventured further out to sea. A dolphin met him, and swam one moment in front of him, one moment behind, then swam round him, finally dived underneath to take him on, then moved him off, then took him on again and first took him terrified further out, then turned shorewards and brought him back to his companions on dry land.

The rumour spread through the town: everyone ran up, regarded the boy as a wonder, asked, listened, and reported the tale. . . . It is known that Octavius Avitus, the proconsular legate, poured unguent on the dolphin while it was ashore, misled by some craven superstition, but it fled out to sea to escape the unfamiliar odour, and only after a number of days did it appear, languid and out of sorts, but soon recovered its strength and rediscovered its former sense of fun and the tricks it used to perform. . . . You will . . . adorn the events with great sympathy and no lack of words. Not that there is any need to add or enhance anything; it will be enough not to detract from the facts themselves.[19]

The first account reduces the matter to a unit of information on the part of a scholar whose purpose is primarily to amass just that; but Pliny the Younger humanizes the story considerably, heard it himself as an oral dinner party story, includes information about how word had got around in the first place, and prepares for a third party, his correspondent Caninius Rufus, to produce a literary account in verse. There is emphasis at more than one point on its "stranger than fiction" quality. Although we ourselves would now accept without hesitation the authenticity of Pliny's account—dolphins are conventionally noted for their philanthropic qualities—we still have the notion of a popular story "going the rounds" and gathering momentum as it travels.[20]

If all that has been reported above about the dolphin is taken as true, the lore related to the hyena demonstrates just how far out intelligence could be about a rather less well-known creature. The hyena is singled out by Pliny the Elder as particularly prized by the Magi for its healing properties; this after he has already mentioned inter alia its annual change of sex. If it swerves to the right in a pursuit, it will derange a human pursuer; a swerve to the left will bring the prospect of capture, aided by seven knots in the hunter's girdle and horsewhip.[21]

> Then, with their skilful pretence in equivocation, the Magi tell us that the hyena should be captured when the moon is passing through Gemini, but that this should be done with practically all its hairs intact; that the skin of its head is useful as a poultice for relieving headache . . . they also say that the hyena's teeth are useful for toothache, whether by the touch of a corresponding tooth, or when used as a poultice.

And so the wonders go on: those seeking cures for miscarriage, homosexual orientation, and much else need only appropriate the relevant parts of the hyena's amazing anatomy to procure the desired effect. This does not tell us the age of the information, but the ancient Persia of the original magi was closer to a genuine observation point than the Greek world. One notes other oddities in basic perception: we ourselves see (and hear) the hyena in folkloric terms as a laughing dog; the Greco-Roman world saw it as a talking pig (Gr. *huaina* = "sow").[22]

Perhaps the most sophisticated construction of the animal kingdom in ancient thought lies in its attitudes toward bees: Virgil gives us a humorous but reverent picture of their miniature culture in his agricultural poem the *Georgics* and connects their supernatural quality to their services to Zeus.[23] The sexual arrangements of bees was misunderstood in antiquity: because worker bees lack the means of reproduction, the relationship of drones and queen could not be readily understood either so that bees were thought not only not to die but not to be born in any normal way either; rather were they (mis)observed to come into being by some kind of process of spontaneous generation from a rotting carcass. For Virgil this is etiological myth ("how the pioneering discoverer Aristaeus learned the facts about bees"); for the author of the Old Testament *Book of Judges* many centuries before it was already the material of a riddle ("out of the strong [in this case a lion's carcass] came forth sweetness"). With such an observation Samson could taunt the Philistines in a folktale about a clever wager to be terribly avenged.[24] In a text likely to be close in date to Hesiod this ranks as wisdom.

PLANTS

As in the case of animals, we have to do with observation and its misapplications. A tree with branches and roots exposed only needs strategically placed gnarls before it too can be seen as humanoid: it grows and dies and so has its own life cycle, while its foliage responds to the wind with imagined shivers or whispers. It is naturally conceived as a living being only restricted in movement by its roots. If an oak tree is struck by lightning and thunder is heard, the tree itself may be just as readily credited as the place where the power of the lightning subsists, rather than being seen as the victim of a force in the atmosphere.

Further, trees and other plants can be seen to flourish in places where corpses are buried, hence the sense that any animate survival of the person has passed into the plant; once a parallelism exists between humans and plants, the tree or wood can possess the life-force of an external soul—cut the tree, and the tree nymph, too, will die.[25] On the other hand, the amazing endurance of trees beyond the life and stature of humans can invest them with a numinous quality: the cults of sacred graves loom large in prehistoric rural religion.[26] One example par excellence embodies a great deal of these associations: the mandrake was not unreasonably invested with the appearance of a woman, and by sympathy, was associated with fertility.[27]

Many of Pliny's observations on plants, as on animals, are concerned, once more, with their sympathies and antipathies, real or imagined, to other species: timber from hornbeam, box, and service-tree has an aversion for cornel wood; fig and rue are sympathetic, radishes and vines antipathetic.[28] There is also a natural association between plants and healing, as between plants and poisons: they are credited with apotropaic powers for the warding off of evil or, indeed, may possess a signature against this or that specific illness or evil force. We have already noted Pliny on ash trees as an apotropaic against the snake[29]; Apuleius, for his part, notes the use of ragwort against the evil eye. Strongly-odored plants, such as garlic, will also serve such a function[30]: "it wards off snakes and scorpions by its smell, and according to some, every kind of wild beast." Once more, antipathies play their part also[31]: as cabbage is an enemy of the vine, it is said to counteract wine and consequently, if taken in food beforehand, it prevents intoxication, while if taken after drinking, it neutralizes the effects. More elaborate associations are also possible: noxious plants with demonic associations include the fig tree (hence Christ's blasting it?); otherworldly people assemble under trees and can be overheard; and plants themselves could be felt as chthonic, like parsley. The yew tree, in particular, already enjoyed a reputation for toxicity, confirmed by modern medicine.[32]

Pliny's remarks on plants drew substantially on old Roman *ars herbaria,* with emphasis on the use of *simplicia* ("simples"), most usually plants, for healing and preventive purposes, though their effects could be felt to be intensified by ritual or magical procedures. In spite of his contempt both for Greek doctors and, more particularly, for the magi, he will resort to their remedies when traditional Roman ones fall short.[33] Much of Pliny's pharmacopia included long-standing traditional folk remedies, some still in use (allium, anethum, ruta, salvia), but he also knows oriental exotica, including pepper, ginger, cinnamon, myrrh, and frankincense; animal products such as hyena dung or lizards' eyes have dropped out of use, but goose grease and goat's milk, among others, survive.[34] Not only the substances themselves, but even their preparation (digging, cutting, and processing), could be mingled with ritual or magical procedures, such as protective procedures in the extrication of a plant. In the case of *selago,*

> It is collected by the right hand, without the use of iron, and put through the left arm-hole under the tunic, as if the gatherer were performing a theft. He has to wear white, and have bare feet thoroughly washed; there has to be a sacrifice of bread and wine beforehand. The plant is then placed in a fresh napkin.[35]

Pliny is our most detailed source for incantations in association with plants (for example, *reseda*).[36] And in any case, compilers, critical and uncritical, have to be carefully sifted in order to try to prize superstition from medical common sense and experience: Theophrastus approves of the common sense practiced in cutting *thapsia* "standing to windward and rubbing one's self with oil." But he ridicules the practice of digging up glykyside at night: "for if a man does it during the day and is seen by a woodpecker while gathering the fruit, he runs the risk of losing his eyesight, and if he is in the act of cutting the root at the time, he suffers prolapse of the anus."[37] When Pliny, for his part, discusses glykyside,[38] he expresses skepticism at only the latter of Theophrastus' comments. One tradition has perhaps a claim to have traveled better than most, concerning the potency of the mistletoe: Pliny comments on the sacral significance of the plant to the Druids (themselves magi in his perception) and the ceremonial manner in which it is gathered (*NH* 16.249f.). Even in a secular context:

Pliny, *NH* 24.12

Some credulously suppose that it is more effective if gathered from the oak at the new moon without employing iron, and without letting it touch the ground; and that it offers a cure for epilepsy, helps women in conception, even if they simply have it about them, and that when chewed and put on sores it is most effective in healing them.

Perhaps there is a clue here in the distinction reserved for mistletoe that has not touched the ground: like the mole among animals, it can be felt as an outsider to the overall scheme of things since in this case its parasitic attachment to trees gives it an existence belonging to neither land, sea, nor air.

MINERALS

The folklore of minerals is more restricted by nature than that of animals and plants: not only are they much less easily observed, but mineralogy and, in particular, its commercial aspects demanded as close to scientific precision as possible. But there is still a great deal of material that we should be able to assign to the domain of folklore. Sacred stones offer a natural overlap between folklore and religious cult.[39] They can be actually embedded in the earth as rock formations or be freestanding, even encompassing a tradition of having fallen from the sky. The former might include the stones of the Theban Cabirion, the rock altars at Samothrace, or the so-called mirthless stone at Eleusis. Such rocks might be seen as forming a connection between the upper and lower worlds, and indeed, we find Apollonius of Tyana hailing the pillars of Heracles in a similar way.[40] Freestanding stones that provided a focus of worship included the Omphalos at Delphi, the reputed center of the world as the "navel" of the earth; numbers of unhewn rocks were also to be found in sanctuaries. Various rocks occur at house doors and crossroads and were held to have a talismanic function, as apotropaics against evil. While the whole business is probably less significant for Greeks, who could see it as a symptom of *deisidaimonia,* it looms large in Roman cults, as, for example, around the boundary god Terminus, to say nothing of the black volcanic stone imported from Pessinus in Phrygia during the Second Punic War as the embodiment of Cybele. Apuleius, always alert for matters of worship and cult, freely admits his propensity for pouring libations over sacred stones.[41]

It is often difficult to classify lore relating to minerals in modern terms: ancient views could be based on color, shape, and provenance rather than chemical properties, even before deep-rooted misconceptions can be treated. One of the most notable false inferences from observation is the notion that stones are attracted to one another, yet another consequence of the notion of sympathies and antipathies.[42] And the fact that metals are mined from underground renders them naturally chthonic, and to religious association is often added strong moral disapproval, which Pliny directs unreservedly at gold. A good deal of his mineralogy is soundly based on reliable authorities, but he can still deviate into the folklore of metals, as when *adamas,* including diamonds, cannot be broken on an anvil, even with the heaviest of iron hammers, or in fire: it takes the warm blood of a goat with the properties of antipathy[43] to split it. The most priceless of objects, in Pliny's natural scheme of things, should be antipathetic to the vilest of animals . . . it is also antipathetic to lodestone, hence sympathetic to iron.

Indeed, iron itself enjoyed a special status in ancient folklore, originating no doubt with the Bronze Age cultures, which experienced it as something extraordinary. It had an early association with meteorites, naturally a rare and of course supernatural source prior to the adoption of smelting in the Near East and the Balkans circa 1200 B.C. It was used as an apotropaic against the evil eye and against hostile supernatural powers such as witches, and it was also wrongly thought to protect against lightning before conductivity was established in the eighteenth century. Iron was also held to protect babies or adults when a circle was traced around them or a pointed weapon was carried around them three times.[44] Water warmed with white-hot iron was credited with medicinal properties, as was rust, able to unite wounds; placed in coffins, it was held to protect the dead against demons. Pliny already warns against gathering a herb with contact with it; he notes that the Druids gather mistletoe with a golden sickle (that is, not iron).[45]

THE FOLKLORE OF GIANT BONES

There is one perhaps exceptionally interesting field of mineral lore: bones do calcify, and this has its place in the notion that bones, the hardest part of the human body, transform into the correspondingly hardest part of the earth, stones. The story of Deucalion and Pyrrha has the bones of Mother Earth, stones, cast behind them to repopulate the human race; the bones of Atlas turn to stone, as does the skeleton of Echo.[46] In recent years it has proved possible as never before to make a link with the progress of modern paleontology. There had been a tendency through most of the twentieth century to regard accounts of giant bones in antiquity as purely fanciful and to judge reports of evidence in terms of mythological stories about dragons, monsters, and the like. But it is the service of Mayor to emphasize the genuine archaeological dimension to the evidence and indeed to note its part in the generation of monster myths themselves.[47] This can be seen in the Elder Pliny's account of a Triton[48]:

> An embassy from Olisipo (Lisbon) was sent to the emperor Tiberius to report that a Triton had been sighted and heard playing on his shell in a particular cave, and that he had the familiar appearance of such a creature. . . . I have as my authorities distinguished men of equestrian rank who say they saw a man of the sea, in the gulf of Gades, human in every part of his body: he climbs aboard ships at night, and at once weights down the parts of the vessel he sits on; if he stays too long, the vessel sinks below the waterline . . . the skeleton of the monster to which they would say Andromeda had been exposed was brought to Rome from Joppa in Judaea and exhibited among the rest of the wonders by M. Scaurus in his aedileship: it was forty feet long, and the height of the ribs was greater than Indian Elephants; the spine was one and a half feet thick.

We note that Pliny evidently approves the social eminence of his source, as though a Roman *eques* could not lie, where a common peasant or slave might well do so; but as we have seen in the case of ghosts or dolphins, lore could be transmitted by all social classes. Aelian later quotes an earlier account from Demostratus, who served on a provincial council that investigated the phenomenon on behalf of an early emperor and himself wrote a treatise on sea monsters, now lost. Even here, the features were too degraded to allow serious investigation, but of course, to us, a hoax seems inevitable in this instance.[49] Pliny also provides evidence on the petrifaction of animal bones,[50] having had access to Theophrastus' lost, two-book work *On Petrifactions*. A recurrent source of comment in antiquity was the giant bones of Pallene,[51] as testified by Solinus:

> Before there were any humans on Pallene, the story goes that a battle was fought between the gods and the giants. [Evidence of destruction] continues to be seen to this day, whenever torrents swell with rain and excessive water

breaks their banks and floods the field. They say that even now in gullies and ravines the people discover bones of immeasurable enormity, like men's carcases but far bigger.

This was still the case in 1994, when teeth were found traceable to *Deinotherium giganteum* and Miocene mastodons. It is difficult to draw lines between folklore, myth, and observation of what to us are paleontological facts. Much evidence of a similar kind has been assembled in Philostratus' *Heroicus,* where a vinedresser in the Troad describes a whole catalog of finds of giant bones, some of them very close to the date of the dialogue itself in the third century A.D., and some of them are still said to be exposed to public view, where others were exposed for a short time before being further eroded into the sea.[52] Accounts are furnished of how the emperor Hadrian had had a skeleton reassembled: of course, it is possible, mistakenly, to reassemble mammal bones, in particular, in human terms, especially if the skeleton is defective or seriously damaged and not systematically excavated in the first place. Each society will interpret such remains in terms of its own stereotype: anyone familiar with the cinema blockbuster *Alien* in the first instance would be able to see monstrous bones in terms of an alien spacecraft.

One motif recurs in a number of such accounts: the religious interpretation of the remains. The available consultant is most often an oracle, but on one occasion at least we find the versatile philosopher and mystic Apollonius of Tyana reported as pronouncing extensively on the whole subject[53]:

> For they say that someone called Typho or Enceladus is lying bound under the mountain [Etna], and that he is breathing out this fire in his death agony. I do acknowledge that giants have existed and that in many places over the earth bodies of this nature appear when their tombs have been broken open; but I do not agree that they came into conflict with the gods.

Pausanias, for his part, lists a host of hero discoveries in Asia Minor—Asterios, Geryon, Hyllos, and Koresus—but it is symptomatic of his mind-set that the dispute is not so much about whether these are giants' bones, but rather which giant they are the bones of. There were attempts at what would now be termed taxonomy of bones and attempts at comparison with previous finds: the whole range of perceptions from mythological through folkloric to semiscientific treatment were already in play.[54] But antiquity seems to have had its share of hoaxes as well, and fakelore concerned with natural history has the feel of an industry. Lucian gives a detailed description of the snake-god Glycon, manufactured as a hybrid snake with a human papier-mâché head; the Tritons examined by Demostratus or Pliny may well have been of the same order. The latter describes exhibitions of an embalmed centaur and of an Egyptian Phoenix, while Aelian speaks explicitly of the falsification of nature by those who use wax in the bogus construction of species.[55] But others were presented live: Sulla's troops were said to have surprised a sleeping satyr in a meadow and captured it.[56]

LEGENDS ABOUT PLACES

We have already noted beliefs about specific kinds of stone; this can be extended to whole places and landscapes.[57] What qualifies a place to be "numinous"? It might be a mountaintop, a grove in a wood, or some similarly remote place, where the supernatural can be readily evoked or imagined or where previous associations can be drawn on. It might be geographically exceptional, like Delphi as the *omphalos* or navel stone of the earth; it might be a place where the natural world is exceptionally dominant over or independent of a man-made landscape, as might be felt, in particular, of parts of Arcadia. The following responses of Pausanias in that region are revealing:

Pausanias 8.29.1

As you come down from Trapezous to the Alpheius, on the left hand side not far from the river is a site called Bathos ["The Depth"], where they hold a rite every second year in honour of the Great goddesses. And here there is a spring called Olympias, which only runs every other year, and near the spring fire rises up. According to the Arcadians it was here and not in Thracian Pallene that the battle of the giants and the gods took place, and they sacrifice there to lightning, tornadoes and thunder.[58]

Legends of buried golden treasure (a gold sword and 12 gold piglets) attached to the site.[59] Pausanias does not arbitrate on the rival claims of Pallene and the Arcadian Bathos in this instance, but he does have a telling aside on the rites of Mount Lykaion:

Pausanias 8.38.6

Mount Lykaion offers among other wonders the following above all: there is on it a precinct of Zeus, which men are not allowed to enter; if anyone disregards the custom and enters, he inevitably dies within the course of the next year. And this too is said, that anything within the precinct, be it man or beast, does not cast a shadow; so if a beast takes shelter there, the hunter is unwilling to follow, but remains outside observing the beast, and sees no shadow cast by it.

There is a clear hint elsewhere that human sacrifice still takes place at this mountain, and Pausanias passes it over in deliberate silence. He is able to pass on a much more common type of tradition in relation to Marathon[60]:

> There it is possible each night to hear the sound of horses neighing and men fighting. If someone deliberately sets out to get a clear view of this, it has no good outcome, but the *daimones* are not angry if someone chances on it unawares. The people of Marathon designate those who died at Marathon heroes, and Marathon after whom the community takes its name, and Heracles, declaring that they were the first of the Greeks to acknowledge him as a god. And they say that there chanced to be a figure present in the battle, of rustic appearance and clothing. This man killed many of the barbarians with his plow and disappeared after the battle. The Athenians asked the oracle, but the god only told them to honour the Hero Echetlaeus ["Plow-Tail"].

We are in the same territory as the West European Wild Hunt, associated in British folklore with the savior figure King Arthur.

THE FOLKLORE OF METAMORPHOSIS

Aside from the conventional problems of distinguishing between folklore and (pseudo-) science in antiquity, there is one phenomenon that affects human relationships with animal, vegetable, and mineral alike. The belief in metamorphosis is legion, as a glance at Ovid's *Metamorphoses* will show: the range of possibilities includes mutations as diverse as maidens into trees, pirates into dolphins, and rulers into stars. Of course, in Ovid's case we are dealing with a deliberately all-inclusive catalog of metamorphoses so that it would be surprising if changes were not prominent. But it might still surprise us that he could lay his hands on 15 books' worth of examples, and we are entitled to ask why.[61]

The foregoing sections are a reminder that in the ancient world, biology was a relatively undeveloped science. Since Darwin at least, we are conditioned to think of "forward" evolution of species, where apes can "evolve" into men, but not vice versa, whereas in the ancient world this was by no means felt to be the case. In a Greco-Roman mythological world view, there is no reason for a man not to regress into what we should regard as a lower species. All ancient man has to go on is the apparent resemblances between species: most men will change into mammals of some sort. What we should regard as evolutionary development backward causes no problems, and in Ovid's stories it is simply no sooner said than done. We might also find it useful to transport ourselves into a world of metamorphoses by seeing the world as the first hunter might see it. If someone puts on an animal skin, does he take on the animal's identity as well? If one makes oneself a dress of bark or leaves, is one, in some sense, on the way to becoming a tree?

The folklore of metamorphosis is certainly able to flourish where popular fable already accepts the convention of talking animals. These are already embedded in Sumero-Babylonian and Egyptian literature and appear as early in the Greek world as Achilles' talking horses in the *Iliad*,[62] in Hesiod's fable of the "Hawk and the Nightingale,"[63] or where fable and myth converge, as in the Aesopic fable of the frogs asking Zeus for a king.[64] This belief is able to interact with scientific (mis)observation, as when Ovid gives us a picture of animals born from the mud after the Flood.[65] But nothing quite prepares us for the profusion of metamorphosed species that seem to come into being in the same semimythical period, and often on a one-off basis: Daphne becomes a laurel, and after that, all laurels are sacred to Apollo; Scylla cuts off her father's hair and then becomes the cutter-bird, *ciris,* the shear water cutting the waves.[66] In both these cases we can evoke the mechanism of a simple charter myth: one change fixes and explains a phenomenon of the natural world for all time. But in some other cases we may be able to invoke a more rationalizing approach. In the story of Actaeon, Ovid's version has him actually changing into a stag. But a Greek relief sculpture from a metope at Selinus shows what might be an earlier version, where instead of actually being changed into a stag, Actaeon is only *wearing* a fawn's skin.[67] This, at any rate, would make for a possible explanation of the story that might actually work in a credible way. Suppose we have a man who decides to spy on a goddess bathing: How might he remain inconspicuous? By covering himself in a stag skin disguise, readily available, of course, since he himself actually hunts stags. With or without the instigation of the goddess, his hounds, trained to attack stags, will savage anything in a stag skin.[68]

In other cases we can note that the motivations for a specific metamorphosis are not always consistent. In Ovid's version the story of Tereus, Procne, and Philomela runs as follows[69]:

> Tereus, the Thracian king, husband of Procne raped her sister Philomela [in Ovid the girls are reversed], and cut out her tongue to prevent her telling the tale. She wove the scene on a tapestry and revealed the deed [thereby suggesting a preliterate source?] Philomela took her revenge by serving up his son Itys as a

dinner. All three change into birds: Philomela into the Nightingale, Procne to the Swallow, and Tereus to the Hoopoe.

Ovid's version is, as usual, unpredictable, but with a certain appetite for the grotesque: he concentrates, for example, on Philomela's indecision as to how she is to punish her wicked husband. But we are given nothing more than the insatiable lust of a tyrant to motivate the action. An earlier Hellenistic Greek poet Boio's version of the story was considerably different: he has the married pair under different names, boasting that their marriage is better than that of Zeus and thus exciting divine envy. The husband's occupation is that of a weaver *(philotechnos)*.[70] It is easy enough to conjecture why his victim might then revenge herself by using her ravisher's own skill against him, and we have here at least the explanation, or indeed the "justification," for such grotesque suffering: the couple's own arrogance brought about their misfortune.

Other, less rationalizing explanations can be offered for some other instances: Forbes Irving points out the extent to which metamorphoses tend to follow sexual license in the wild and suggests that the whole business is a kind of metaphor for female sexuality. Sometimes this leads to inconsistency: he points out how many of the rapes in Ovid take place in the country because it is a place of wildness, then says that in some cases, like that of Io, it is the place of conspicuous chastity—but we might not be able to have things both ways, and the seductions may have nothing to do with the rural background at all.[71] But there may be more to it still. We do know of stories, like some early incestuous versions of Cinderella, for example, where some sexual assault is followed by the construction of garments of animal skin; one hears of garments of lice, animal pelts, fur, or the like to conceal the shame of having been wooed by her father. It would not take too much effort to envisage that a girl in the plight of Io or Daphne should ask for a skin of calf or bark. One might think, also, of Adam and Eve in the garden: after the shame of sexual awareness they cover themselves with garments of leaves. If Ovid had retold the tale, might they not simply have changed into trees?

Of course, the gods themselves can exercise a prerogative of continually changing shapes. It is perhaps unsurprising that the sky god Zeus turns out also to be the shapeshifter par excellence—one only needs to look at the vast possibilities of cloud formation to imagine why—or Poseidon has predictably similar powers, given the changing colors and moods of the sea. But the belief extends also to sorceresses: we are still left asking questions about the folktale behind the story of Circe, changing Odysseus' crew to swine, as she had changed others before them into tame animals.[72] Now there is a strong tradition of this kind of sorcery in oriental tales: Ishtar had a reputation of changing her lovers into beasts once they were discarded; the Sumero-Babylonian hero Gilgamesh takes her to task for exactly that and recites a whole catalog of the shapes into which she had turned her lovers.[73] Where sorcery is involved, the metamorphosis can be activated magically by a potion or ointment or reversed by a "natural" cure of roses.[74] One type of story extends this magical aspect still further, or seems to: we are aware of a number of stories involving someone who practices shapeshifting, the classic example being the Egyptian demigod Proteus.[75] But there are others: there is Mestra or Hypermestra, who keeps changing her shape and selling herself to feed her father,[76] as a privilege granted by Poseidon. It may be that the changes naturally associated with water deities offer the common factor.

CONCLUSION

How, then, are we to view the folklore of the natural world overall? It is clearly a world pullulating with possibilities but where not all the connections are as wrong as was once assumed: prehistoric bones, or their fossilized remains, will point more readily to conflicts of the gods and giants or to metamorphosis from animal to stone. But there *were* giants in those days, and calcification is indeed a form of metamorphosis. We must more often think in terms of distortion of the natural world rather than total invention in every case.

NOTES

1. For an illuminating analysis of Greek assumptions, see Lloyd (1983), 7–57.
2. Pliny, *NH* 9.27.
3. French (1994), 202f; for Pliny's general attitudes to animals and their instincts, see Beagon (1992), 33–44.
4. French (1994), 206.
5. Pliny, *NH* 16.24.
6. As in Philostratus, *Life of Apollonius* 3.45; for a different description, Aelian, *NA* 4.20 (as manticore).
7. Note esp. the role of the snake-god Glycon in Lucian's *Alexander.*
8. For the geese on the Capitol, Livy 5.47.
9. French (1994), 181.
10. Plutarch, *Mor.* 968F–969A; cf. Pliny, *NH* 8.103, only a matter of the fox's superior hearing.

11. French (1994), 216ff.

12. As amply attested in Pliny, *NH* 28–32, passim.

13. Aelian, *NA* 11.109.

14. Pliny, *NH* 5.34; cf. Lucian, *de Electro* 4f, *LCL* 1.76–79.

15. Pickering, *The Cassell Dictionary of Folklore* (London, 1999), s.v. Phoenix; for unicorns, sphinxes, griffins, and the like, see Cherry (1995).

16. For Phoenix lore in general, see van den Broek (1972). The emperor Claudius was sent a presumably fraudulent one, as Pliny himself surmises, but convincing enough to be exhibited in the *Comitium, NH* (10.5).

17. van den Broek (1972).

18. Mayor (1993, 1994).

19. *NH* 9.26; *Ep.* 9.33.

20. For the evident popularity of dolphin *mirabilia* in Pliny's age, cf. 9.25: a tale from the reign of Augustus is purveyed, Maecenas, Fabianus, and Flavius Alfius, among others.

21. For the folk-healing properties of the Hyena, see Pliny, *NH* 28.94f., with *LCL* additional note, 573.

22. For this role, as the *corocotta,* see, e.g., Aelian, *NA* 7.22, Pliny, *NH* 8.107, has it as a hybrid between hyena and lion.

23. Virgil, *Georgic* 4.1–280; on Pliny's attitude, of similar enthusiasm, see Beagon (1992), 141f.

24. *Georgic* 4.281–558; *Judges* 14:8–14.

25. This form of the external soul is at least as old as the ancient Egyptian form of the "Two Brothers' Tale," Lichtheim, *AEL* (1976), 208.

26. Note esp. the sacred trees representing Philemon and Baucis, Ovid, *Met.* 8.715–724.

27. On the properties of the mandrake, see Raven (2000), 38f.

28. French (1994), 206.

29. Pliny, *NH* 16.24; Krappe (1930), 237, no. 31.

30. Pliny, *NH* 20.50.

31. Ibid., 20.84.

32. Major (1998–1999), 187–191.

33. Stannard, *Helmantica* (1986), 95–106.

34. Ibid.

35. Pliny, *NH* 24.103.

36. Pliny, *NH* 27.131.

37. Theophrastus, *de causis Plantarium* 9.8, 8.7.

38. Pliny, *NH* 27.85; *HP* 9.8.6; Lloyd (1983), 145; further instances follow in 9.8, on kentauris, mandragora, and others, though he concedes that "there may be nothing out of place in saying a prayer when cutting a plant" (8.7).

39. Price-Kearns s.v.

40. Philostratus, *Life of Apollonius* 5.5.

41. Apuleius, *Florida* 1.

42. For the supposed erotic attraction embodied in magnetism, Achilles Tatius 1.17.

43. French (1994), 239.

44. Pliny, *NH* 34.44f.

45. Ibid., 16.251.

46. Mayor (2000), 208.

47. Ibid.

48. Pliny, *NH* 9.9ff.

49. Mayor (2000), 228–231.

50. Mayor (2000), chapter 2.

51. Solinus 9.6f., tr. Mayor.

52. Mayor (2000), 116–120.

53. *Life of Apollonius* 5.16.

54. Pausanias 1.35.4ff., 7.2.4.

55. Examples of natural and mythological curiosities exhibited in Casson (1974), 243ff.

56. Plutarch, *Life of Sulla* 27.2 (exhibit of a live "satyr" to Sulla); cf. the account of satyrs in Pausanias 1.23.7.

57. For the interaction of landscape and memory, see Alcock (2002).

58. For "geomyths," extraordinary phenomena such as earthquakes, volcanoes, and the like, see Vitaliano (1973).

59. Pausanias 8.29.1, with Levi ad loc.

60. Ibid., 8.38.7, 1.32.3f.

61. On the whole subject of Metamorphoses, see Forbes Irving (1990).

62. *Iliad* 19.404–423.

63. Hesiod, *Works and Days* 202–212.

64. Phaedrus 1.2.

65. Ovid, *Met.* 1.416–437.

66. Ibid., 1.548–567, 8.151f.

67. Carpenter (1991), no. 130 (Actaeon in a fawn skin), in contrast to no. 133 (Actaeon with the head of a stag).

68. For Actaeon, Ovid, *Met.* 3.174–252; cf. the curious case of Apollonius and the beggar-turned-hound, *Life of Apollonius* 4.10.

69. Ovid, *Met.* 6.412–674.

70. For further discussion, see Forbes Irving (1990), 80–90.

71. Forbes Irving (1990), 63–90, passim.

72. *Odyssey* 10.233–240.

73. Wide range of examples in Page (1973), 57–64.

74. Apuleius, *Met.* 3.24, 11.13.

75. *Odyssey* 4.455–458.

76. Ovid, *Met.* 8.871–874.

Nine
Medicine and Magic

The application of animal, vegetable, and mineral in the last chapter to serve the needs of superstition leads us naturally to consider the whole apparatus of medicine and magic. It is in these two naturally overlapping areas that our sources for ancient folklore are probably best documented and yet probably most prone to be studied from any perspective other than that of a folklorist. Magic can be presented as an entity almost in its own right and apart from the contexts of folklore at all,[1] while ancient medicine, even where it does rely on folk remedies, is at least as likely to be seen as part of the history of philosophy, or of medicine itself.[2] Moreover, "magic" as such is not easily defined or definable in ancient theory or practice. Early (and indeed, late) association with the Persian magi could be used to confer both antiquity and respectability,[3] while much in between goes to the other extreme of charlatanism, wonder working, or quackery.[4] In the late antique magical papyri, in particular, the boundaries with religion and science are difficult to draw: prayer, formula, and ritual practice seem to intermingle in a way that fosters confusion rather than conceptual clarity.[5] H. Versnel plausibly suggests "manipulation" as the key word: there is an attempt to enlist supernatural forces to achieve an end, more by compulsion than persuasion. And confusions of categorization seem to arise almost inevitably, given the ancient precaution of trying as many approaches as possible to ensure the desired result[6]: R. Gordon[7] notes the polarization between magic as specious show ("prestidigitation") and as a special power to achieve real effects of good and ill, and he points to the ability of the Greco-Roman world to accept or question both positions and a variety in between, with constant legal difficulty about locating what might be criminal about them.[8]

THE NATURE OF FOLK REMEDY

Perceptions apart, it could be very difficult to separate medicine and magic in practice: even Theophrastus' *Enquiry into Plants* is not exempt from irrational elements, as in book 9, where the views of the *rhizotomoi* (rootcutters) themselves are embodied.[9] We frequently find that in popular Greek medicine of any period, and in Roman popular medicine generally, there is a mixture of proprietary remedies and magical rituals and incantations. The latter could and still can at least supply a degree of psychosomatic help, if nothing else, by allaying in some measure the anxiety of the patient and so indirectly contributing to the promotion of well-being. That there were charlatans or fringe doctors who won the disapproval not just of the Elder Cato but of Pliny as well there is no doubt, though we find that even a sometimes questionable practitioner, such as Scribonius Largus, obviously does possess experience and practical skills, in contrast to Pliny, who is so often only as reliable as his "authorities."[10] Pliny himself jumbles reserved reports about incantations, amulets, or rituals, which still mention those obtaining relics from executed criminals or the drinking of blood.[11] Animal remedies rather than plant ones are more prone to sympathetic cures: Pliny is not above recommending ringing a plant with iron, carefully gathering it at night, intoning its purpose and the name of the recipient, and using the magic number three for its application by leaves or dosages.[12]

Magic makes itself felt early on in Greek literature: into her mixture of cheese, barley, honey, and Pramnian wine, the semidivine Circe of the *Odyssey* mixes *pharmaka lugra* ("baleful drugs"); the recipients immediately assume the outward features of swine.[13] But when the word *pharmakon* itself occurs here, it is difficult in the context to distinguish its meaning clearly as "drug" as opposed to "spell,"[14] all the more so when Circe uses a *rhabdos* ("staff") with all the force of a magic wand. And the protective drug *moly*, which Hermes gives to Odysseus, is specifically described, with its black root and its flower like milk: unfortunately, its application is not altogether clear, unsurprisingly in a story so selectively told to underplay the magical implications. We should also bear in mind the Egyptian drug known to Helen herself in *Odyssey* 4 (the opium poppy?), already apparently alluded to as a medicinal cure for a wound in battle in the *Iliad*.[15] Overall, it is not straightforward to explain Homeric medicine in relation to some assumption of theurgy,[16] the more or less mechanical working of the divine. There was some speculation as to the drug used by Medea to lull the serpent (*arkeuthos*, prickly juniper, as early as Musaeus?). By Pindar's time we have a sense of "combined therapies," on the part of the healing deity Asklepius, including incantation, surgery, soothing drinks, and amuletic drugs[17]: Sophocles himself actually wrote a lost *Rhizotomoi*—Macrobius actually quotes it in some detail ("cutting poisonous herbs with her face turned away lest she perish from the strength of their noxious aromas, then pouring the herbs' juices into bronze jars, the herbs themselves being cut with bronze sickles").[18] This and further fragments hint at the possibility of *thapsia garganica,* deadly carrot, specifically dangerous to cattle in Attica and ranked with hemlock as a dangerous root. Allusion is made both in the *Homeric Hymn to Demeter* and in Aristophanes' *Lysistrata* to pennyroyal, thought of as a female abortifacient and contraceptive (with an obscene pun between *glechon/ blechon*)[19]: it would have been familiar both to midwives and prostitutes and presumably to any supposedly mixed audience of Aristophanes.

We have our fair share of magical operations alluded to in literature. Later in the *Odyssey,* we find a flow of blood stopped by an incantation,[20] while Hesiod is able to catalog miracles of Hecate and so provide an early example of aretalogy, "wonder catalog."[21] The Greek theater, both comic and tragic, provides magical scenes, including the conjuring up of the ghost of Darius[22] as well as fun at the expense of magicians (Menander's lost *Deisidaimon*). Two works were particularly influential: Theocritus's sketch of an erotic magic performance and Medea's role in Apollonius of Rhodes.[23] Later, the novel takes up where epic leaves off, particularly in the magical operations in Thessaly that begin Apuleius' *Metamorphoses* and the description of necromancy in Heliodorus.[24] Philosophers early and late tend to show some susceptibility to magical experiment (Apuleius himself is by no means exempt from suspicion in his *Apology*), and indeed, mainstream philosophy from Plato onward remains suspicious until the theurgists of late antiquity: Plato's own description in the *Republic* affords a reasonable outsider's view of their activities[25]:

> And mendicant priests *(agurtai)* and seers *(manteis)* come to the doors of the rich and convince them that they have acquired from the gods by sacrifices and incantations the power to heal some wrongdoing of their own or their forebears, through games and festivals. And if someone wants to injure an enemy, for a modest expense they will harm a just man as much as an unjust with evocations and magic bonds, by persuading the gods, so they declare, to help them.[26]

The *Laws* is set to punish those who despise humans to the point of capturing the spirits of a good number of the living by claiming that they can raise the ghosts of the dead and promising to seduce even the gods, whom they bewitched by sacrifices, prayers, and incantation, who out of a love of money, make every effort to ruin individuals, whole families, and cities from top to bottom.[27] Not long afterward, the Derveni papyrus is already linking such persons with the powers to placate *daimones* by means of incantations (*epoidai*).[28]

As before, we tend to find a bewildering mixture of the proprietary and the arbitrary. Take the following prescription for a contraceptive agent[29]:

> Take as many bitter vetch seeds as you want for the number of years you wish to remain sterile. Steep them in the blood of a menstruating woman. Let them steep in her own genitals. And take a frog that is alive and throw the bitter vetch seeds into its mouth so that the frog swallows them, and release the frog alive at the place where you captured him, and take a seed of henbane, steep it in mare's milk; and take the nasal mucus of a cow with grains of barley, put these into a [piece of] leather skin made from a fawn and on the outside string it up with a mulehide skin, and attach it as an amulet during the waning of the moon [which is] in a female sign of the zodiac on a day of Kronos or Hermes. Mix in also with the barley grains cerumen from the ear of a mule.

This contains a cross section of magical procedures and reflexes, but it also contains two staples of (nonmagical) medical practice, vetch and henbane, whose properties were well documented and understood. We can see in the recipe the interaction of the two and the success of the one in producing an aura of efficacy in the perception of those attuned to magical procedures, while having at least a predictable pharmacological effect.

All in all, John Scarborough points to a general confusion: in spite of Medea and Circe, there is no female monopoly on the practice of plant lore, and there is a sense of continuity to be suspected from older Sumero-Babylonian and Egyptian traditions as well. It is once more difficult to separate religious and scientific (that is, empirically observed) notions about the pharmacology of plants.[30] People who held generally religious or flawed overviews of the world were still capable of rational deductions about them. Theophrastus himself is capable of fudging his notion of an herb because of the folkloric assumptions of the root cutters who supply his information: he can combine Aristotelian classification with "sympathetic" pharmacology of bulbous roots[31]; Pliny the Elder is still more obviously prone to such mixtures of perception and attitude. Again, Theophrastus will suggest why squill might be a good "averter": it is the long-lived quality of plants growing from bulbs reinforced by analogy of the pomegranate being preserved if set in squill. But he is not above quoting squill as a purificatory remedy for the *deisidaimon,* without necessarily condemning the superstition itself.[32] Squill was certainly known for its distinctive pungency and may, on that account, have figured prominently in such religio-magical rites as those connected with expelling a scapegoat. The same sort of muddle as

Theophrastus is able to produce on the properties of squill can be paralleled by Lucian's descriptions of some of the remedies of Alexander of Abonouteichos:

> To other people he prescribed regimes and diets, aware, as I said at the outset, of many useful cures. And he had a great fondness for *kytmides*—a term he made up for a restorative cure put together from bear's grease.[33]

The intervention of psychological factors is illustrated by another observation of Lucian's about Alexander. The latter issued an oracle prescribing a prophylactic verse against the plague under Marcus Aurelius[34]:

> And there was one oracle, another spontaneous utterance, addressed to all nations, which he dispatched during the plague: it consisted of a single verse:
> "Phoebus, the unshorn one, wards off the cloud of the plague."
> and this it was possible to see all over, written over doorways as an averter of the plague. But for the most part it had the opposite effect: for by some stroke of fortune it was these very houses in particular on which the verse was inscribed that were devastated. Don't think I'm claiming that they died because of the verse, but by some coincidence that was how it turned out. And perhaps most people, reassured by the verse, were careless and lived rather too complacently, not supporting the oracle against the disease, since they had the syllables working on their behalf and the unshorn Apollo shooting off the plague!

It is difficult for modern Westerners to think themselves into a society that takes magic for granted, not only as something that actually works in its own right, but that works so predictably and certainly that it can be used to regulate society as a whole. The idea may be dismissed as superstition by the highly educated or philosophically inclined but can still penetrate to the highest echelons of society:

> At any rate Cleodemus said "If then someone takes from the ground in the left hand the tooth of a weasel killed in the manner I have mentioned, and wraps it in the skin of a newly-flayed lion, then binds it about the legs, the pain stops at once." "Not in the skin of a lion," said Deinomachus, "but of a hind still virgin and unmated; and that has a more convincing rationale, for the hind is swift and its greatest strength is in its feet. The lion is brave of course, and his fat and right forepaw and the stiff bristles from his chin are very effective if a person knows how to use each of them with its own proper incantation; but it has very little to offer as a cure for the feet."
> "I too was long of that persuasion," Cleodemus rejoined, "that it had to be a hind's skin because the hind is swift; but not long ago a Libyan knowledgeable on these matters convinced me otherwise, reminding me that lions are quicker than hinds. 'The fact is,' he said, 'they actually chase and catch them!'"[35]

Such a passage abounds in the insights it affords on how a basic folk-magical principle of "sympathy" can be applied—and subverted—by the same imperfect logic that is used to generate it in the first place. (Lucian goes on to suggest that a doctor present recommends cures for gout based on lifestyle and diet, much as a modern doctor might be expected to do.) Much emphasis in the learned exchange is on the proper and traditional grammar of folk remedies; they will work, like magic spells, if they are carried out to the letter, and not otherwise (always a useful "let-out" in accounting for failure in any given instance).

CURSING

More unambiguously "magical" in its operations is the notion of the curse[36]: this embodies and extends the sympathetic principle in that it purposes to "bind its intended victim, and frequently employs gestures of twisting and binding in the preparation and execution." The subject of cursings is by no means confined to erotic and erotically related magic; rather, we find scenarios of curses against legal opponents, in a variety of instructive social situations. No fewer than some hundred such curse tablets have been excavated from the spring of Sulis Minerva at Bath alone: someone who has typically lost a cloak at the baths will dedicate it to the goddess so that simple theft now becomes sacrilege.[37] Sometimes a revealing social narrative may emerge[38]:

> One Epaphroditus has lured away my slaves. He has taught them evil ways. He has put ideas into their heads, he has given them advice, he has seduced them. He has laughed at me, he has given them wings to waste time in the marketplace. He gave them the idea of running away; he himself bewitched my slave-girl, so that he could take her to wife against my will. For this reason he bewitched her to run away along with the others. Lady Demeter, being the victim of these things, and being on my own, I take refuge with you. May I find you propitious, and grant that I should find justice. Grant that the one that has done such things to me should find no peace in body or mind anywhere, whether still or moving. May he not be served by slaves or slave-girls, by small people or a large person. May he fail to accomplish his aims. May a bind-curse seize hold of his house and hold it fast. May no child cry.[?] May he not lay a happy table. May no dog bark. May no cockerel crow. May he not harvest after he has sown. . . . May neither the land nor the sea bear fruit for him. May he not have blessed joy, and may he himself perish miserably, and all that is with him.

The remainder, a direct prayer to Demeter, makes it clear that it is the laughter of enemies that is the driving force behind the curse. It seems very clear in this instance that the situation is one characteristic of daily life in a slave-owning society, a case of enticement: it is instructive to compare the subject matter of one of Alexander of Abonouteichos' oracles, which seems to hint at a similar situation.[39] There is the clear implication that erotic magic has been practiced by the enticer himself, and it is certainly not excluded that the slave master who makes the curse is jealous of the man who has obtained sexual favors from his own property. The characteristic consequences of the curse reflect an agricultural society: crop failure will strike to the heart of any enemy.

The success, or supposed success, of cursing is attested by the frequency of widespread *katadesmoi/defixiones* throughout the area of the Roman Empire, and the actual topics themselves reflect a wider range of everyday activities, where a rival might be expected, whether in trading activities, lawsuits, athletic competitions, or sexual rivalries. Topics on justice with names as opposed to anonymous curses tend to elevate the motivation from simple hatred or rivalry to a sense of unfairness and the desire for wrongs righted.

AMULETS AND DOLLS

In a sense, amulets[40] and their formulae constitute a form of counteraction to curses: a wide range of materials and formulae were used to protect the beneficiary and were often worn about the person. Body parts of the prematurely dead figure prominently, as do symbols of life-forces such as phalloi, but no more than simple thread could be called upon, as it is in the antiimpotence charm administered by Proselenus to Encolpius.[41] In amulets the distinction between magical and medical application is at its slimmest in this area: materials bound to any injury might have known and genuinely medical efficacy in our sense or they might, as in the Lucian example of the lions' skin, embody some supposed "sympathetic" effect. We are fortunate in having a number of late testimonia relating Apollonius of Tyana to the supply of amulets in Byzantium[42] to avert a plague of insects. One thinks likewise of Moses' aversion of the Egyptian plagues[43] and the ambiguous reputation of Moeses/Musaeus outside biblical tradition as a powerful magician in his own right.

Dolls of a variety of substances could be "activated" to perform sympathetic results, as when the Magical Papyri prescribe[44] the fashioning of a Hermes figure out of wax and plant extracts, which will promote any amount of trade when three non-Greek names are attached to it; Apuleius had just such a Hermes doll, which he rather implausibly claims against his accusers to be nonmagical.[45] Erotic magic could likewise make use of voodoo-type dolls, and to Lucian's well-known story of Chrysis and Glaukias, which involves just such a sending and summoning, Ogden compares a very detailed prescription for a pair of Eros and Psyche dolls with the same object in mind of summoning the beloved.[46] Erotic cursing could also be practiced, by the same means, by piercing a female clay figurine with bronze needles and similarly by compelling the lover thus symbolized to obey and accede to erotic demands: it is to be put beside the grave of someone who has died a violent or premature death.[47] A relatively rare operation is the use of magic for the sending of dreams: the Leiden Papyrus[48] includes a detailed prescription for the drawing of a four-winged figure in myrrh on a linen sheet; demons to be named receive written instruction to furnish whatever dream the victim is to have, and the demons are conjured in the name of Seth, the archenemy of the Egyptian Osiris, under (appropriate) threat of dismemberment if they disobey (he it was who treacherously dismembered the body of Osiris himself).

The persistence of such procedures presupposes that either they were perceived to have at least the possibility of success, whether at first hand or by report—a few well-publicized coincidences might easily ensure the latter—or that they were sufficiently entrenched in traditional practice to be able to continue automatically, regardless of degrees of skepticism. Lucian's presentations, in particular, suggest a market among those with more money than sense (including the implied dupe Glaukias above). But we might also accept an element of therapy in the cursing of an enemy: when one earths the tablet, one is earthing one's anger.

EROTIC MAGIC

A high proportion of broadly magical activity in antiquity is concerned with attracting the services of a lover or some similarly sexually nuanced operation. An extensive repertoire of surviving magical papyri emphasizes the scope and scale of operations. Many of these once more entail a sympathetic principle. Aside from the normal common sense prescriptions of this or that item of diet on general recommendation (many bulbous and therefore testicular in implication), there is a distinctive class of so-called *agogai* spells: typically an item, such as hair, from the lover, bound with a prescription "make X love me." Fire may be used literally in the execution of the spell to replicate the fire of passion to be aroused in the beloved. Besides the sympathetic techniques as such come a marked degree of rhetorical melodramatics and psychological manipulation. Rooftops at night are favorite venues, from which it is easy to make contact with the moon or the planet Venus; a light may be included in the proceedings, and the progress of the seduction or attraction may be monitored; the spell has to deprive the beloved of sleep before a feeling of lust for the agent of the magic.[49] Winkler notes the social and psychological reality of the situation: the victim of infatuation is putting himself in a position of control and is transferring his own erotic desperation fancifully to the beloved.[50]

The magical papyri find their narrative counterpart quite closely in the details of the celebrated witch transformation[51] of the Thessalian witch Pamphile, operating in Hypata:

> Now first of all Pamphile took all her clothes off, then she unfastened a little chest and took a number of small jars from it; she removed the lid of one of these, scooped out some of the ointment, and for some time rubbed it in the palms of her hands, then anointed herself with it from the tips of her toenails right to the very top of her hair; she had a long and secret colloquy with the lamp, then she shook her limbs with a tremulous movement. As her body gently went into motion soft feathers grew and powerful wing feathers; her nose hardened and took on a curve, while her nails became hooked. Pamphile had turned into an owl. She gave out a strident screech and already began to test herself in flight by leaping little by little off the ground. Soon she was off skywards and flew out of the house in full flight.

A witch's flying ointment has been reconstructed from a medieval recipe: the effect it has is not to cause the subject to fly, but so to disarrange the subject's perception of distances and planes as to give the illusion of flying; in other words, it offers a hallucinogenic "trip."[52] It will only take a third-hand account to turn such an illusion into a "factual" experience, unrestrained by the question "did anyone actually see you?"

Apuleius' contemporary Lucian offers us a useful construction on how a witch might be presented in the rumor mill between two courtesans[53]:

Bacchis: There is a very handy witch (pharmakis), a Syrian, still fresh and firm: when Phanias was annoyed with me . . . just as Charinus with you, she brought us together after all of four months, when I had already given up on him, and he came back to me again drawn by incantations.

Melissa: What did the old girl charge, if you can still recall?

Bacchis: She doesn't call for a huge fee, Melissa, only a drachma and a loaf; and you have to have seven obols, sulphur, and along with the salt a torch. These the old woman takes; she has to have a bowl of wine mixed, and she has to drink it on her own. You'll have to have something from the man, like clothes or boots, or a few hairs or something of the sort.

Melissa: I've got his boots.

Bacchis: She hangs these up and fumigates them with the sulphur, and
             sprinkles salt on the fire, and she adds both your names, his
             and yours. Then from her bosom she brings out a wheel, and
             spins it round chanting some spell rapidly off her tongue with
             weird and spine-chilling names. That's what she did that time.
             And before long Phanias, although his friends criticised him
             and Phoebis, his lover, kept pleading with him, he came back
             to me, and it was because of the charm in large measure that he
             came back. And also she taught me this spell for making him
             hate Phoebis, to watch out for any footprints she left, wipe
             them out, put my right foot in the place of her left and vice
             versa (with my feet pointing the other way) with "I trample on
             you and I am on top of you." And I did as instructed.

Melissa: Don't delay, Bacchis. Call the Syrian right now, and you,
             Acis, get the bread and sulphur and all the rest of the ingre-
             dients for the spell.

This little mime-like performance preserves a wealth of detail, and although
Lucian sometimes gilds the lily somewhat, he succeeds here in producing
something of a documentary quality of an operator of routine love magic in
operation. In the first place, this is an instance of everyday erotic magic: the
pharmakis is cheap and characteristically foreign (to an action notionally set
in Athens). The main point is the association of the names and the possession of objects that are part of or associated with the beloved. Most of the rest
may be for show, including the incantation and the magic wheel, though it is
worth noting the association between wisewomen and the circular motion of
wheels, as in the case of the prophetic Fates themselves. Some at least of the
process is done by the measure of belief on the part of the beneficiary: it never
occurs to her that the lover may simply have tired of the rival. The desperation of the present client is a cliché of characterization: lovers will not wait.

    There is little need in these contexts to draw a distinction between Greek
and Roman: it is rather the case that whatever was felt to work could be and
was diffused, often from the fringes of the Greco-Roman world (the nation-
alities of practitioners mentioned by Lucian are revealing in this respect). But
it is perhaps surprising to note that even the Elder Cato has his own magically
operating superstitions:

    In the event of any dislocation, the following incantation will heal it: take
    a green reed, four or five feet long, and split it down the middle. Have two

men hold it to the hips: Start to chant *moetas vaeta daries dardaries astataries dissunapiter,* until the parts come together. Hold iron over them, and when they come together and touch, hold the join and cut right and left. Bind the pieces to the dislocation or the break and it will heal. But chant every day, and for a dislocation as follows: *huat huat huat ista sisatas sistardannabou dannaustra.*[54]

There are similar prescriptions in Varro and Marcellus Empiricus.[55] It is also useful to bear in mind that Pliny was aware that many herbs were known only to illiterate country folk so that many of the plants were not actually named, and of course, those conversant with their properties were not necessarily disposed to pass on their unique knowledge.[56]

THE MAGICAL PROFESSION

Pliny himself reserves a good deal of venom for the magi as a profession, and his indictment of them certainly goes to the root of his view of superstition[57]:

> None will doubt that magic began from medicine, and that it crept in under the guise of healing, as if it were a higher and more sacred form of medicine; that to the most flattering and desirable promises it added the force of religion, over which even today the human race is absolutely in the dark; and meeting with success there too, it added astrology, as no-one is not greedy to hear his destiny, and convinced that it is to be sought most accurately from the heavens. And so it held human sense in a threefold binding and rose to such a lofty height that it holds sway over the great part of all nations, and in the east it gives orders to the King of Kings.

Just how readily magic and medicine can be associated within this bond is well illustrated from a personal reminiscence of Pliny himself[58]:

> Should anyone ask what lies the ancient magi told—when in my youth I saw Apion the grammarian, he handed down to me that the herb cynocephalia, known in Egypt as osiritis, was a divine plant and an apotropaic against all poisons, but if it were wholly uprooted, the perpetrator would die; he also claimed to have called up shades to find out from Homer the name of his country and parents; but he did not dare to reveal the replies he received.

Pliny attributes magic to a Persian origin and, indeed, to a named author for the earliest surviving book: Ostanes, frequently cited in quotations from the Greek Democritus.[59] This might be felt to fuel his xenophobia, already given free rein against Greeks and doctors, and a list is furnished of the Greek philosophers (including Plato) who picked magic up abroad; it is also associated with contemporary druidism and its repellent human sacrifices. But in fact, Greek myth is hardly short of magicians in itself: not only Hermes and Hecate are involved, but at the Grimms' fairy tale level, there are the Telchines, who know magic as well as metalworking, to say nothing of little people like the Idaean Dactyls[60] and such more respectable figures as Musaeus, Melampus, and Orpheus, all perhaps with a touch of pied piper characteristics. . . .

There is early on a tendency to join the term *magos,* with its oriental and originally respectable overtones, with the term *goes,* a figure concerned with mourning, healing, and prophecy, but amounting in context often to little more than "charlatan, conjurer."

An unusual anecdote serves to illustrate the contrary force, whereby charges of magic could be subverted by simple common sense:

Pliny, *NH* 18.41ff

The freedman C. Furius Chresimus was greatly hated, as he had a much larger yield from quite a small holding than those around him from much larger estates, as if he was using spells to entice other people's crops. And so he feared condemnation in an action at the hands of the curule aedile Spurius Albinus, and on the appointed day when the tribes had to cast their votes, he assembled all his agricultural tools in the forum, and brought his sturdy farm household, according to Piso well looked after and well turned out, as well as his well-wrought iron implements, weighty mattocks, heavy ploughshares, and well-fed oxen. Then he said: "Citizens, these are my magic spells, but I cannot show you or produce in court my late nights and early rises and sweaty toil"; and so he was unanimously acquitted.

Such a case, probably from 186 B.C., suggests a general enough belief in magic in a sociolegal context: there is genuine belief that someone of low status and Eastern origin could practice an abuse condemned as early as the Laws of the Twelve Tables of transferring crops from a neighbor's field to his own.

CONCLUSION

The overlap between traditional remedies and magical procedures enabled a wide gray area to flourish: the general urge to leave no stone unturned to secure and maintain health and happiness underlay the inclination to "try anything," whether to obtain social justice or revenge on the one hand, or amorous fulfillment on the other. In such a climate Pliny's analysis of the remedies of the magi, or Lucian's of Alexander's drugs, is acutely revealing. Anyone could chance his arm, and the rewards for a shrewd commercial entrepreneur like Alexander in a conservative and superstitious community are hardly surprising.

NOTES

1. The recent accessible bibliography on magic is considerable: among many, Graf (1997); Faraone and Obbink (1991); Flint et al. (1999); Dickie (2001); Ogden (2002).

2. Note, however, the excellent treatments by Lloyd (1979, 1983).

3. On the magi, Pliny, *NH* 30.1.1f.; also Apuleius, *Apology* 25f.

4. For charlatanism in general, see Anderson (1994), 131–150.

5. Versnel in Faraone and Obbink (1991), 92.

6. Ibid., 93.

7. In Flint et al. (1999), 162.

8. Ibid., 168.

9. Scarborough in Faraone and Obbink (1991), 138; cf. also Raven (2000), 33f.

10. Scarborough in French and Greenaway (1986), 62f.

11. For example, the abhorrence of using gladiators' blood as a cure for epilepsy, Pliny, *NH* 28.5; for detailed assessment of Pliny's drug lore, see Scarborough in French and Greenaway (1986), 59–85.

12. For Pliny's limitations in relation to plants, see Morton in French and Greenaway (1986), 86–97.

13. *Odyssey* 10234ff., with Scarborough in Faraone and Obbink (1991), 139, to whom I owe much of the detail of the following discussion.

14. Scarborough in Faraone and Obbink (1991), 139.

15. *Odyssey* 4.220–230; cf. *Iliad* 8.306f.

16. Scarborough against Smith in Farraone and Obbink (1991), 142.

17. Pindar, *Pythian* 3.51ff.; Scarborough in Faraone and Obbink (1991), 143.

18. Scarborough in Faraone and Obbink (1991), 144, citing Macrobius 5.19.9 (his translation).

19. On pennyroyal, in *Homeric Hymns and Apocrypha*, 209; Aristophanes, *Lysistrata* 89; Scarborough in Faraone and Obbink (1991), 144f.

20. *Odyssey* 19.457.

21. Hesiod, *Theogony* 411–452.

22. *Persae* 619–842.

23. Theocritus 2; Apollonius Rhodius 3.528–533, passim.

24. Apuleius, *Metamorphoses* 1–3, passim; Heliodorus 6.15.

25. Graf (1997), 22.

26. Plato, *Republic* 364B.

27. Graf (1997), 25, citing *Laws* 909B.

28. Ibid., 23.

29. Scarborough in Faraone and Obbink (1991), 158; *PGM* 36.320-32, tr. Scarborough.

30. e.g., Scarborough in Faraone and Obbink (1991), 161f.

31. Theophrastus 9.18.3–11, after Scarborough in Faraone and Obbink (1991), 149.

32. cf. Scarborough in Faraone and Obbink (1991), 147.

33. Lucian, *Alexander* 22.

34. Lucian, *Alexander* 36; a fragment of the verse (*Iliad* 20.39) has indeed been found in an inscription at Antioch on Orontes in combination with the seven prophylactic vowels and in honor of Apollo *Alexikakos* (warder off of ills); see Caster (1938) ad loc.

35. Lucian, *Lover of Lies* 7.

36. Ogden (2002), 210–226; Versnel in *OCD,* 3; Strubbe in Faraone and Obbink (1991), 33–59, 60–106; Gager (1992).

37. Tomlin (1988).

38. Tr. Ogden (2002), no. 188, after Homolle *BCH* (1901), 25, 412–56.

39. Lucian, *Alexander* 50.

40. Pliny, *NH* 28f.; *OCD,* 3 Versnel; Kotansky in Faraone and Obbink (1991), 107–137.

41. Petronius, *Satyrica* 131.

42. e.g., Dulière (1970); Anderson (1994), 194.

43. Exodus 5:1–12:30.

44. *PGM* 4.2359–72.

45. Ogden (2002), 251ff.

46. Ibid., 256ff.

47. For defensive use of voodoo dolls, see Faraone (1991).

48. *PGM* 2.66f.

49. cf. the scenario in Apuleius, *Met.* 3.21, where Pamphile performs a magical metamorphosis before flying off to a lover.

50. Winkler in Faraone and Obbink (1991), 224ff.

51. Apuleius, *Met.* 3.21f.

52. Harper in *Folklore* (1977), 88, 105f.; *Met.* 3.21.4.

53. *D. Meretr.* 4.1f.

54. *De Agricultura* 160.

55. Similar references in Cato, *De Agri Cultura* 1.2.27; Marcellus Medicus 15.11.

56. Pliny, *NH* 25.4, and "further on"?; Beagon (1992), 112.

57. Pliny, *NH* 31.2; for a useful short overview, see Beagon (1992), 99–113.

58. Pliny, *NH* 31.18.

59. On Pliny's Ostanes, see Ogden (2002), text 45; cf. 46.

60. Note also Burkert (1985), 281–285, on the Samothracian Kabeiroi.

Ten
Conclusion

We should conclude our survey on ancient folklore by suggesting some summaries for the present and some prospects for the future. At more than double the length of Halliday's introduction, we still have a sense of how much has had to be left out. Our first impression is that definition and categorization themselves remain, and will remain, difficult: I have aimed throughout to avoid rigidity. Once all the caveats are offered, I hope I have attempted to explain, to myself as much as to the reader, how some of ancient folklore must have worked and how we can accustom ourselves to sifting evidence of bewildering diffuseness. Often, the most telling evidence, in this author's view, is about how a rumor might have started or how a supposedly remarkable occurrence was reported and just a little exaggerated.

We might describe the available picture of Greek and Roman folklore as follows in terms of what it is like to inhabit the thought world of Greco-Roman folk. Theirs is a world where old wives' tales told by old women or nurses will stay with their charges for the rest of their lives, though they may graduate from a belief in child-eating witches or the like to a thought-world in which nymphs and satyrs still roam the countryside, demons are part of the management structure of the supernatural, and anyone, from god to slave, can be invested with the trickery needed to survive. Beliefs can be consolidated by myths of generations of gods who generate heroes by mortal women to found cities ruled by legendary rulers; virtuous heroines will find ideal husbands with the help of magic objects and supernatural helpers; Cinderella is already on hand in some form or other, even if there is no grand ball or pumpkin coaches to convey her to it, and already, she has a slipper for a king to find. People are already celebrating births, comings of age, marriages, and deaths and are taking holidays and festivals at gaps in the yearly cycle. There are rather more divinities or semidivinities to placate, and perhaps, too, rather more taboos to be negotiated, and many more unlucky days than Friday the 13th. And as if there were not enough folklore to be getting on with, there is always some more fakelore to replace any that is lost, before becoming folklore in turn, if it survives long enough. There is plenty of proverbial wisdom in fables and proverbs, jokes about numskulls, and the rest to fortify us with the common sense and survival skills to cope. And there are plenty of quacks, false prophets, magicians, wisewomen, and the rest to be guarded against. You may be confident enough in reason and science to stand outside the world of hearsay, rumor, and the rest, but there will always be a friend of a friend to make you wonder, the exotic foreign priest to tell you otherwise, or the tale from your great grandfather's day to act as a warning. And what you heard long ago may linger longer than what you read in a learned treatise yesterday. You had better take care. . . .

There is one abiding impression in all this: that there are sufficient correspondences to affirm that the Greco-Roman world represents a continuity, in many respects, from the traditional culture of the Near East and that it does not stand too far apart from the picture we might now gather of the traditional folklore of modern Europe. It is perhaps still too tempting to assume continuities rather than revivals where we find a gap in tradition, but it flies in the face of geography and the normal processes of transmission to assume gaps in continuity every single time there is a gap in evidence.

We are reminded time and again of the limits of observation in the ancient world, sometimes underlined by class divisions: Pliny the Elder may believe an *eques* where he would not accept the word of a peasant or a slave. Such a tendency is in accord with a still wider gulf between the credulous and the rational (or supposedly so). What peasants believe is somehow of less consequence, as are the way they speak and the tales they tell. Pliny and his class do not really see themselves most of the time as "folk." And yet what we might think of as superstitious reflexes, of believing what we want to uncritically, is never too far away. Here is Pliny's own nephew writing to a well-educated and aristocratic correspondent on the problem of the existence of ghosts:

> And so I should be very keen to know whether you think that there are such things as ghosts, and that they have their own shape and some supernatural quality, or whether they are empty figments and take their shape only from our own fears. I myself am led to believe they exist from what I hear happened to Curtius Rufus. . . .[1]

It is all too clear from two of the ghost stories that follow that Pliny has a vested interest in the prophetic power of dreams: in Curtius' case they confirmed his personal ambition, while in Pliny's case a dream had a convenient (but unconvincing) bearing on his own political fortunes. The psychology of superstition is central to an understanding of the frameworks of belief that underlie the attitudes of even the most highly educated. The world of the dead naturally accounts for a high proportion of ancient cult practice: not only do remains have to be ensured either by cremation or inhumation or some other means of reaching the next world, but precautions have to be taken to placate the spirits or ghosts of that world, especially if they haunt the living through failure to obtain access, and they must be placated until they do. This offers the mainspring for a high proportion of ancient ghost stories,[2] and curiosity on the matter unsurprisingly was not confined to the lower orders of society.

There is also an abiding gulf between the folklorist and the classicist in perception, assumption, and general approach. We can suggest a final illustration of this in relation to a modern urban myth. Recent scholarship has tended to regard abduction by aliens, with or without return to earth, as a modern variety of folklore, which can only take its impetus and color from the UFO preoccupations from the 1940s onward and which belongs as much to science fiction as to folklore itself. But it has, of course, a natural counterpart in the numerous journeys to the Otherworld in both ancient and medieval semipopular literature. One instance that stands out from antiquity and has not, so far as I am aware, been cited in this context is the dream in which Lucian encounters first Sculpture and then Paideia, each of whom tries to entice him to her own way of life; Paideia then takes him aloft in her celestial chariot and allows him to sow something (words as seeds, presumably) before setting him down on earth again.[3] If we think of it in terms of soul-flights or dreams alone, we shall miss the analogy, but classicists think in those terms, not in terms of abduction by aliens, and folklorists, in general, are likely to be unaware that it is there.

We began with a visit to a site where an oral story had been told, and we may wish to refresh our memories with another of the same. The Greek philosopher and man of letters Dio of Prusa, wandering in exile in the Peloponnese in the late first century A.D., gives an account of a woman from whom he claims to have heard an oral story:

> Now as I was on my way from Heraea to Pisa beside the river Alpheus, I was able to find the road for part of the way, but in the course of coming on some woodland and rough country and more than one path leading to various herds

and flocks, I met no-one and was unable to ask the way, so that I was lost and at high noon I was wandering aimlessly. So when I saw on some high ground a clump of oaks that looked like a sacred grove, I made for it in the hope of seeing some road or house from there. So I found some stones set together after a fashion, and animal pelts from sacrificed animals hanging and clubs and sticks, offerings from some shepherds, so it appeared; a little further off I saw a woman sitting, big and strong, getting on in years; she had a generally rustic dress and locks of white hair hanging down. I addressed all my questions to her. And she, in a Doric dialect, gently and kindly told me that the place was a grove sacred to Heracles, and about herself, that she had a son who was the shepherd and that often she looked after his flocks. She also claimed to have been endowed with the art of prophecy from the mother of the gods, and that all the shepherds round about made use of it, and the farmers, about producing and safeguarding harvests and flocks. . . . "At some time you will meet a great man, the ruler over a great many land and peoples; you must not hesitate to tell them this story, even if some people take you for a wandering babbler . . . listen then to the following tale and pay careful attention so that you recall it clearly and can tell it to the man I say you will meet: it is about the god before whom we are at this moment. . . ."[4]

The story told is an unusual version of the traditional allegory "the choice of Heracles," this time to choose between queenship and tyranny. The setting is the authentic one for a country fairy tale: here we have another *anilis fabula*, told by a local and ageing wisewoman in a remote rural setting and with prophetic connotations. In some ways she is presented as little more than a (suspiciously eloquent) fortune-teller. But one way or another, her story was passed on.

It is fitting to end, however, with a traditional tale of our own, the man who set out to find the folklore of the ancients:

Once upon some other time there was or there was not a man who did not know the folklore of the ancients, and he set out to find it. First of all he met a crowd of people who said they knew, so he listened as they pointed out primrose paths going out in all directions; but none of the signposts seemed to say anything very helpful, and so he followed his instinct along an unbeaten track with no signpost except "they say this leads to where the folk speak." Along this route he met all sorts of people, and he only listened to those who began their answers to his questions with "they say. . . ." So he noted down what they said, and especially if they said, "I heard this from a friend of a friend once upon a time." If they said "I read this in a book," he didn't listen. He listened to children and old men and women for the most part. In course of time he noticed that everyone was looking much older, and he was feeling the same. Eventually he could travel no further, so he stopped at a well, and beside it sat an ancient man: "I have been waiting for you," he said, "you will find what you are seeking down at the bottom of the well. There you will meet the first man; he was my great-grandfather, or so they tell me, who will tell you what he says is the first tale, but you also must perform a ritual." "Must I do that before or after I hear the first tale?" he asked. "The choice is yours," said the ancient man. So the traveller went down and met the even more ancient man, who told him the tale before he performed the ritual, as the traveller was all agog to hear it. No sooner had he finished listening, than the ancient man said: "the ritual is to drink from this cup." So he drank from the cup. "What spring is this?," he asked: "they say it's called Leth-. . . ." He couldn't remember the rest, not even the next syllable, and he realised he'd forgotten the first tale, or so he told me. . . .

And having tried to find out the folklore of the ancients, I know how he felt.

NOTES

1. Pliny, *Ep.* 7.27.1f.; on attitudes to the supernatural, see Dodds (1971).
2. For the genre, see Felton (1999).
3. *Lucian's Dream* 15f.
4. Dio, *Or.* 1.52–58.

Glossary

Aarne-Thompson. The joint authors of the revised edition of *The Types of the Folktale,* the principal directory of folktales related to the historic-geographic method.

Aesopic. Associated with the fables attributed to Aesop, and so involving instruction through simple folk narrative.

Analogue. In folktale scholarship, used of a tale that closely resembles another, whether as a variant or simply as a similar product.

Anecdote. A short, realistic account, often of an actual happening in the everyday and here and now and often initially in oral transmission.

Animal Tale. Any story in which animals are the protagonists: it can include fantastic tales of talking animals following Aesopic convention, or more realistic tales, where animals are simply the principle characters, without doing any impossible actions (for example, Androcles and the Lion).

Archetype. The original form to which all other versions may be traced back. Archetypes of ancient manuscripts are notoriously difficult to reconstruct from subsequent textual variants, and those of folktales subjected to oral transmission wellnigh impossible, though that was the aim of the historic-geographic method (q.v.).

Belief. The conviction that any given information is true. It is often used as a criterion for classification of myths as opposed to folktales but cannot be consistently maintained.

Bogeyman. An English term for usually trivial but malevolent sprites and the like used to scare children and so corresponding to Greek terms such as Mormo, Akko, Alphito, and similar creatures.

Cautionary Tale. A story whose moral acts as a warning, very often in a nursery context.

Collective Composition. A folk narrative that has been developed at the hands of a succession of (usually anonymous) authors: the range might extend from adding new verses to a nursery rhyme to adding whole episodes or reshaping a (generally oral) epic.

Contamination. The conflation or confusion of two tales, or two versions of a single tale: the merging of the "stupid ogre blinded" and the "false name Noman" in Homer's *Odyssey* offers an example of the first.

Contemporary Legend. A popular, generally untrue tale occurring and receiving transmission in a modern, generally urban environment. Its counterpart rarely survives antiquity because its natural channels of transmission have been most vulnerable at the end of the ancient world.

Cumulative Tale. A tale that relies for its effect on the accumulation of similar or parallel details contrived to end in a climax; often the text is of a nonsense or jingle character.

Curse. A malevolent wish against another party, whether to avenge wrong or obtain justice, or to exercise power or fear, through divine or magical means.

Cursing Tablet. A tablet of lead buried in the ground, in a tomb, or other strategic location to communicate a curse to powers of the world below.

Custom. In the context of folklore a traditional practice, usually relating to a whole community, though it might be practiced in a private or family context (such as shaving the heads of brides in Sparta). Ancient perspectives sometimes tended to amass reports of "curious customs" of barbarian peoples, and the implicit prejudice persisted well into the twentieth century. Anthropological scholarship stresses the constructive understanding of the meaning of a custom in its ethnological context and increasingly notes the susceptibility of traditional and supposedly timeless customs to change over time.

Diffusion. The process by which folkloric material is transmitted from one center to another. It is central to the so-called historic-geographic method, which attempts to map the process of distribution of popular, especially oral, material over time. It may be stimulated by such factors as proximity, invasion, or trading patterns over long distances; it is generally prevented only by insuperable barriers, such as untraversed ocean, isolation by natural disasters, and the like. It is usually accepted as the only explanation for sophisticated and complex tales to reproduce themselves in widely separated localities.

Epic. A large-scale work, usually in verse and often of traditional and anonymous character, embodying the experience of a whole community; its theme is often, but not always, the lofty exploits of a hero or heroes in a "heroic age" in the dimly remembered past. It thus may function as a repository for layers of folklorically significant material.

Etiological Tale. A tale that purports to explain the cause of some feature of the human or natural world, often with the aid of an arbitrary metamorphosis.

Exemplum. A tale intended to instruct and frequently used in Christian sermons but also featuring in rhetorician's manuals and other literature of "persuasion."

Fable. A usually short wisdom story, normally fictitious and often featuring talking animals; it offers a basic vehicle for folk wisdom.

Facetia. A witty saying, joke, or tale, usually short enough to be included in collections of *facetiae*.

Fairy. A traditional supernatural being of limited power as well as limited morality and often only having local influence.

Fairy Tale. A loosely definable category within folktale relying heavily on magic and its operators and typically with a romantic theme and happy outcome.

Fakelore. Material purporting to be or mistakenly believed to be traditional but being, in fact, of recent or spurious manufacture; the distinction is hard to make in the case of oracles, for example, where the integrity of the original producers is almost by definition open to doubt.

Finnish School. A group of nineteenth- and twentieth-century scholars working within the methodologies developed in the 1880s onward by Karl and Julius Krohn on mapping the development and diffusion of folktales. Their exacting techniques, often frustrated by lack of critical mass in early evidence, tended to lose momentum around 1960 but served to generate the key indexing tools to which professional folktale study is still bound.

Friend of a Friend. The proverbial source of much urban or contemporary legendary material, the point being that the teller or reporter has no direct, firsthand knowledge of the source of the information.

Folklore. Popularly transmitted material in either verbal or nonverbal form, stretching to include traditional crafts and techniques as well as tales, jokes, and so on.

Folktale. A traditional and usually anonymous story, typically embodying stereotypical content, broader than but encompassing fairy tale (q.v.).

Fool Tale. An entertaining, sometimes didactic tale featuring the behavior of simpletons who misunderstand basic logic or human relationships, often to an incredible degree.

Formula. A traditional and repeated verbal or thematic unit in the construction of a folktale: "there is and there is not" would serve as an opening formula of a doubtfully believable tale; "the hero obtains a magic object" would serve to illustrate a thematic formula, which is scarcely distinguishable from the term "motif."

Frame Tale. A story that acts as a container for another or a series of others. It is a particular feature of oriental collections, which sometimes employ more than one frame arranged concentrically, challenging the memory skills of both an oral storyteller and his audience in the first instance.

Function. A significant action marking a structural feature of a tale. The term is especially associated with the "31 functions" held by Vladimir Propp to constitute the irreducible building blocks of traditional fairy tales.

Genealogy. An account of ancestry to establish individual identity: "I am braveheart son of Fearless son of Valourlove" illustrates the purpose of genealogy in "heroic" contexts, but others are also found, such as the brief parental histories on tombstones.

Ghost Story. A tale of the supernatural, especially concerning revenants returning from the world of the dead.

Incantation. A religious or magical formula that derives its power or distinctive character from being sung or intoned.

Jack Tale. A traditional story in which an ordinary and unexceptional hero is enabled, with the help usually of magic or supernatural powers, to achieve results beyond his hopes or expectations. An element of the simpleton is often implied, as in Jack's trading of a cow for the beans that grow the beanstalk. Lucius fulfils the function in Apuleius' *The Golden Ass.*

Joke Book. A collection of gags, often as part of the professional stock-in-trade of an itinerant jester. The *Philogelos* serves as a rare surviving example from antiquity.

Legend. A story now seen as implausible but elaborated from a historical or supposedly historical base.

Lie. A falsehood told in folkloric contexts, most often for entertainment purposes ("it was this big. . . .").

Literary Tale. A story which, while it may use traditional elements, treats them in a sophisticated and culturally anachronistic way. A folktale hero does not, in ordinary folklore, expect to go to university, but in a literary tale he can. The language of a literary tale can expect to be much more elaborate or multifaceted than the simple, straightforward presentation of a folktale.

Local Legend. A legend that is confined to a particular locality, often tied to an individual feature of a landscape.

Magic. Supernatural power or procedure capable of overriding or controlling the natural and divine order through the often mechanical harnessing of forces by a practitioner for good or ill.

Märchen. German term for a folk- or fairy tale (q.q.v.).

Merry Tale. A pleasant, often jocular story, sometimes in a contemporary setting, which may entail sexual adventure/misadventure. It overlaps a good deal with the early character of the *novella.*

Metamorphosis. The transformation of one species into another, featuring frequently in myth, in folktale, and less often, in legend; it is often linked to explanatory motives ("why the laurel is sacred to Apollo. . . .").

Migratory Legend. A story of quasi-historical basis capable of moving from one locality to another: the "Sorcerer's Apprentice" tale can appear in second-century Egypt or eighteenth-century Germany, with only slight adaptation to its surroundings.

Monogenesis. The doctrine that a folktale has only a single origin and replicates itself in order to diffuse, as opposed to *polygenesis,* by which it is held to originate independently from more than one source.

Monomyth. A term associated, in particular, with Joseph Campbell's *The Hero of a Thousand Faces,* which argues that heroic material draws, despite its many superficial variations, on a standard template.

Morphology. The study of the appearance of a phenomenon or object, borrowed from the natural sciences. It is applied specifically to folktale in the English title of Propp's classic, *The Morphology of the Folktale.* The term evokes an air of scientific precision which is not always fulfilled.

Motif. A constituent part of a popular tale, capable of recurring in variants of the same tale or in other tales: *Cinderella* would constitute a whole tale, where the "slipper test" would constitute a single motif. Finding the most satisfactory way to describe a motif poses one of the major problems in tale classification. ("Glass slipper" is likely to be unhelpful as it would be confined to Perrault's version and its derivatives—a more verbal notion such as "test involving uniquely fitting object (ring, tight slipper)" would be more satisfactory).

Myth. A story which is not necessarily true but which may nevertheless be widely believed. But the meaning shifts so frequently in discussion that no single definition is likely to command universal approval. In an ancient context it tends to suggest association with the canon of Greek mythology from creation to the death of Odysseus, much of which might be more comfortably described in other terms.

Noodle. An idiot or fool, often the focus of so-called numskull stories: the late antique *Philogelos* relies heavily on such a figure.

Novella. A short narrative usually reporting "hot news"—generally of a realistic, everyday, gossipy, and most often sexual kind. *The Widow of Ephesus* as told by Petronius offers the classic ancient paradigm.

Oecotype. Von Sydow's term for a distinctively local version of a folktale, embodying some distinctive identifying motif or motifs (for example, the allusion to Ashville or equivalent in Balkan versions of *Cinderella*). The theory threatens the single archetype theory of the historic-geographic school as it suggests, in some respects, more than one origin for a tale, even within a diffusionist theory.

Old Wives' Tale *(Anilis Fabula).* The kind of story to be associated with elderly female narrators, usually, in antiquity, felt to be unreliable and childish, hence association with the nursery. *Cupid and Psyche* is so described by its elderly female narrator.

Oral Narrative. Any storytelling material conveyed by word of mouth. In illiterate societies this is the only medium of transmission (other than pictures), but in any others it may alternate with written transmission of some kind.

Periegesis. A guided tour of sites, into which an author may incorporate traditional or folkloric material attached to individual places.

Polygenesis. The process according to which tales are held to be of multiple origin, generated by similar circumstances rather than by the diffusion of a complex model. It is now generally thought to be confined only to the simplest materials: it enjoyed approval at the turn of the nineteenth and twentieth centuries before the full impetus of diffusionist scholarship could be felt.

Proverb. A short popular saying, usually incorporating some element of common sense or folk wisdom.

Religious Tale. Any tale in which piety toward a deity or deities is the motivating force: it will embrace the miracle accounts in honor of Asclepius as readily as the deeds of Christian saints.

Riddle. A rudimentary puzzle of often deliberately elusive or ambiguous solution and typically susceptible to oral transmission.

Structuralism. A loosely conceived later twentieth-century method of analysis inter alia of narrative forms which sets out to demonstrate the basic motives and motifs that underlie the most elementary materials. It shows preference for often simple binary contrasts and frequently generates controversy in the manner in which it endeavors to reduce narratives to such contrasts.

Superstition. A survival from the beliefs of a generally less sophisticated age. The term is of limited use because of the degree of subjectivity entailed ("religion is what I believe; what you believe is old-fashioned and irrational. . . .").

Survival. Anything that properly belongs to a previous age, whether belief, verbal construct, artifact, or some other form. Its association with the emotively loaded term "primitive" once more restricts its value.

Tall Tale. A narrative that relies on deliberate exaggeration and shameless falsehood as the mainspring of entertainment ("with a mighty leap I jumped over the moon. . . . I was not surprised to find a herd of athletic cows on the other side. . . .). Lucian's *True Histories* offers an ancient paradigm.

Trickster Tale. A story that relies on the resourcefulness and lateral thinking of an (often lovably) villainous character, who somehow survives his miscalculations and tricks his way out of trouble, though society may catch up with him in the end.

Type. The basic unit of classification for folktales in Aarne and Thompson's *The Types of the Folktale*. It should be noted that the system acknowledges overlaps between type numbers, a source of dissatisfaction to Propp, and no type is completely isolated from all others and not subject to "contamination."

Unfinished Tale. Applied in folktale contexts not to a story accidentally uncompleted by its author, but one ingeniously and jocularly contrived to repeat itself indefinitely or to keep breaking off.

Urban Legend. A specialist term for a contemporary legend that presupposes a modern urban, as opposed to a traditional rural, environment.

Variant. A version of a story that differs from others or from a central standard version, for example, in which Cinderella is recognized not by a slipper, but by a ring.

Wonder Tale. A tale whose effect is to engender amazement (and usually credulity) in its audience.

Bibliography

TEXTS, TRANSLATIONS, COMMENTARIES, AND ANTHOLOGIES

Items placed in this section may often contain elaborate commentary or prefatory material as well as texts.

Achilles Tatius, *Leucippe and Clitophon*, ed. J.-P. Garnaud, Paris: Les Belles Lettres (1991).

———. *Loves of Clitophon and Leucippe*, S. Gaselee, LCL (1917).

Aelian, *Historical Miscellany (Varia Historia)*, N. J. Wilson, *LCL* (1997).

———. *De Natura Animalium*, A. Scholfield, *LCL*, 3 vols. (1958–1959).

Apollodorus, *The Library (Bibliotheca)*, J. G. Frazer, *LCL*, 2 vols. (1921).

Apollonius of Rhodes, F. Vian (Budé, 1974–1981)

———. tr. R.L. Hunter, *Jason and the Golden Fleece (The Argonautica)*, New York: Oxford University Press (1995).

Apuleius, *Metamorphoses,* ed. D. S. Robertson, tr. P. Vallette, 3 vols., Paris: Les Belles Lettres (1940).

———. *Cupid and Psyche,* ed. E. J. Kenney, New York: Cambridge University Press (1990).

———. *The Golden Ass,* tr. P. G. Walsh, Oxford: Clarendon (1994).

———. *Apulei Apologia,* ed. R. Helm (Leipzig: Teubner 1905)

———. *Apulei Florida,* ed. R. Helm (Leipzig: Teubner 1910)

———. *The Apologia and Florida of Apuleius of Madaura,* tr. H.E.Butler, Oxford: Clarendon Press, (1909).

Argenti, P., and H. J. Rose, *The Folklore of Chios,* vols. I–II, New York: Cambridge University Press (1948).

Aristophanes, bilingual texts and commentaries by A. Sommerstein, Warminster: Aris and Philips (1980–), (*Peace,* 1985; *Lysistrata* 1990).

Athenaeus *LCL* by C.B. Gulick, 7 vols. (1927–1943).

Augustine, *City of God, LCL* by G.E. McCracken et al., 7 vols. (1957-1972).

Aulus Gellius, *The Attic Nights of Aulus Gellius, LCL* by J.C. Rolfe, 3 vols., New York (1927), rev. Cambridge, MA (1946).

———. *Noctes Atticae*, ed. P.K. Marshall, 2 vols., Oxford Classical Texts, Oxford (1968), rev. (1990)

Babrius, B. E. Perry, *LCL* (1965) (with Phaedrus).

Basile, G., *The Pentamerone of Giambattista Basile,* tr. N. M. Penzer, London: John Lane (1932). From Benedetto Croce's Italian version.

Betz, H. D. (ed.), *The Greek Magical Papyri in Translation, Including the Demotic Spells,* 2nd ed., Chicago: University of Chicago Press (1992).

Briggs, K. M., *A Dictionary of British Folk-Tales in the English Language,* vols. I–II, Bloomington: University of Indiana Press (1970).

Callimachus, *Hymns, LCL* by A.W. Mair (1921).

Carmina Popularia: Campbell, D., *Greek Lyric LCL* 5 (1993).

Cato, *De Agri Cultura,* ed. W. Hooper and H. Ash, *LCL* (1967).

———. *De Agri Cultura,* A. Mazzarino, Stuttgart: Teubner (1982).

Celoria, F. (tr.), *The Metamorphoses of Antoninus Liberalis: A Translation with a Commentary,* New York: Routledge (1992).

Cicero, *Tusculan Disputations,* ed. A. E. Douglas, Warminster: Aris and Phillips (1985).

———. *de Natura Deorum,* ed. A. S. Pease, Cambridge, Mass: Harvard University Press (1955).

———. *de Divinatione,* ed. A. S. Pease, Urbana: University of Illinois (1920–23).

Dawkins, R. M., *Modern Greek in Asia Minor,* Cambridge: Cambridge University Press (1916).

———. *Forty-Five Stories from the Dodekanese,* Cambridge: Cambridge University Press (1951).

———. *Modern Greek Folktales,* Oxford: Clarendon (1953).

———. *More Greek Folktales,* Oxford: Clarendon (1955).

van Dijk, G.-J., *Ainoi, Logoi, Mythoi: Fables in Archaic, Classical, and Hellenistic Greek Literature*, Leiden: Brill (1997).

Dio Cassius, *LCL* by E. Cary, 9 vols. (1914–1927).

Dio Chrysostom, *LCL* by W. Cohoon and H.L. Crosby, 5 vols. (1932–1951).

Dionysius of Halicarnassus, *Roman Antiquities, LCL* by E. Cary, 7 vols. (1937–1950).

Downing, C., *Armenian Folk Tales and Fables,* London: Oxford University Press (1972).

El-Shamy, H. M., *Folktales of Egypt,* Chicago: University of Chicago Press (1980).

Euripides, *Cyclops,* ed. R. Seaford, Oxford: Clarendon Press (1984).

Grimm, J., and W. Grimm, *The Complete Fairy Tales of the Brothers Grimm,* tr. J. Zipes, New York: Bantam (1992), of the 1857 collection, with 40 additional tales.

Halm, C. *Rhetores Latini minores,* Leipzig (1803), repr. Frankfurt am Main (1964).

Hansen, W. (ed.), *Anthology of Ancient Greek Popular Literature,* Bloomington: Indiana University Press (1998).

Heliodorus, *Aethiopica,* ed. R. M. Rattenbury and T. J. Lumb, tr. J. Maillon, Paris: Les Belles Lettres, 3 vols. (1935–1943).

Heraclides Ponticus, ed. F. Wehrli, Die Schule des Aristoteles 7, Basle: Schwabe (2nd ed. 1969).

Herodotus, A. D. Godley, *LCL,* 4 vols. (1920–1925).

———. *Historiae,* ed. K. Hude, Oxford: Oxford University Press (3rd ed. 1940).

———. *The Histories,* tr. A. de Sélincourt, rev. J. Marincola, New York: Penguin (1996).

Hesiod, *Works and Days,* ed. M. L. West, Oxford: Clarendon (1978).tr. M.L. West, Oxford (1998).

———. *Theogony,* ed. M.L. West, Oxford: Claredon Press (1966).

Hierocles, *The Philogelos, or Laughter-Lover,* tr. B. Baldwin, Amsterdam: J. C. Gieben (1983).

Hock, R. F., and E. N. O'Neil (eds.), *The Chreia in Ancient Rhetoric: The Progymnasmata,* Atlanta: Scholars Press (1986).

Homeric Hymns and Apocrypha, M. L. West, *LCL* (2003).

Hyginus, *Fabulae,* ed. H. J. Rose, Leiden: A.W.Sythoff (1933).

Juan Manuel, *El Conde Lucanor,* tr. J. York (as *Count Lucanor* or *The Fifty Pleasant Stories of Patronio*), London: Gibbings (1899).

Julian, *LCL* by W.C. Wright, 3 vols (1914–1923).

Lewis, G. (ed., tr.), *The Book of Dede Korkut,* Harmondsworth: Penguin (1974).

Lichtheim, M., *Ancient Egyptian Literature,* vols. I–III, Berkeley: University of California Press (1973–1980).

Livy, *LCL* by B.O. Foster et al., 14 vols. (1919–1959).

Longus, *Daphnis and Chloe,* P. Turner, Harmondsworth: Penguin (1968).

———. *Daphnis and Chloe,* ed. M. D. Reeve, Leipzig: Teubner (1987).

Lucan, J.D.Duff, *LCL* (1928)

Lucian, *LCL,* A.M. Harmon, K.F. Kilburn, and M.D. Macleod, 8 vols. (1913–1967).

Lucian, *Alexander.* M. Caster, *Études sur Alexandre ou le Faux Prophète de Lucien,* Paris, Les Belles Lettres, (1938).

Maximus of Tyre, *The Philosophical Orations,* tr. M. B. Trapp, New York: Oxford University Press (1997).

Megas, G. A., *Folktales of Greece,* Chicago: University of Chicago Press (1970).

Ovid, *Fasti,* J.G. Frazer (with commentary), London: Macmillan (1929).

———. *Fasti,* J. G. Frazer, *LCL* (1931).

———. *Die Fasten,* ed. F. Bömer, Heidelberg: Winter (1958).

———. *Metamorphoses.* F. J. Miller, *LCL* (1916).

———. *Metamorphoses,* ed. W. S. Anderson, Cambridge: Teubner (1977).

———. *Metamorphoses,* ed. R. J. Tarrant, New York: Oxford University Press (2004).

———. *Metamorphosis VIII*, with commentary by A. Hollis, Oxford: Claredon Press (1970).

Paroemiographici Graeci, tr. E. V. Leutsch and P. Schneidewin, Goettingen: Vandenhoeck and Ruprecht, (1839–1851), repr. by G.Olms: Hildesheim (1958).

Pausanias, *Pausanias's Description of Greece*, commentary by J. G. Frazer, London: Macmillan (1898).

———. W. Jones, *LCL* (1918–1935).

———. *Guide to Greece*, tr. P. Levi, Harmondsworth: Penguin (1971).

———. *Pausaniae Graeciae Descriptio*, ed. M. H. Rocha-Pereira, Leipzig: Teubner (1973–1981).

Perrault, C., *The Fairy Tales of Charles Perrault*, tr. A. Carter, London: Gollancz (1977).

Petronius, *Cena Trimalchionis*, ed. M. S. Smith, Oxford: Clarendon (1975).

———. *Satyrica* 3rd ed., ed. K. Müller, Munich: Heimeran (1978).

———. *Satyricon* rev., tr. J. P. Sullivan, Harmondsworth: Penguin (1986).

Phaedrus, B. E. Perry, *LCL* (1965, with Babrius).

Philip, N., *The Cinderella Story*, New York: Penguin (1989).

———. *The Penguin Book of Scottish Folktales*, Harmondsworth: Penguin,(1995).

Philostratus Senior, *Vitae Sophistarum*, W. C. Wright, *LCL* (1922).

———. *Imagines*, tr. A. Fairbanks, *LCL* (1931).

———. *Imagines*, ed. K. Kalinka and O. Schoenberger, Munich: Heimeran (1968).

———. *Heroicus*, ed. L. de Lannoy, Leipzig: Teubner (1977).

———. *Vita Apollonii*, C. P. Jones, *LCL*, 2 vols. (2005).

Phlegon of Tralles, *Book of Marvels*, tr. W. Hansen, Exeter: Exeter University Press (1996).

Plato, *Selected Myths*, tr. C. Partenie, Oxford: Oxford University Press (2004).

———. *Republic*, ed. J. Adams, Cambridge: Cambridge University Press (2nd ed. 1963).

Plautus, *LCL*, by P. Nixon, 5 vols. (1916–1938).

Pliny the Elder, H. Rackham and W. H. S. Jones, *LCL* (1938–1963).

———. *Histoire Naturelle* ed. J. Beaujeu et al., Budé: Les Belles Lettres (1947).

———. *Naturkunde*, ed. R. König and G. Winkler, Munich: Heimeran (1973).

Pliny the Younger, *Epistularum Libri Decem*, ed. R. A. B. Mynors, Oxford: Clarendon (1963).

———. *The Letters of the Younger Pliny*, tr. B. Radice, Baltimore: Penguin (1963).

Plutarch, *Lives*, B. Perrin, *LCL* (1914–1926)

———. *Moralia*, F. C. Babbitt et al., *LCL*, 17 vols. (1927–2004).

———. *The Greek Questions of Plutarch*, tr. W. R. Halliday, Oxford: Clarendon (1927).

———. *The Roman Questions of Plutarch*, tr. H. J. Rose, Oxford: Clarendon (1924).

Pollux, *Onomasticon*, ed. E. Bethe, *Lexicographici graeci* 9.1-3, Teubner (1900–1937), repr. Stuttgart (1967).

Preisendanz, K., and A. Henrichs (eds.), *Papyri Graecae Magicae: Die griechischen Zauberpapyri*, 2nd ed., Stuttgart: Teubner (1973).

Reardon, B. P. (ed.), *Collected Ancient Greek Novels,* Berkeley: University of California Press (1989).

Solinus, ed. Mommsen (1895), repr. (1958).

Stephens, S. A., and J. J. Winkler (eds.), *Ancient Greek Novels: The Fragments,* Princeton: Princeton University Press (1995).

Strabo, *LCL,* by H.L. Jones, 8 vols. (1917–1932).

Straparola, G. F., *The Nights of Straparola,* vols. I–II, tr. W. G. Waters, London: Lawrence and Bullen (1894).

Tales from the Thousand and One Nights, tr. N Dawood, Harmondsworth: Penguin (1973).

Tertullian, *de Anima,* ed. J. H. Waszink, Amsterdam: North Holland Publishing Company (1947).

Theocritus, A. S. F. Gow, Cambridge: Cambridge University Press (2nd ed. 1952).

Theophrastus, *Characters,* R.C. Jebb and J.M. Sandys, Cambridge: Cambridge University Press (1909); Steinmetz, P., Munich: Hüber (1960); R.G Ussher, London: Macmillan (1960).

———. *de Causis Plantarum, LCL,* by B. Einarson and G. K. K. Link, 3 vols. (1976–1990).

Varro, *De re rustica,* R. G. Kent, *LCL* (1951).

Vergil, *Eclogues,* ed. R. Coleman, Cambridge: Cambridge University Press (1977).

———. *Georgics,* commentary by R. A. B. Mynors, Oxford: Clarendon Press (1988).

Xenophon, *Hellenica, LCL* by C. L. Brownson, 2 vols. (1918, 1921).

Zipes, J. (tr.), *Beauties, Beasts, and Enchantment: Classic French Fairy Tales,* New York: New American Library (1989).

———. *Spells of Enchantment: The Wondrous Fairy Tales of Western Culture,* New York: Viking (1991).

SECONDARY LITERATURE

Basic Research Tools

Aarne, A., and S. Thompson, *The Types of the Folktale,* Helsinki: Suomalainen Tiedeakatemia (1961).

Ashliman, D. L., *A Guide to Folktales in the English Language,* New York: Greenwood (1987).

Bolte, J. and Polivka, G., *Anmerkungen zu den Kinder- und Hausmärchen der Brüder Grimm,* vols. I–V, Leipzig: Dieterich'sche Verlagsbuchhandlung (1913–1932).

Carnes, P., *Fable Scholarship: An Annotated Bibliography,* New York: Garland (1985).

Christiansen, R. T., *The Migratory Legends: A Proposed List of Types with a Systematic Catalogue of Norwegian Variants,* Helsinki: Suomalainen Tiedeakatemia (1958).

Crum, R. H., Additions to the Bibliography of Greek and Roman Folklore, *Classical Weekly* vol. 42, 234 (1949).

Gantz, T., *Early Greek Myth: A Guide to Literary and Artistic Sources,* Baltimore, Johns Hopkins University Press (1993)

Hansen, W. (ed.), *Anthology of Ancient Greek Popular Literature,* Bloomington: Indiana University Press (1998).

———. *Ariadne's Thread: A Guide to International Tales Found in Classical Literature,* Ithaca: Cornell University Press (2002).

Macartney, E. S., A Bibliography of Collections of Greek and Roman Folklore, *Classical Weekly* vol. 40, 99–101 (1947).

Opie, I., and M. Tatem (eds.), *A Dictionary of Superstitions,* Oxford: Oxford University Press (1989).

Ranke, K. (ed.), *Enzyklopädie des Märchens,* Berlin: Walter de Gruyter (1977–). Eleven volumes published to date.

Sanile, R. W., and F. Maltomini, *Papyrologica Coloniensia,* 16.1–2, *Supplementum Magicum,* Opladen (1990–1992).

Thompson, S., *Motif-Index of Folk Literature,* vols. I–VI, Bloomington: Indiana University Press (1955–1958).

Walz, C. *Rhetores Graeci,* (9 vols., Stuttgart/Tübingen: Cotta 1832-1836 (repr. Osnabrück: Zeller 1968).

Zipes, J. (ed.), *The Oxford Companion to Fairy Tales,* Oxford: Oxford University Press (2000).

Folklore Methodology

Ashliman, D. L., *Folk and Fairy Tales: A Handbook,* Westport: Greenwood (2004).

Cocchiana, G., *The History of Folklore in Europe,* tr. J. N. McDaniel, Philadelphia: Institute for the Study of Human Issues (1981). Italian original published 1952.

Dorson, R.M., *Folklore and Folklife: an Introduction,* Chicago: University of Chicago Press (1972).

Dégh, L., *Folktales and Society: Storytelling in a Hungarian Peasant Community,* Bloomington: Indiana University Press (1969, 1989).

Dundes, A. (ed.), *The Study of Folklore,* Englewood Cliffs: Prentice-Hall (1965).

———. *Interpreting Folklore,* Bloomington: Indiana University Press (1980).

———. The Motif-Index and the Tale Type Index: A Critique, *Journal of Folklore Research* vol. 34, 195–202 (1997).

Foley, J. M., Ancient Greek Studies and Folkloristics, *Journal of American Folklore* vol. 107, 437–449 (1994).

Georges, R.A. and M. Owen Jones, *Folkloristics: An Introduction,* Bloomington: Indiana University Press (1995).

Goldberg, C., The Historic-Geographic Method: Past and Future, *Journal of Folklore Research* vol. 21, 1–18 (1984).

Halliday, W. R., *Folklore Studies, Ancient and Modern,* London: Methuen (1924).

———. *Greek and Roman Folklore,* New York: Longmans Green (1927).

———. *Indo-European Folk-Tales and Greek Legend,* Cambridge: Cambridge University Press (1933).

Hansen, W., An Ancient Greek Ghost Story, in N. Burlakoff and C. Lindahl (eds.), *Folklore on Two Continents: Essays in Honor of Linda Dégh,* pp. 71–77, Bloomington: Indiana University Press (1980).

———. Verbal Folklore of Ancient Greece, *Journal of Folklore Research* vol. 20, 97 (1983).

———. Greek Mythology and the Study of Ancient Greek Oral Story, *Journal of Folklore Research* vol. 20, 97–112 (1983).

———. Mythology and Folktale Typology: Chronicle of a Failed Scholarly Revolution, *Journal of Folklore Research* vol. 34, 275–280 (1997).

———. Homer and the Folktale, in I. Morris and B. Powell (eds.), *New Companion to Homer,* pp. 442–462, New York: Brill (1997).

———. Idealisation as a Process in Ancient Greek Story-Formation, *Symbolae Osloenses* vol. 72, 118–122 (1997).

Henderson, J., The Homing Instinct: A Folklore Theme in Phaedrus, app. Perott. 16 Perry/14 Postgate, *Proceedings of the Cambridge Philological Society,* vol. 23, 17–31 (1977).

Jason, H., and A. Kempinsky, How Old Are Folktales? *Fabula* vol. 22, 1–27 (1981).

Jones, S. S., The Innocent Persecuted Heroine Genre: An Analysis of Its Structure and Themes, *Western Folklore* vol. 52, 13–41 (1993).

———. *The Fairy Tale: The Magic Mirror of the Imagination,* New York: Routledge (2002).

Krappe, A. H., *The Science of Folklore,* New York: Norton (1964).

Krohn, K., *Die folkloristische Arbeitsmethode,* Oslo: Instituttet for sammenlignende kulturforskning (1926).

———. *Uebersicht ueber einige Resultate der Märchenforschung* (*Folklore Fellows Communications* 96), Helsinki: Academia Scientiarum Fennica (1931).

Lawson, J. C., *Modern Greek Folklore and Ancient Greek Religion: A Study in Survivals,* Cambridge: Cambridge University Press (1910).

Levin, I., Vladimir Propp: An Evaluation on his Seventieth Birthday, *Journal of the Folklore Institute* vol. 4, 32–49 (1967).

Nicolaisen, W. F. H., Why Tell Stories about Innocent Persecuted Heroines? *Western Folklore* vol. 52, 61–71 (1993).

Propp, V., *Morphology of the Folktale,* Austin: University of Texas Press (1968).

———. *Theory and History of Folklore,* Minneapolis: University of Minnesota Press (1984).

Scobie, A., Some Folktales in Graeco-Roman and Far Eastern Sources, *Philologus* vol. 121, 7–10 (1977).

———. Storytellers, Storytelling and the Novel in Graeco-Roman Antiquity, *Rheinisches Museum für Philologie* vol. 123 229–259 (1979).

Stinton, T. F. C., Phaedrus and Folklore: An Old Problem Restated, *Classical Quarterly* vol. 29, 432–435 (1979).

Taylor, A., The Biographical Pattern in Traditional Narrative, *Journal of the Folklore Institute* vol. 1, 114–129 (1964).

Thompson, S., *The Folktale,* Bloomington: Indiana University Press (1946).

Trubshaw, B., *Explore Folklore*, Loughborough, Heart of Albion Press, (2002).

Utley, F. L., Folk Literature: An Operational Definition, in A. Dundes (ed.), *The Study of Folklore,* pp. 7–24, Englewood Cliffs: Prentice-Hall (1965).

Zipes, J., *Breaking the Magic Spell: Radical Theories of Folk and Fairy Tales,* Austin: University of Texas Press (1976).

A special volume of the *Journal of Folklore Research* (vol. 34, 1997) is devoted to the issue of tale type indexing.

Mythology

Borgeaud, P., *The Cult of Pan in Ancient Greece,* tr. K. Atlass and J. Redfield, Chicago: University of Chicago Press (1988). French original published 1979.

Bremmer, J. (ed.), *Interpretations of Greek Mythology,* London: Croom Helm (1987).

Bremmer, J., and N. Horsfall, *Roman Myth and Mythography,* London: University of London (1987).

van den Broek, R., *The Myth of the Phoenix, according to Classical and early Christian Traditions,* Leiden: Brill, (1972).

Buxton, R. G. A., *Imaginary Greece: The Contexts of Mythology,* Cambridge: Cambridge University Press (1994).

Carpenter, T. H. *Art and Myth in Ancient Greece,* London: Thames and Hudson, (1991).

Cherry, J. (ed.), *Mythical Beasts,* San Francisco: Pomegranate Artbooks (1995).

Clader, L. L., *Helen: The Evolution from Divine to Heroic in Greek Epic Tradition,* Leiden: Brill, (1976).

Clauss, J. J., and S. Iles Johnston (eds.), *Medea: Essays on Medea in Myth, Literature, Philosophy, and Art,* Princeton: Princeton University Press (1997).

Csapo, E., *Theories of Mythology,* Malden: Blackwell (2005).

Detienne, M., and J.-P. Vernant, *Cunning Intelligence in Greek Culture and Society,* tr. J. Lloyd, Hassocks: Harvester (1978).

Dowden, K., *Death and the Maiden: Girls' Initiation Rites in Greek Mythology,* London: Routledge (1989).

———. *The Uses of Greek Mythology,* New York: Routledge (1992).

Edmunds, L. (ed.), *Approaches to Greek Myth,* Baltimore: Johns Hopkins University Press (1990).

———. Myth in Homer, in I. Morris and B. Powell (eds.), *New Companion to Homer,* pp. 415–441, New York: Brill (1997).

Faraone, C. A., *Talismans and Trojan Horses: Guardian Statues in Ancient Greek Myth and Ritual,* New York: Oxford University Press (1992).

Farkas, A. E., P. O. Harper, and E. Harrison (eds.), *Monsters and Demons in the Ancient and Medieval Worlds,* Mainz: von Zabern (1987).

Forbes Irving, P. M. C., *Metamorphosis in Greek Myths,* Oxford: Clarendon (1990).

Gantz, G., *Early Greek Myth: A Guide to Literary and Artistic Sources,* Baltimore: Johns Hopkins University Press (1993).

Gardner, J. F., *Roman Myths,* Austin: University of Texas Press (1993).

Greene, M. T., *Natural Knowledge in Preclassical Antiquity,* Baltimore: Johns Hopkins University Press (1992).

Halliday, W. R., The Superstitious Man of Theophrastus, *Folklore* vol. 41, 121–153 (1930).

Hansen, W. F., Greek Mythology and the Study of the Ancient Greek Oral Story, *Journal of Folklore Research* vol. 20, 101–111 (1983).

Hartland, E. S., *The Legend of Perseus: A Study of Tradition in Story, Custom, and Belief,* London: D. Nutt (1894–1896).

———. *Mythology and Folktales; Their Relation and Interpretation,* London: D. Nutt (1900).

Kirk, G. S., *Myth: Its Meaning and Functions in Ancient and Other Cultures,* Cambridge: Cambridge University Press (1970).

———. *The Nature of Greek Myths,* Harmondsworth: Penguin (1974).

Kramer, S. and J, Maier, *Myths of Enki, The Crafty God,* New York: Oxford University Press, (1989).

Larson, J., *Greek Nymphs: Myth, Cult, Lore,* New York: Oxford University Press (2001).

Rose, H. J., *A Handbook of Greek Mythology,* London: Methuen (1928).

Schrempp, G., and W. Hansen, *Myth: A New Symposium,* Bloomington: Indiana University Press (2002).

Segal, R. A. (ed.), *The Myth and Ritual Theory: An Anthology,* Oxford: Blackwell (1998).

Terpening, P. H., *Charon and the Crossing: Ancient, Medieval, and Renaissance Transformations of a Myth,* Lewisburg: Bucknell University Press (1985).

Vernant, J.-P., *Myth and Society in Ancient Greece,* tr. J. Lloyd, New York: Zone Books (1990). French original published 1974.

Veyne, P., *Did the Greeks Believe in Their Myths?: An Essay on the Constitutive Imagination,* tr. P. Wissing, Chicago: University of Chicago Press (1988).

Von Hendy, A., *The Modern Construction of Myth,* Bloomington: Indiana University Press (2002).

Wiseman, T. P., *Remus: A Roman Myth,* New York: Oxford University Press (1995).

———. *Roman Myths,* Exeter: Exeter University Press (2004).

Yarnall, J., *Transformations of Circe: The History of an Enchantress,* Urbana: University of Illinois Press (1994).

Folk- and Fairy Tale

Anderson, G., *Fairytale in the Ancient World,* New York: Routledge (2000).

———. 'Old Tales for New: Finding the First Fairy Tales', pp. 85-98 in Davidson and Chaudhri (2003).

Anderson, W., *Kaiser und Abt,* Helsinki: Swomalainen Tiedeakatemia (1923).

Bettelheim, B., *The Uses of Enchantment: The Meaning and Importance of Fairy Tales,* New York: Knopf (1976).

Bottigheimer, R. B. (ed.), *Fairy Tales and Society: Illusion, Allusion, and Paradigm,* Philadelphia: University of Pennsylvania Press (1986).

Braginton, M. V., *The Supernatural in Seneca's Tragedies,* Menasha: George Banta (1933).

Davidson, H. E., and A. Chaudhri (eds.), *A Companion to the Fairy Tale,* Cambridge: D. S. Brewer (2003).

Falassi, A., *Folklore by the Fireside: Tex and Context of the Tuscan Veglia,* Austin, Texas: University of Texas Press, (1980).

Felton, D., *Haunted Greece and Rome: Ghost Stories from Classical Antiquity,* Austin: University of Texas Press (1999).

Hynes, W.J. and W.G.Doty, *Mythical Trickster Figures: Contours, Contexts, and Criticisms,* Tuscaloosa: University of Alabama Press, (1993).

Johnston, S. I., Defining the Dreadful: Remarks on the Greek Child-Killing Demon, in P. Mirecki and M. Meyer (eds.), *Ancient Magic and Ritual Power,* pp. 355–381, New York: Brill (1995).

Luethi, M., *Once Upon a Time: On the Nature of Fairy Tales,* Bloomington: Indiana University Press (1976).

Matthew, J., Macsen, Maximus, and Constantine, *Welsh Historical Review* vol. 11, 431–448 (1983).

Mayor, A., What Were the Griffins? Who Were the Arimaspeans? *Folklore* vol. 104, 40–66 (1993).

———. Guardians of the Gold, *Archaeology* vol. 1994, 52–59 (1994).

Nilsson, M.P., *Greek Folk Religion,* Philadelphia: University of Pennsylvania Press, (1940).

Opie, P., and I. Opie (eds.), *The Classic Fairy Tales,* New York: Oxford University Press (1974).

Purkiss, D., *Troublesome Things: A History of Fairies and Fairy Stories,* Cambridge: Cambridge University Press (2000).

Radin, P., *The Trickster: A Study in American Indian Mythology,* New York: Schocken Books (1972).

Swann Jones, S., *The Fairy Tale: The Magic Mirror of the Imagination,* New York: Routledge (2002).

Tatar, M., *The Hard Facts of the Grimms' Fairy Tales,* Princeton: Princeton University Press (1987).

———. *The Classic Fairy Tales: Texts, Criticism,* New York: Norton (1999).

von Franz, M.-L., *Problems of the Feminine in Fairy Tales,* Dallas, Texas: Spring Publications (1983; original 1972).

———. *Shadow and Evil in Fairy Tales,* Zurich: Spring Publications (1974).

Zipes, J., *Fairy Tales and the Art of Subversion: The Classical Genre for Children and the Process of Civilization,* New York: Wildman (1983).

Individual Tales

Snow White

Böklen, E., *Sneewittchenstudien,* vols. I–II, Leipzig: Mythologische Bibliothek (1910, 1915).

Jones, S. S., The Structure of Snow White, *Fabula* vol. 24, 56–71 (1983).

———. *The New Comparative Method: Structural and Symbolic Analysis of the Allomotifs of Snow White,* Helsinki: Suomalainen Tiedeakatemia (1990).

Cinderella

Cox, M. E. R., *Cinderella: Three Hundred and Forty-Five Variants of Cinderella, Catskin, and Cap o'Rushes,* London: Folklore Society (1893).

Dundes, A. (ed.), *Cinderella: A Casebook,* New York: Wildman (1983).

Pantajja, E., Going Up in the World: Class in *Cinderella, Western Folklore* vol. 52, 85–104 (1993).

Perco, D., Female Initiation in Northern Italian Versions of *Cinderella, Western Folklore* vol. 52, 73–84 (1993).

Philip, N., *The Cinderella Story,* New York: Penguin (1989).

Rooth, A. B., *The Cinderella Cycle,* Lund: Gleerup (1951).

Sierra, J., *Cinderella,* Phoenix: Oryx (1992).

Cupid and Psyche

Fehling, D., *Amor und Psyche,* Wiesbaden: Steiner (1977).

Swahn, J.-Ø., *The Tale of Cupid and Psyche,* Lund: Gleerup (1955).

Wright, J. R. G., Folktale and Literary Technique in Cupid and Psyche, *Classical Quarterly* vol. 21, 273–284 (1971).

Oedipus

Edmunds, L., *Oedipus: The Ancient Legend and Its Later Analogues,* Baltimore: Johns Hopkins University Press (1985).

Edmunds, L., and A. Dundes (eds.), *Oedipus: A Folklore Casebook,* 2nd ed., Madison: University of Wisconsin Press (1995).

Johnson, A. W., and D. Price-Williams, *Oedipus Ubiquitous: The Family Complex in World Folk Literature,* Stanford: Stanford University Press (1996).

Polyphemus

Calame, C., Les légends du Cyclops dans le folklore Européan et extra-Européan: Un jeu de transformation narrative, *Études de Lettres, Bulletin de la Faculté des Lettres,* vol. 3.2.2, 45–79 (1977).

Glenn, J., The Polyphemus Folktale and Homer's *Kyklopeia*, *Transactions of the American Philological Association* vol. 102, 133–181 (1971).

Hackman, O., *Die Polyphemsage in der Volksüberlieferung*, Helsinki: Frenckellska Tryckeri-Aktiebolaget (1904).

Mundy, C. S., Polyphemus and Tepegoez, *Bulletin of the School of Oriental and African Studies* vol. 18, 279–302 (1956).

Röhrich, L., Die mittelalterlichen Redaktionene des Polyphem-Märchens (*AT* 1137) und ihr Verhältnis zur ausserhomerischen Tradition, *Fabula* vol. 5, 48–71 (1962).

The Poor Man of Nippur

Gurney, O., The Tale of the Poor Man of Nippur, *Anatolian Studies* vol. 6, 145–162 (1956).

———. The Tale of the Poor Man of Nippur, *Anatolian Studies* vol. 7, 135 (1957).

———. The Tale of the Poor Man of Nippur and Its Folktale Parallels, *Anatolian Studies* vol. 22, 149–158 (1972).

Jason, H., The Poor Man of Nippur: An Ethopoetic Analysis, *Journal of Cuneiform Studies* vol. 31, 189–215 (1979).

Magic, Religion, Science

Anderson, G., *Sage, Saint and Sophist: Holy Men and Their Associates in the Early Roman Empire*, New York: Routledge (1994).

Beagon, M., *Roman Nature: The Thought of Pliny the Elder*, New York: Oxford University Press (1992).

Beard, M., J. North and S. Price, *Religions of Rome*, 2 vols., Cambridge: Cambridge University Press, (1998).

Bodson, L., and D. Marcolungo, *L'oie de bon aloi: Aspects de l'histoire ancienne de l'oie domestique*, Vise: Musée régional d'Archéologie et d'Histoire de Vise (1994).

Burkert, W., *Structure and History in Greek Mythology and Ritual*, Berkeley: University of California Press (1979).

———. *Homo Necans: The Anthropology of Ancient Greek Sacrificial Ritual and Myth*, tr. P. Bing, Berkeley: University of California Press (1983). German original published 1972.

———. *Greek Religion*, tr. J. Raffan, Cambridge: Cambridge University Press (1985). German original published 1977.

———. *The Orientalising Revolution: Near Eastern Influence on Greek Culture in the Early Archaic Age*, Cambridge, MA: Harvard University Press (1992) (German original published 1984).

Dickie, M. W., *Magic and Magicians in the Greco-Roman World*, New York: Routledge (2001).

Dodds, E. R., Supernatural Phenomena in Classical Antiquity, *Proceedings of the Society for Psychical Research* vol. 5, 189–271 (1971).

Dowden, K., *Arkteia: Death and the Maiden: Girls' Initiation Rites in Greek Mythology,* London: Routledge (1989).

Dulière, W.L., *Protection permanente contre des animaux nuisibles assurée par Apollonius de Tyana dans Byzance et Antioche, Évolution de son mythe, Byzantinische Zeitschrift* 63 (1970), 247-277.

Faraone, C., Binding and Burying the Forces of Evil: The Defensive Use of "Voodoo Dolls" in Ancient Greece, *Classical Antiquity* vol. 10, 165–220 (1991).

Faraone, C. A., and D. Obbink (eds.), *Magika Hiera: Ancient Greek Magic and Religion,* New York: Oxford University Press (1991).

Flint, V., R. Gordon, G. Luck, and D. Ogden, *The Athlone History of Witchcraft and Magic in Europe,* vol. 2, *Greece and Rome,* London: Athlone (1999).

Fontenrose, J. *Python: A Study of Delphic Myth and its Origins,* Berkeley: University of California Press (1959).

French, R. K., *Ancient Natural History: Histories of Nature,* New York: Routledge (1994).

French, R., and F. Greenaway (eds.), *Science in the Early Roman Empire: Pliny the Elder, His Sources and Influence,* Totowa: Barnes and Noble (1986).

Gager, J. G. (ed.), *Curse Tablets and Binding Spells from the Ancient World,* New York: Oxford University Press (1992).

Graf, F., *Magic in the Ancient World,* tr. F. Philip, Cambridge: Harvard University Press (1997).

Grant, F.C., *Ancient Roman Religion,* Indianapolis: Bobbs-Merrill (1957).

Harper, N. N., The Witch's Flying Ointment, *Folklore* vol. 88, 105 (1977).

Hedreen, G., 'The Cult of Achilles in the Euxine', *Hesperia* 60 (1991), 313-330.

Henig, M., *Religion in Roman Britain,* New York: St. Martin's (1984).

Herbert-Brown, G., *Ovid and the Fasti: An Historical Study,* Oxford: Clarendon (1994).

Homolle, T., Inscriptions d' Amorgos, *Bulletin de Correspondence Hellénique* vol. 25, 412–456 (1901).

Hutton, R., *The Pagan Religions of the Ancient British Isles: Their Nature and Legacy,* Oxford: Blackwell (1991).

Johnston, S. I., *Restless Dead: Encounters between the Living and the Dead in Ancient Greece,* Berkeley: University of California Press (1999).

Kramer, S.N., *History Begins At Sumer: Thirty-Nine Firsts in Man's Recorded History,* Philadelphia: University of Philadelphi Press, (1981).

Kronenberg, A., The Fountain of the Sun: A Tale Related by Herodotus, Pliny and the Modern Teda, *Man* vol. 55, 74 (1955).

Kurtz, D. C., and J. Boardman, *Greek Burial Customs,* London: Thames and Hudson (1971).

Lloyd, G. E. R., *Magic, Reason and Experience: Studies in the Origin and Development of Greek Science,* New York: Cambridge University Press (1979).

———. *Science, Folklore, and Ideology: Studies in the Life Sciences in Ancient Greece,* New York: Cambridge University Press (1983).

Luck, G. (tr.), *Arcana Mundi: Magic and the Occult in the Greek and Roman Worlds: A Collection of Ancient Texts,* Baltimore: Johns Hopkins University Press (1985).

Major, A., The Yew Tree in Antiquity: Superstition or Science? *Acta Classica Universitatis Scientiarum Debreceniensis* vols. 34–35, 187–191 (1998–1999).

Mayor, A., Grecian Weasels, *Modern Ferret* vol. 15, 17–21 (1998).

———. *The First Fossil Hunters: Paleontology in Greek and Roman Times,* Princeton: Princeton University Press (2000).

Merrifield, R., *The Archaeology of Ritual and Magic,* London: Batsford (1987).

Ogden, D., *Greek and Roman Necromancy,* Princeton: Princeton University Press (2001).

———. *Magic, Witchcraft, and Ghosts in the Greek and Roman Worlds: A Sourcebook,* New York: Oxford University Press (2002).

Ogilvie, R. M., *The Romans and Their Gods in the Age of Augustus,* London: Chatto and Windus (1969).

O'Neill, H. E., and J. M. C. Toynbee, Sculptures from a Romano-British Well in Gloucestershire, *Journal of Roman Studies* vol. 48, 47–55 (1958).

Parke, H. W., *The Oracles of Zeus: Dodona, Olympia, Ammon,* Oxford: Blackwell (1967).

———. *Festivals of the Athenians,* London: Thames and Hudson (1977).

Parry, H., *Thelxis: Magic and Imagination in Greek Myth and Poetry,* Lanham: University Press of America (1992).

Price, S., and E. Kearns, *The Oxford Dictionary of Classical Myth and Religion,* Oxford: Oxford University Press (2003).

Raven, J. E., *Plants and Plant Lore in Ancient Greece,* Oxford: Leopard's (2000).

Rose, H. J., *Religion in Greece and Rome,* New York: Harper (1959).

Russell, D.A., *Plutarch,* London: Duckworth (1972).

Russell, W. M. S., Greek and Roman Ghosts, in H. R. E. Davidson and W. M. S. Russell (eds.), *The Folklore of Ghosts,* pp. 193–213, Cambridge: Brewer (1981).

Scullard, H. H., *Festivals and Ceremonies of the Roman Republic,* Ithaca: Cornell University Press (1981).

Shepard, O., *The Lore of the Unicorn,* New York: Houghton Mifflin (1930).

Stannard, J., Herbal Magic and Herbal Medicine in Pliny's Time, *Helmantica* vol. 37, 95–106 (1986).

Tomlin, R.S.O., 'The curse tablets', in B. Cunliffe (ed.), *The Temple of Sul Minerva at Bath, vol. 2: The Finds from the Second Spring,* Oxford: Oxford University Press (1988).

Toynbee, J. M. C., *Genii Cucullati in Roman Britain, Hommages à W. Deonna,* Brussels, Collection Latomus (1957), 456–469.

———. *Death and Burial in the Roman World,* Ithaca: Cornell University Press (1971).

———. *Animals in Roman Life and Art,* Ithaca: Cornell University Press (1973).

Vanggaard, J. H., *The Flamen: A Study in the History and Sociology of Roman Religion,* Copenhagen: Museum Tusculanum (1988).

Vitaliano, D. B., *Legends of the Earth: Their Geologic Origins,* Bloomington: Indiana University Press (1973).

Wolters, X. M. F. G., *Notes on Antique Folklore on the Basis of Pliny's Natural History 1, XXVIII, 22–29,* Amsterdam: H. J. Paris (1935).

Zaidman, L. B., and P. S. Pantel, *Religion in the Ancient Greek City,* tr. P. Cartledge, New York: Cambridge University Press (1992).

Miscellaneous

Alcock, S. E., *Archaeologies of the Greek Past: Landscape, Monuments, and Memories,* New York: Cambridge University Press (2002).

Alcock, S. E., J. F. Cherry, and J. Elsner (eds.), *Pausanias: Travel and Memory in Roman Greece,* New York: Oxford University Press (2001).

Aly, W., *Volksmaerchen, Sage und Novelle bei Herodot und seinem Zeitgenossen,* Göttingen: Vandenhoeck and Ruprecht, 2nd ed. 1969 (original 1921).

Anderson, G., *Studies in Lucian's Comic Fiction,* Leiden: Brill (1976).

———. *Philostratus: Biography and Belles Lettres in the Third Century* A.D., London: Croom Helm (1986).

Bourboulis, P. P., *Studies in the History of Modern Greek Story-Motives,* Thessalonica (1953).

Casson, L., *Travel in the Ancient World,* London: Allen and Unwin (1974).

Cummins, W.A., *King Arthur's Place in Prehistory: The Great Age of Stonehenge,* Stroud, Gloucestershire: Alan Sutton (1992).

Fehling, D., *Herodotus and his 'Sources': Citation, Invention and Narrative Art,* Leeds: Francis Cairns (1989).

Ginzberg, L., *The Legends of the Jews,* Philadephia: The Jewish Publication Society of America (1948).

Goldberg, C., *Turandot's Sisters: A Study of the Folktale AT 851,* New York: Garland (1993).

Gould, J., *Herodotus,* London: Weidenfeld and Nicolson (1989).

Habicht, C., *Pausanias' Guide to Greece,* Berkeley: California University Press (1985).

Holzberg, N., *Die antike Fabel. Eine Einfuehrung,* Darmstadt: Wissenschaftlich Buchgesellschaft (1993).

Houlihan, P. F., *Wit and Humour in Ancient Egypt,* London: Rubicon Press (2001).

Hutton, R., *Druids, Witches and King Arthur,* London, Hambledon and London (2003).

Johns, C., *Sex and Symbol: Erotic Images of Greece and Rome,* London: Book Club Associates (1982).

Kakrides, J. T., *Homeric Researches,* Lund: Gleerup (1949).

Kramer, S. N., *The Sumerians: Their History, Culture, and Character,* Chicago: University of Chicago Press (1963).

———. *History Begins at Sumer: Thirty-Nine Firsts in Man's Recorded History,* Philadelphia: University of Pennsylvania Press (1981).

Kramer, S. N., and J. Maier (eds.), *Myths of Enki, the Crafty God,* New York: Oxford University Press (1989).

Laistner, M. L. W., *Christianity and Pagan Culture in the Later Roman Empire,* Ithaca: Cornell University Press (1951).

Lefkowitz, M., *The Lives of the Greek Poets,* Baltimore: Johns Hopkins University Press (1981).

Lord, A.B., *The Singer of Tales,* Cambridge (Mass.): Harvard University Press (1960).

Megas, G., Die Sage von Alkestis, *Laographia* vol. 25, 158–191 (1967).

————. *Folktales of Greece,* Chicago: University of Chicago Press (1970).

Merrifield, R., *The Archaeology of Religion and Magic,* London: Guild Publishing (1987).

Millar, F. *A Study of Dio Cassius,* Oxford: Oxford University Press (1964).

Momigliano, A.D., *Alien Wisdom: The Limits of Hellenization,* Cambridge: Cambridge University Press (1975).

Mossman, J. (ed.), *Plutarch and his Intellectual World,* London: Duckworth (1997).

Mullen, P. B., *I Heard the Old Fisherman Say: Folklore of the Texas Gulf Coast,* Austin: University of Texas Press (1978).

Murray, O., Herodotus and Oral History, in H. Sancisi-Weedenburg (ed.), *Achaemenid History,* vol. 2, pp. 93–115, Leiden: Brill (1987).

Ogden, D., Aristomenes of Messene: *Legends of Sparta's Nemesis,* Swansea: The Classical Press of Wales, 2004.

Opie, P. And Opie, I., *The Lore and Language of Schoolchildren,* Oxford: Oxford University Press (1959).

Page, D. L., *The Homeric Odyssey,* Oxford: Clarendon (1955).

————. *Folktales in Homer's Odyssey,* Cambridge: Harvard University Press (1973).

Perry, B. E., *Aesopica: A Series of Texts Relating to Aesop or Ascribed to Him or Closely Connected with the Literary Tradition That Bears His Name,* Urbana: University of Illinois Press (1952).

Radin, P., *The Trickster: A Study in American Indian Mythology,* 2nd ed., New York: Shocken (1972).

Ranke, K., *Die Zwei Brüder: Eine Studie zur vergleichenden Märchenforschung* (*Folklore Fellows Communications* 114), Helsinki: Academia Scientiarum Fennica (1934).

Rappoport, A. S., *The Folklore of the Jews,* London: Soncino (1937).

Russo, J., Greek Proverbs, *Journal of Folklore Research* vol. 20, 121–130 (1983).

Sabar, Y. (tr.), *The Folk Literature of the Kurdistani Jews: An Anthology,* New Haven: Yale University Press (1982).

Salles, C., *Assem para et accipe auream fabulam:* quelques remarques sur la littérature populaire et le répertoire des conteurs publics dans le monde romain, *Latomus* vol. 40, 3–20 (1981).

Salway, P., *Roman Britain,* Oxford: Clarendon Press (1981).

Scobie, A., *Apuleius and Folklore,* London: Folklore Society (1983).

Sifakis, G. M., The Structure of Aristophanic Comedy, *Journal of Hellenic Studies* vol. 112, 123–139 (1992).

Sourvinou-Inwood, C., *"Reading" Greek Death: To the End of the Classical Period,* Oxford: Clarendon (1995).

Swift, E., *The End of the Western Roman Empire: An Archaeological Investigation,* Stroud, Gloucestershire: Tempus Publishing (2000).

Treggiari, S., *Roman Marriage: Iusti Coniuges from the Time of Cicero to the Time of Ulpian,* Oxford: Clarendon (1991).

Walcot, P., *Hesiod and the Near East,* London: Athlone Press (1966).

Walsh, P.G., *The Roman Novel,* Cambridge: Cambridge University Press (1970).

Warner, M., *No Go the Bogeyman: Scaring, Lulling, and Making Mock,* New York: Farrar, Straus, and Giroux (1999).

West, M. L., *The East Face of Helicon: West Asiatic Elements in Greek Poetry and Myth,* Oxford: Clarendon (1997).

Wiedemann, T. E. J., *Adults and Children in the Roman Empire,* New Haven: Yale University Press (1989).

Zipes, J. (ed.), *The Trials and Tribulations of Little Red Riding Hood,* New York: Routledge (1993).

———. Spinning with Fate: Rumpelstiltskin and the Decline of Female Productivity, *Western Folklore* vol. 52, 43–60 (1993).

———. *When Dreams Came True: Classical Fairy Tales and Their Tradition,* New York: Routledge (1999).

Web Resources

The Internet is well provided with resources for folklore study in general. Ashliman's bibliography of Web resources for folk- and fairy tales alone stretches for 16 pages and is scarcely exhaustive. The resources for the classical world are equally rich, but as in the case of books, materials on ancient folklore tend to be less well covered, and the same problems of categorization occur: much searching may have to be done under such rubrics as mythology and religion. Searchers are warned that Web sites are much less controlled than scholarly books and journals and that folkloric, mythological, and biblical sites may contain outlandish or ideologically driven materials.

SEARCH ENGINES

The first resort is Google (http://www.google.com); other sites include All the Web (http://www.alltheweb.com); Alta Vista (http://www.altavista.com); DMOZ (http://dmoz.org); Excite (http://www.excite.com); Lycos (http://www.lycos.com); Teoma (http://www.teoma.com); WebCrawler (http://www.webcrawler.com); WiseNut (http://www.wisenut.com); and Yahoo! (http://www.yahoo.com).

RESEARCH LIBRARIES

COPAC (http://copac.ac.uk/copac): union catalog including the British Library and principal university library holdings in the United Kingdom and Republic of Ireland.

Gabriel (http://www.kb.nl/gabriel): European National Libraries.

Library of Congress (http://www.loc.gov): includes also the Folklife Sourcebook (http://www.loc.gov/folklife/sourcebk.html).

Libweb (http://sunsite.berkeley.edu/Libweb): Internet resources from libraries of over 115 countries.

ELECTRONIC TEXT INDEXES

Especially valuable is Online Books (University of Pennsylvania), listing over 20,000 titles of electronic books and shorter resources available free. This can also be accessed through World eBook Library, with links to other resources (http://www.netlibrary.net); the Digital Book Index combines free texts together with commercial sites.

DIRECTORIES OF ELECTRONIC TEXTS

DMOZ directory of electronic text archives (http://dmoz.org/Arts/Literature/Electronic_Text_Archives).
Google directory of electronic text archives (http://directory.google.com/Top/Arts/literature/Electronic_Text_Archives).
Yahoo! guide to collections of literary texts in languages other than English (http://www.lib.virginia.edu/wess/etexts.html).
Google directory for fairy tales (http://directory.google.com/Top/Society/Folklore/Literature/Tales/Fairy_Tales).
Yahoo! directory for folk- and fairy tales (http://dir.yahoo.com/Society_and_Culture/Mythology_and_Folklore/Folklore/Folk_and_Fairy_Tales).
DMOZ directory for myths and folktales (http://www.dmoz.link-ex.net/index.php?c+Arts/Literature/Myths_and_Folktales/Myths).

LIBRARIES OF ELECTRONIC TEXTS

Folktexts, D. L. Ashliman, folklore and mythology texts (http://www.pitt.edu/~dash/folktexts.html).
Online Books (http://digital.library.upenn.edu/books).
Perseus Digital Library, specializing in Greek, Roman, and Renaissance materials (http://www.perseus.tufts.edu).
Project Gutenberg, long-established series of online, free, downloadable texts (http://www.gutenberg.net).

BIBLIOGRAPHICAL AIDS

A useful starting point for exploration of relevant classical sites is A. Mayor, "Bibliography of Classical Folklore Scholarship, Myths, Legends and Popular Beliefs of Ancient Greece and Rome" (http://www.worldagesarchive.com/Reference_Links/Myth_Bibliograpgy.htm); so also the "Internet Classics Archive" (http://classics.mit.edu/).

ORGANIZATIONS AND JOURNALS

American Folklore Society (http://afsnet.org).
Folklore Fellows' Communications (http://www.folklorefellows.fi).
Folklore Society (http://www.folklore-society.com).
Trickster's Way (online journal of trickster research) (http://www.trinity.edu/org/ tricksters/TrixWay).
A wide range of academic journals can be accessed through **JSTOR** (http://www. jstor.org).

FOREIGN LANGUAGE SITES

DMOZ (selection of sites with links) (http://dmoz.org/Arts/Literature/Myths_and_ Folktales).
Contes (http://fr.dir.yahoo.com/Art_et_culture/Litterature/Genres/Contes).
Europäische Märchengesellschaft (the European Fairy Tale Society) (http://www. maerchen-emg.de).
Il était une fois . . . les contes de fées (http://expositions.bnf.fr/contes).
Projekt Gutenberg–DE (http://www.gutenberg2000.de), large library of electronic texts, including fairy tales (http://www.gutenberg2000.de/maerchen/index.htm) and legends (http://www.gutenberg.org).
Russian Folklore (http://www.folklore.ru).
Usyal-Walker Archive of Turkish Oral Narrative (Texas Technological University) (http://aton.ttu.edu).
There are Yahoo! directories inter alia for Danish (dk), Italian (it), Norwegian (no), Swedish (se), and Spanish (es) mythology and folklore, following the formula http://[country code].dir.yahoo.com.

Index